AARP

AARP

America's Largest Interest Group and Its Impact

Christine L. Day

American Interest Group Politics
Matt Grossmann, Series Editor

An Imprint of ABC-CLIO, LLC
Santa Barbara, California • Denver, Colorado

Library of Congress Cataloging-in-Publication Data

Names: Day, Christine L., 1954– author.
Title: AARP : America's largest interest group and its impact / Christine L. Day.
Description: Santa Barbara, Calif. : Praeger, [2017] | Series: American interest group politics | Includes bibliographical references and index.
Identifiers: LCCN 2017032319 (print) | LCCN 2017042237 (ebook) | ISBN 9781440834110 (ebook) | ISBN 9781440834103 (alk. paper)
Subjects: LCSH: American Association of Retired Persons. | Senior power—United States. | Older people—Political activity—United States. | Retirees—Political activity—United States.
Classification: LCC HQ1064.U5 (ebook) | LCC HQ1064.U5 D3897 2017 (print) | DDC 306.3/80973—dc23
LC record available at https://lccn.loc.gov/2017032319

ISBN: 978-1-4408-3410-3 (print)
978-1-4408-3411-0 (ebook)

21 20 19 18 17 1 2 3 4 5

This book is also available as an eBook.

Praeger
An Imprint of ABC-CLIO, LLC

ABC-CLIO, LLC
130 Cremona Drive, P.O. Box 1911
Santa Barbara, California 93116-1911
www.abc-clio.com

This book is printed on acid-free paper ∞

Manufactured in the United States of America

Contents

Acknowledgments

"Piece of cake" I thought to myself about writing a book on AARP. "It's a book about a single organization." I should have known better; AARP is anything but simple. The first book I wrote about interest groups and the politics of aging was published in 1990, when I was still years away from being AARP age-eligible myself. During the 1980s, AARP had been growing by millions per year and, by the end of the decade, had become a household name. But I had never heard of AARP in the early 1980s when James Swann, now professor of applied gerontology at the University of North Texas, told me about his research on aging policy and about AARP. I have studied the role of interest groups in the politics of aging off and on since then, and thought I was pretty familiar with AARP. I have learned a great deal more about this complex organization while working on this book, and I hope I have properly conveyed that knowledge here. If not, it is all on me, and certainly not on those who have so generously aided me along the way.

Everyone currently and formerly at AARP was most gracious and forthcoming with their time and information. I am especially grateful to David Certner, James Dau, Kevin Donnellan, Jo Ann Jenkins, Peggy Laramie, Nancy LeaMond, Cindy Lewin, Cheryl Matheis, Lynn Mento, Sarah Mika, William Novelli, Joshua Rosenblum, John Rother, Barbara Shipley, Jason Weinstein, Jessica Winn, and Jason Young in Washington, D.C., and to Denise Bottcher and Jason Tudor at AARP Louisiana. Alexander Guerin and Charles Caston at AARP were very helpful in providing annual membership numbers. Also generous with their time and their reflections about AARP's role in rebuilding New Orleans's Hollygrove neighborhood after Hurricane Katrina were Paul Baricos, Kevin Brown, and Pam Jenkins.

Connie Phelps and Janet Crane of the University of New Orleans Library faculty were tremendously helpful to me in digging up information through government documents and interlibrary loan. My current and former colleagues at the University of New Orleans have made this a most pleasant and stimulating environment for doing this research. Fellow political scientists Claire Abrams and Albert Ringelstein helped me out by keeping their ears to the ground and their eyes on the news for anything about AARP. Beth Boles, another great friend among political scientists, provided both excellent accommodations and thought-provoking conversation while I was in Washington.

My editor at Praeger, Steve Catalano, has been both tremendously helpful and extremely patient as I labored at this longer than intended. Series editor Matt Grossmann provided encouragement and helpful comments on early chapter drafts.

Finally, a million thanks to my husband Steve Schmitt, whose patience and encouragement and amazing culinary talents powered me through this project.

CHAPTER ONE

Introduction

People have different ideas about AARP and what it is. I heard this in people's reactions whenever I mentioned that I was writing about AARP. "It's too liberal." "It's too conservative." "It's an insurance company." "It's a money machine." One reaction I never got, however, was: "AARP? I've never heard of it." Surveys show that 98 percent of Americans are aware of AARP, Barbara Shipley, the organization's senior vice president of brand integration, told me.[1] I believe it. But it is a complex, multifaceted organization, and many people are not quite sure what to make of it. One thing everyone seems to know, though, is that when you turn 50 years old, AARP finds you and invites you to join.

"Many bad things happen when you turn 50," writes funnyman Dave Barry in *Dave Barry Turns 50*. "But . . . the worst thing is that, soon after your 50th birthday, you get The Letter. You older individuals know what letter I'm talking about: It's the one inviting you to join the AARP, which stands for 'American Association of Retired Persons Who Are Always Ahead of You in Line Asking if They Get a Discount.'"[2]

Humorist Bill Geist has a similar reaction to The Letter in his own book about turning 50. "Ahhhhhh!" The Letter is "the worst thing one can receive in the mail, now that a Unabomber suspect has been apprehended and the military has stopped sending out draft-induction letters."[3]

Old-age stereotypes and AARP turn up in the jokes of late-night comedians as well, reports the *Washington Post* in an article reflecting on AARP's own 50th birthday in 2008:

> David Letterman, for one, suggested that Sylvester Stallone's latest geriatric version of Rambo should qualify for "an AARP discount on ammo." Jon Stewart joked that presidential candidates at an AARP-sponsored debate embraced the organization's principles, including that "your grandchildren

> are, in fact, adorable." The AARP debate was like others, Conan O'Brien observed, "except the moderator asked the same question over and over."[4]

Presidents joke about it too. Presidents Bill Clinton and Barack Obama both turned 50 while in office. "I'm going to be all right until I get my A.A.R.P. card in the mail," Clinton said at his birthday bash. "And there will be a couple of bad hours there."[5] Obama, on his own 50th birthday, told a 2011 campaign fund-raiser audience that "by the time I wake up, I'll have an email from AARP asking me to call President Obama and tell him to protect Medicare."[6]

The jokes resonate with people because both AARP and the aging process are so familiar. The jokes reflect anxiety about getting older, perhaps even feeling one's mortality. Jo Ann Jenkins, AARP's chief executive officer (CEO) since 2014, wants to "disrupt aging." "I want to give people the opportunity to embrace aging as something to look forward to; not something to fear; to see it as a period of growth, not decline; to recognize the opportunities, not just the challenges and, perhaps most importantly, to see themselves and others as contributors to society, not burdens."[7]

Her words reflect the thinking of AARP's founder, Ethel Percy Andrus. Andrus, retired from a distinguished career as an educator and the first woman urban high school principal in California, was shocked to witness the meager living conditions of so many retired teachers. Volunteering with the California Retired Teachers Association, she realized that pensions were inadequate and health insurance often unattainable.[8] Like most people over the age of 65 in the 1940s, those retired teachers were destitute. Craig Walker and Bret Bradigan tell the story of the moment that Andrus decided to organize on a national level:

> One day a local grocer asked Dr. Andrus if she would check on an old woman he hadn't seen in several days. He gave Ethel the woman's address. The people who lived there didn't recognize the name, but then said, "Oh, you must mean the old woman living out back." That's when Andrus discovered that one of her retired teachers was living in a chicken coop. The woman was gravely ill, but had no money to visit a doctor. It was a moment that would charge Ethel Percy Andrus' life with a new purpose.[9]

Andrus founded the National Retired Teachers Association (NRTA) in 1947, believing that organizing nationally would increase retired teachers' clout and help them help each other. It was not only about aiding those in dire need but also about smashing stereotypes of old age as a time to wind down or disengage. Andrus took her vision of positive aging nationwide.

Older people have much to contribute to society, through meaningful work, voluntarism, helping others, exploring the world, and finding new adventures. "To serve, not to be served," was one of her founding slogans for AARP; "what we do, we do for all," was another.[10]

One common, widespread need among retirees, she discovered, was access to health care. Medicare was still over a decade away, and private insurers viewed older people as too risky. Andrus spent years trying to persuade insurance companies to sell group health insurance to NRTA members. Insurance agent Leonard Davis finally took her up on it, and demand for the wildly popular health insurance policies spread beyond retired teachers. In 1958, Andrus founded the American Association of Retired Persons (AARP) with Davis's help, selling health insurance to members through the mail, which ultimately earned Davis hundreds of millions of dollars. His company, Colonial Penn, attracted plenty of competition once other insurance companies realized what a profitable market retirees provided, and after Andrus died in 1967, Colonial Penn's policies were not such a good deal any more. In fact Colonial Penn's control over the organization became rather scandalous, especially after Andy Rooney's 1978 exposé on the CBS news show *60 Minutes*.[11] But AARP severed ties with Davis and Colonial Penn and moved on by the early 1980s, experiencing something of a renaissance, returning to the principles laid down by Ethel Andrus, and growing by leaps and bounds.[12]

Many people know AARP for the numerous membership benefits—the myriad product and service discounts, *AARP The Magazine* and other publications and websites abounding with information and calls to action, and, still the association's primary source of funds, the insurance products. AARP is not an insurance company, but it licenses with third-party providers and receives royalties for the use of its name and its logo. Proceeds from AARP's business operation support its member services and political advocacy, keeping the dues low and continuing to attract members by the tens of millions, making it the largest interest group in the country. In 1984, the association dropped its eligibility age from 55 to 50, and it grew even faster. In 1999, with half of its members still working and not yet retired, the association dropped the "Retired" and changed its name simply to the now familiar initials, AARP.

Many people know AARP for its political power, satirized by Dave Barry:

> AARP is a large and powerful organization, similar to the Mafia but more concerned about dietary fiber. AARP is greatly feared in Washington, D.C.,

> because of the fierce way it lobbies for issues of concern to senior citizens, such as Social Security, Medicare, and the constitutional right to drive without any clue where the actual road is. Whenever Congress is considering legislation that in any way affects these programs, AARP sends trained commando squadrons of elderly people to visit the congresspersons who disagree with the official AARP position. If these congresspersons do not change their minds, their bodies are later found bound hand and foot with support stockings, their skin covered with ugly round welts from being viciously jabbed with cane tips. So, AARP is not an organization to mess with.[13]

Serious observers of Washington politics agree that AARP is a visible and important presence, but more often characterized as pragmatic and responsible than as extremist or inflammatory. In today's polarized political environment, AARP is sufficiently pragmatic in its politics to be both a valued coalition partner and an adversary to groups on both the right and the left. Its policy expertise and well-established connections with policy makers enhance its influence, but the major source of AARP's influence is its enormous membership base. Some call it powerful, some call it dangerous; others suggest that its power is more symbolic than real. But in a political system dominated by business and corporate interests, AARP is one of the few consumer groups that pop up in lists of most powerful, most influential, and big-spending advocacy groups, big enough to be dubbed, frequently, a political "800-pound gorilla."

It is also an elephant. John Rother, AARP's long-time policy director, invokes the famous Indian fable of the elephant and the blind men to describe AARP's complexity.[14] In the story, six blind men touch an elephant to find out what it is. One touches the leg and thinks it is a pillar; another touches its tail and thinks it is a rope; a third man touches its trunk and thinks it is a tree branch; the fourth feels its ear and thinks it is a fan; the fifth feels its belly and thinks it is a wall; and the sixth man believes its tusk is a solid pipe.[15]

AARP is like that, and supporters and critics alike focus on different aspects of the complex organization. It is more than an advocacy group, more than a seller of insurance, more than a membership behemoth offering a wide array of services and product discounts for its $16 annual membership dues. "The integrated approach is what's important to understand about AARP," says Rother, who now serves as CEO of the National Coalition on Health Care, of which AARP is a member. "It's all important to what AARP does."[16]

The chapters that follow examine the various aspects of AARP and how they relate to the whole. Following a history of AARP in Chapter 2, Chapter 3 describes the member benefits and services along with the growth and maintenance of AARP's enormous membership; Chapter 4 discusses AARP's evolving and pragmatic approach to politics; Chapter 5 examines the nature and extent of its political influence; and Chapter 6 assesses the relationship between AARP's nonprofit and business divisions, in the context of conflict-of-interest charges leveled by AARP's critics across the partisan spectrum. The book finishes with a look to the future of AARP and the challenges faced by the organization and the 50+ constituency it represents.

CHAPTER TWO

AARP's History: Growing Up and Branching Out

AARP has a unique history among interest groups. Neither fish nor fowl, it is not easily classified in the political or business realms. Much criticism of the group arises from this difficulty in figuring out just where it fits—and thus how it should be regarded, regulated, consulted, and taxed. For its 38 million members, it provides a wide array of products, discounts, publications, and information as well as an influential voice in Washington. It is, in the words of Charles R. Morris, "a warm and fuzzy eight-hundred-pound gorilla."[1]

A variety of external and internal factors fueled AARP's growth and expansion into the political realm after the group's founding in 1958. The population was aging, the interest group universe was expanding, and age-based programs and benefits gave older Americans a political identity and a stake in government. Thus the expansion of the aging enterprise—the "programs, organizations, bureaucracies, interest groups, trade associations, providers, industries, and professionals that serve the aged in one capacity or another"[2]—was both cause and consequence of AARP's growing size and influence. But it was Ethel Percy Andrus who provided the foundation onto which AARP's political, service, and charitable ventures were built.

The Founding

When Dr. Andrus retired from her job as California's first woman urban high school principal at the age of 62, she had yet to embark on the career that would be her most famous and enduring legacy.[3] It was 1944, and her plan was to care for her mother, who had been in poor health, and to volunteer with the California Retired Teachers Association (CRTA). Although she had other income to supplement her teachers' pension of $60 per month, the meager pension led her to wonder how other retired teachers fared on so little money. As her mother's health improved, Andrus stepped up her work with the retired teachers. Their poverty-stricken existence shocked her on the numerous visits she paid as the director of welfare for the Southern Section of the CRTA. Finding one retired teacher languishing in a chicken coop was the famous last straw—one that still tugs at heartstrings in AARP's televised commercial that begins: "A chicken coop—the unlikely birthplace of a fundamental idea."[4] That idea was to organize retired teachers at the national level. She founded the National Retired Teachers Association, AARP's precursor, in 1947.

Social consciousness was nothing new to Ethel Andrus. Born in 1881, she grew up in the Gilded Age of extreme inequality, the fabulous wealth of monopoly industrialists contrasting with the abject poverty of factory and farm workers. She earned her first college degree and began her teaching career in Chicago, becoming an active volunteer with the settlement house movement, founded by her mentor Jane Addams to provide community and social services to the urban poor. She continued her teaching career in California after moving there with her family, and in 1916, at the age of 35, she began a 28-year run as the principal of Lincoln High School.

Lincoln High School was located in an ethnically diverse, high-poverty area of Los Angeles. Dropout and juvenile delinquency rates were high; English skills were often low; racial and ethnic conflict was endemic. Andrus engaged the students in innovative educational and community-service programs for learning skills, building confidence, and forming cross-cultural alliances. She established adult education programs to engage the parents as well. Crime and dropout rates fell dramatically, and test scores and graduation rates rose. At the same time she furthered her own education and became one of the first women to earn a PhD at the University of Southern California in 1930. Her efforts earned widespread recognition and reward, and her programs were adopted by the National Education Association to serve as models to be adopted by other schools.

The same zeal for social reform, combined with innovative and practical solutions drawing on business and community connections, drove Ethel Andrus to establish the National Retired Teachers Association (NRTA). Collectively, she believed that retired teachers could help themselves and each other to overcome the insecurity of meager retirement incomes. Older people, she insisted in speeches and conversations across the country, are vital and productive with much to contribute through voluntarism and civic participation. One of her goals was to establish retirement facilities that would provide health care as well as outlets and networking opportunities for engagement in community activity.

Andrus recognized health care access as one of the great unmet needs of older retirees. Like the woman she had found in the chicken coop, many suffered from illness or disability and could not afford health care or insurance payments. Retirement generally meant the end of employer-provided insurance. Private insurers considered older people to be high actuarial risks, and the federal government would not establish Medicare until 1965. Andrus approached more than 40 private insurance companies about providing group insurance for members of the NRTA. All of them turned her down.

Frustration turned to positive action when Ethel Andrus met Leonard Davis, a 31-year-old insurance broker in Poughkeepsie, New York, in 1955. She sought him out upon hearing that he had established a group insurance plan with Continental Casualty Co. for some retired teachers in New York. Davis, a pioneer in direct-mail marketing, arranged a group plan for the members of the NRTA the following year, one that could be sold through the mail. This turned out to be a boon for Davis, Continental Casualty, and the NRTA, which grew to the tens of thousands on the popularity of the policies. Retired teachers were profitable customers after all. Indeed, older Americans, shunned by insurers until Andrus teamed up with Davis, proved to be an insurance-market gold mine.

The NRTA Health Plan was so popular that word spread to other aging and retired Americans who could not find anyone to insure them. Large numbers of people prevailed upon Andrus and Davis to make their policies available to nonteachers through a broader-based organization. Davis persuaded Continental Casualty to provide a group plan, investing $50,000 of his own money, for the members of the new American Association of Retired Persons. The AARP was chartered and swung into action in 1958.

Ethel Andrus was now, at the age of 76, the founding president of both NRTA and AARP (which merged officially in 1982, having long shared facilities and staff).[5] Partnering with Davis, she launched *Modern Maturity* magazine and, the following year, a mail-order discount prescription service for AARP members. Still more benefits followed, enhancing her vision of active and positive aging: a travel service, classes and seminars, opportunities for voluntarism, and a wide array of discounts negotiated with private businesses. Membership soared as people clamored for the insurance and other benefits. The combined membership grew to 130,000 in the first year, 400,000 in 1962, nearly two million in 1962, and over seven million in 1975, which made it one of the largest membership organizations in the country, even at a fraction of the size that it is today.[6] Money rolled in as the membership grew, from the modest dues and from a fixed percentage of the revenue from insurance, prescription drugs, and an expanding number of products and services offered to members.

Service and advocacy, not profit, were Andrus's motives. Based in California, she continued to promote an active, positive view of aging in *Modern Maturity*, in speeches and interviews, and in visits to Washington, D.C., and state capitals around the country. Combating stereotypes of older people as passive, dependent, and debilitated, she promoted lifelong learning, self-fulfillment, and community service in old age and retirement. "Creative energy is ageless," she would insist, as she lobbied to end mandatory retirement and age discrimination.[7] "To serve, not to be served," was her personal motto, and it became AARP's motto as well. She died in 1967 at the age of 85 and remains a revered icon at AARP; her portraits, her words, and her mission permeate AARP headquarters, conferences, and publications.[8]

Leonard Davis is a more controversial figure. His marketing genius and pioneering use of direct mail, coupled with Ethel Andrus's determination to enhance older people's lives, launched AARP into the organizational stratosphere. She identified needs; he turned them into profits. AARP's magazine, *Modern Maturity*, was not only an outlet for Andrus's ideals; it was also an effective marketing tool. In 1963, just five years after Davis invested $50,000 into their fledgling insurance venture, he bought out Continental Casualty's AARP/NRTA policies and formed his own company, Colonial Penn, as the sole insurance provider for AARP/NRTA members. His Colonial Penn Group became the platform for a variety of enterprises: not only health but also life, auto, and homeowners insurance, as well as AARP's travel service, a temporary employment service, and even a trailer park for older people.[9]

Colonial Penn became one of the country's largest insurance companies and Davis became one of the country's wealthiest philanthropists, with a fortune topping $200 million.[10] Before his death in 2001 at the age of 76, he and his wife donated generously in support of education, the arts, and the promotion of quality of life in old age, including their endowment of the Ethel Percy Andrus Gerontology Center at the University of Southern California. Along the way, however, Colonial Penn and AARP ended their association in a swirl of controversy and scandal.

First Brush with Controversy: The Break with Colonial Penn

The insurance policies offered to members of AARP/NRTA had filled a critical need for older Americans previously deemed uninsurable, and Leonard Davis had made it happen. But by the 1970s, two aspects of the relationship between AARP and Davis's company came under increasing scrutiny: (1) the value of Colonial Penn's policies and (2) the extent of Davis's control over AARP.[11]

Leonard Davis embodied the American entrepreneurial ideal: he amassed a fortune selling a much-needed product. Everyone benefited: older Americans finally had access to health insurance, Colonial Penn raked in hundreds of millions of dollars, and AARP expanded its size and influence. But Colonial Penn's success attracted competition from other companies that finally recognized the value of the senior-citizen insurance market. As new and better insurance products entered the market, Colonial Penn retained its clients by holding a virtual monopoly on policies sold through AARP. A Senate subcommittee investigation in 1974, a *Money* magazine report in 1975, and an analysis by *Consumer Reports* in 1976 all found Colonial Penn's insurance products to be among the worst in the market in terms of price and value. At the same time, Morris notes that *Forbes* magazine in 1976 proclaimed Colonial Penn "the most profitable company in the country. (Not the most profitable *insurance* company in the country, but the most profitable *company*.)"[12] Its critics charged that Colonial Penn's success was no longer based on offering the best product at the best price, but rather on using AARP's mailing lists, convention displays, and publications—including advertisements in *Modern Maturity* disguised as articles and editorials—to market an inferior product. The company banked on AARP's reputation for service and advocacy in order to gain customers' trust.

Colonial Penn's virtual monopoly on AARP's business ventures was assured by Leonard Davis's control of AARP's operations and manipulation of its board of directors. Principal partners in the law firm that Davis hired for AARP in the early 1970s included Cyril Brickfield, who had served as AARP's executive director in the late 1960s and returned as executive director in 1977 for another ten years. By the mid-1970s, some staff and board members had started to question Davis's control over operations and the exclusive deal with Colonial Penn. Member complaints about high-pressure sales pitches to buy more insurance made some state chapter leaders suspicious as well. AARP's Executive Director Harriet Miller, a social activist who later served as mayor of Santa Barbara, had started to question the value of Colonial Penn's products for AARP members. Increasingly suspicious that AARP had become primarily a marketing tool for the benefit of Colonial Penn, she moved to expose and weaken the tight relationship between Colonial Penn and AARP. As a result, "she was harassed, overloaded with petty assignments, and eventually ousted from her job" after just a year and a half as executive director.[13]

In 1978, it all came to a head, when Miller sued Davis and the organization for wrongful termination,[14] and the popular CBS television news program *60 Minutes* broadcast an exposé on Colonial Penn and AARP. Settling out of court, AARP agreed to pay Miller $480,000; she agreed to sealing the court records and remaining silent about the suit. But it was not the lawsuit that first grabbed the attention of *60 Minutes* investigative reporter Andy Rooney. Instead, it was a video shoot in front of AARP's Washington office building in 1977, a building chosen simply for its façade as a backdrop for an unrelated televised report. When people emerged from the building demanding an end to the videotaping, as if they had something to hide, Rooney decided to find out who they were and what they were hiding. The resulting *60 Minutes* episode, "Super Salesman," featured interviews with AARP staff and volunteers who appeared to be oblivious, even dumbfounded, about the control exercised by Davis and Colonial Penn. Some disillusioned AARP officers quietly helped Rooney with his investigation, while Rooney attempted repeatedly, in vain, to interview Davis and other top executives at AARP and Colonial Penn.[15] In addition, a U.S. Postal Service official told Rooney that they were investigating AARP's use of the nonprofit-rate mailings to sell insurance for profit. Three years later, postal officials recommended criminal charges, but the U.S. district attorney decided that criminal intent would be too hard to prove.[16]

Demoralized but determined to rescue its reputation, AARP parted ways with Davis in 1979 and began the process of dropping all Colonial Penn products. In 1981, AARP chose Prudential Insurance—the nation's largest insurer at that time—as its group health insurance provider, after seeking competitive bids. Davis retired from Colonial Penn in 1983 to pursue his philanthropic interests, including academic research and advocacy in support of positive aging. As cofounder of AARP, he had struck a "Faustian bargain,"[17] working with Ethel Andrus to improve older people's lives while enriching himself. Andrus remains a constant guiding presence at AARP to this day, while Davis is persona non grata. As AARP's Legislative Director John Rother told Dale Van Atta in 1994, "Leonard Davis is a name that is not uttered within the four walls of AARP anymore."[18]

Having severed ties with Colonial Penn, AARP set about burnishing its image as it continued expanding in size, scope, and political activism—following the twin legacies of Andrus and Davis in service, advocacy, and business.

Membership Surge: AARP Becomes a Household Name

AARP rose within a few decades of its founding from a little-known retiree group to the 38-million-member colossus that it is today. The controversies of the 1970s did not slow its growth; its membership had climbed past 10 million by the time of the 1978 *60 Minutes* broadcast, and to 13 million by the time it dumped Colonial Penn for Prudential in 1981. As its membership grew, so did its lobbying strength.[19] With Leonard Davis gone and the Colonial Penn scandal behind it, AARP more than doubled in size to 33 million by the end of the 1980s, making it the largest voluntary association in the United States, as well as one of the wealthiest and most widely recognized.[20]

AARP's extensive array of products, services, and discounts for its members explains much of its phenomenal growth. External influences also fueled its expansion. AARP was founded on the cusp of an interest group explosion in the 1960s and 1970s, as record numbers of political organizations established headquarters in the nation's capital. Interest groups representing older people arose among them, as both cause and consequence of "the graying of the federal budget," Robert Hudson's phrase for the expansion of aging-related benefits and services.[21] Old-age advocates highlighted the poverty and loss so often accompanying retirement and advancing age. Policy makers responded with policies to reduce those risks and hardships. Older Americans in turn developed a stake in government, as well as an age-group consciousness based on aging-specific programs and benefits, and they stepped up their political mobilization.[22]

There were precursors; older Americans had organized in the past. Early efforts to promote old-age income security arose in the 1920s, in response to surging unemployment and poverty among the elderly, whose proportion of the population was growing. Ideally, aging would lead to comfortable retirement, and some businesses offered private pensions in order to cultivate worker loyalty and encourage retirement to make way for younger workers. But increasingly, old age meant hardship for the aging and their family caregivers, or even a move to the poorhouse. Organizations such as the American Association for Old Age Security and the American Association for Labor Legislation lobbied for public pensions and other social insurance. Older people themselves organized in support of public pensions during the Great Depression years, most prominently the Townsend movement, which claimed some two million members at its peak. Those movements lacked the leadership structure, pragmatism, and policy expertise for long-term stability, and they died out after the passage of the Social Security Act in 1935. Historians downplay their influence on the legislation. But those groups helped to promote sympathy for the aging as well as group consciousness among them, laying the foundation for the rise of old-age advocacy in the 1960s.[23]

Following the passage of the Social Security Act, political organization on behalf of the elderly languished for nearly three decades—a period Pratt calls "the dismal years."[24] Some prominent social scientists in the 1950s doubted that older people would be organizing politically any time soon. Social Security had reduced their level of desperation, and surveys showed little evidence of old-age solidarity and common interest.[25] Other scholars suggest that policies benefiting the elderly have done more to segregate, demobilize, and pacify older people than to mobilize them politically.[26] The doubters were correct in noting the diversity of older Americans and their life situations, a diversity that potentially hampers group solidarity. But the doubters were wrong about the emergence of aging-based political organizations after the 1950s. The creation and expansion of Social Security and other aging-based programs and benefits did not remove the impetus for political mobilization. On the contrary, they enhanced aging group consciousness and a sense of collective interest among older people, whose problems were far from solved. Even after a flurry of legislation targeting aging-related challenges, old-age income insecurity remained a large and daunting problem.

Ethel Andrus had witnessed firsthand the dire situation of many older retirees, and the meagerness of their pension income. When AARP was founded in 1958, the poverty rate for Americans aged 65 years and older was 35 percent, higher than any other age group and more than twice as high as it would be two decades later.[27] Andrus's accomplishments on behalf of the aging were exceptional, but her sympathy for their plight was not, as Americans came to view the elderly as deserving beneficiaries after long lives of hard work. Robert Binstock characterizes the New Deal through the 1970s as the era of "compassionate ageism," based on stereotypes of older people as poor and frail.[28] Given the diversity of older people, many did not match the stereotype. But public compassion, coupled with the notion of deservingness, resulted in the creation of policies to alleviate problems of poverty, illness, and loss in old age, especially during the 1960s and 1970s.

Social Security—more formally, Old Age, Survivors, and Disability Insurance—was amended several times to expand the size and scope of benefits, culminating in automatic cost-of-living increases after 1972. Since then it has lifted more people out of poverty than any other government program. Supplemental Security Income established a minimum income level for older people in 1974. Medicare and Medicaid together cover most health care costs for older people since 1965. The Older Americans Act, passed in 1965 and expanded in later years, provides a network of programs and services, including daily nutrition. The Employee Retirement

Income Security Act of 1974 helps protect private pensions. Two major laws prohibit age discrimination, a cause particularly championed by Ethel Andrus: the Age Discrimination in Employment Act of 1967, passed the same year she died, and the Age Discrimination Act of 1975, banning age discrimination in any program receiving federal assistance. Numerous other policies powered by compassionate ageism have provided housing, energy, and other types of assistance, and have created bureaucratic agencies and congressional committees focused on various aspects of aging. By the late 1970s, the elderly poverty rate was 15 percent—similar to that of adults under 65 and much lower than that of children—and the dream of retirement had become reality for many older adults.[29]

The rise and politicization of aging-based interest groups occurred largely in the wake of these policy achievements. AARP was the first of many aging-based political organizations founded after World War II. In the decades that followed, a trickle of groups became a flood.

Henry Pratt's *The Gray Lobby*, published in 1976, listed "only a handful—ten [groups] at the present time" that "are both engaged in politics at the national level and more or less exclusively preoccupied with old-age problems."[30] These included three mass-membership groups (AARP, the National Council of Senior Citizens, and the National Association of Retired Federal Employees), three professional associations, and four trade associations. Twenty years later, aging-based interest groups numbered in the hundreds, with state- and local-level chapters and standalone groups pushing the number into the thousands.[31]

As AARP emerged from the shadow of Leonard Davis and Colonial Penn in the late 1970s, it also rode the wave of a veritable explosion of advocacy groups in Washington. Political organizations proliferated in the 1960s and 1970s, as social movements—for civil rights, women's rights, environmental protection, and more—evolved into stable interest groups, business and corporate interests engaged in counter-mobilization, education levels increased, new mass communications technologies flourished, government activity expanded, and election campaigns grew increasingly expensive and dependent upon interest-group contributions. In sum, social upheaval and political change, combined with greater organizational opportunities through advances in communication and education, generated large numbers of new groups making demands on government.[32]

Governmental growth, however, is not just a result of interest group demands. The reverse is also true. The rise of old-age advocacy illustrates this reciprocal relationship between public policy and political organization. Government programs like Social Security and Medicare define older people as a beneficiary group and give them a stake in the political system. The agencies administering programs benefiting the elderly encourage older Americans' political mobilization, in order to support the agencies' work as well as the well-being of their clientele.[33] Social Security expansion has increased older Americans' political consciousness and participation, as beneficiaries defend policies that increase their income security and age-based political identity.[34] AARP existed years before the creation and expansion of old-age programs and benefits in the 1960s and 1970s, but did not move its headquarters to Washington from California until 1967, and engaged in limited lobbying there prior to the early 1970s.[35]

Building upon the foundation laid by Ethel Andrus and Leonard Davis, AARP grew rapidly, attracting members by the millions with an expanding array of product and service options and discounts. Starting with the health insurance business, AARP soon developed a wide array of material incentives—products and discounts—for attracting members, including life, auto, and homeowners insurance; low-cost prescription drugs, health aids, and travel benefits; mutual funds and annuities; tax assistance; the 55-Alive seminar on driving skills (now called the Driver Safety Program); a bimonthly newsletter called *The AARP Bulletin* and a magazine called *Modern Maturity*, which became the country's largest-circulated magazine in the late 1980s. The organization renamed it *AARP The Magazine* in 2002, creating three different versions for members in their fifties, sixties, and seventies or older.

Equally famous is the association's ability to track down virtually every American approaching the age of 50 in order to begin the promotional mailings, including the invitation letter that has become a national symbol of reaching the milestone of being 50 years old. The database management process has developed over decades of purchasing and mining lists from voter registration records to subscriptions and product warranties.[36]

The mailing list dates back to AARP's founding and Leonard Davis's savvy use of direct-mail marketing to sell products for Colonial Penn—or, from Ethel Andrus's point of view, to make people aware of products, services, and opportunities to improve their lives and enhance their independence in their later years. Membership dues have always been low—$16 per person or couple today—and they bring in about 20 percent of AARP's revenue. Members then have access to arguably the largest array of perks and discounts available from any membership organization. They also can enjoy social and volunteer activities through thousands of local and state chapters, as well as supporting AARP's political activities.

But most join for the discounts on travel, insurance, prescription drugs, and health aids, and for the publications.[37]

By the late 1970s, the era of "compassionate ageism" was giving way to "scapegoating the aged," as the poor-and-frail elderly stereotype was often eclipsed by a new one: older people as privileged and prosperous, no longer deserving of government aid but in fact draining government coffers and burdening working taxpayers.[38] Policy changes in the 1960s and 1970s had alleviated many of the ravages of aging, and the poverty rate of Americans aged 65 and over, disproportionately high in 1960, fell below the poverty rate of the general population in 1982. But no stereotype—neither the poor-and-frail nor the privileged-and-prosperous—captures older Americans' socioeconomic diversity.

Ethel Andrus recognized this diversity, seeing older people as both a population in need and a resource to be tapped. She sought to protect them against poverty and loss, and to increase their opportunities for serving others while enhancing their own self-worth. "The stereotype of old age as a disease, increasingly costly and troublesome," she wrote, ". . . is contradicted by the host of happy and productive oldsters participating and serving beyond the call of duty."[39]

These sentiments still fuel AARP's multisector social enterprise model. The optimistic view of older people as active, healthy, and prosperous helps to attract members, customers, and private-sector product development for a lucrative older market. At the same time, AARP representatives can portray older people as the "deserving needy" in lobbying for aging-based programs and social services. Its political advocacy has expanded to make it one of the most widely recognized and influential interest groups in national and state politics.

Advocacy Expansion: AARP Becomes a Washington Heavyweight

AARP has long been characterized as one of the most—sometimes *the* most—influential lobbying group in Washington.[40] But AARP did not start out as an overtly political organization or lobbying group. Ethel Andrus sought to improve the well-being of older Americans, but her primary emphasis was on building individual purpose and dignity while fighting stereotypes of the aging as useless and weak. Thus her motto for the organization was "to serve, not to be served." While Leonard Davis was primarily interested in the business aspect of the organization, Andrus emphasized service to—and by—retirees.[41] One of her earliest projects for NRTA was the establishment of the innovative Grey Gables retirement home in Ojai, California. At a time when most older Americans lived in poverty, and the vast majority lived with relatives, Andrus designed Grey Gables not only to provide comfort and care but also to encourage residents to remain actively involved in the community, tutoring local students, serving on local boards, and otherwise volunteering their time, knowledge, and experience. Her hope was for Grey Gables to serve as a model for active retirement centers nationwide.[42]

Ethel Andrus did not eschew political action altogether; indeed, politics was part of her service mission. She wrote of the need for collective action, not only for retirees to encourage and provide for each other but also to lobby state and national governments for causes such as eliminating mandatory retirement, expanding retiree pensions and tax benefits, and generally "improving retirement provisions and removing retirement inequities."[43] While NRTA/AARP was based in Ojai, she spent much of her time lobbying in Washington, and, in 1965, moved organizational headquarters briefly to Long Beach and then to the nation's capital.[44]

AARP did not become a political powerhouse overnight. From the late 1950s to at least the late 1960s—AARP's first decade, and NRTA's second—more energy and resources were put into organization building and membership expansion.[45] By the middle of the 1960s, membership was past the one million mark, and climbing. Money poured in both from membership dues and from affiliated business royalties. As membership dues accounted for only half of the group's revenues, critics began building the case that AARP's politics was overly deferential to its business enterprises, especially, at that time, Colonia Penn. But royalties also provided a steady income, keeping the annual dues low and benefits plentiful, giving its expanding membership substantial bang for the buck.[46]

While AARP was growing in the 1960s and 1970s, government benefits for older Americans were expanding. Great Society policies including the creation of Medicare and Medicaid and the expansion of Social Security greatly improved older Americans' access to health care and income security. But AARP and other mass-membership interest groups representing older Americans had little influence on their passage. Instead, most accounts credit policy experts and activist public officials for the policy initiatives and program enhancements that halved the elderly poverty rate and doubled the proportion of the federal budget devoted to old-age benefits within a couple of decades.[47] Older, more established groups, organized labor in particular, played a more decisive role in lobbying for improvements in the well-being of older and retired persons. AARP's lobbying efforts were, at most, narrowly targeted, defensive rather than innovative, and modest in scope.[48]

As membership continued to grow, so did the political activities of AARP and other aging-based interest groups. If the 1950s and 1960s were the decades of growth and organizational consolidation, the 1970s and 1980s were the decades when AARP came into its own politically. "There's a New Kick in the Step of the Senior Citizen Lobbies," proclaims a *National Journal* headline in 1976; "the voice of the nation's elderly has begun to be heard and noted in the political process."[49] Scholars and journalists began to acknowledge their influence, as AARP developed vastly expanded policy expertise, gaining connections and trust on Capitol Hill and mobilizing its members to contact public officials en masse.[50]

AARP and the labor-affiliated National Council of Senior Citizens (NCSC), the two broad-based mass-membership groups, formed the core of aging-based citizen activism. The National Council of Senior Citizens, a creation of the labor union movement's support for John F. Kennedy's presidential campaign, recruited its largely blue-collar membership from organized labor. NCSC was more overtly political than AARP from the beginning, lobbying actively for Medicare throughout the early and mid-1960s. AARP was generally characterized as anchoring the conservative end of the senior-organization spectrum, with its largely white-collar professional membership base. Agreeing broadly in their defense of Social Security, Medicare, and services supported under the Older Americans Act, the two groups, during the 1970s, nevertheless had some policy disagreements reflecting their different constituencies. AARP, whose members were more likely to continue working later in life, lobbied against mandatory retirement and against the reduction of Social Security benefits for beneficiaries who worked after reaching the age of 65 years, while the more blue-collar union-affiliated NCSC remained ambivalent. NCSC, on the other hand, was a more enthusiastic supporter of comprehensive national health insurance.[51] In fact, NCSC's Executive Director William R. Hutton suggested in 1976 that AARP's resistance to nationalized health insurance was driven by its relationship with Colonial Penn, which would lose business if health insurance were covered by the state.[52]

As the 1970s progressed, the aging-based organizational landscape expanded—with the Gray Panthers organizing on the left in 1971, and the conservative National Alliance of Senior Citizens forming on the right flank in 1974—serving as something of a precursor to numerous conservative senior organizations that would promote themselves as "conservative alternatives to AARP" in subsequent decades. The diversity of aging-based membership organizations that continued to emerge reflects the wide range of political views among older Americans themselves. But by this time, Medicare, Social Security expansion, and other programs benefiting older people had provided the basis for a shared sense of unity in defense of those benefits, and an enhanced sense of age-group consciousness.[53] In 1979, some 30 membership, professional, and service provider groups (excluding the conservative National Alliance) formed the Leadership Council of Aging Organizations to facilitate information sharing and unified advocacy.[54] AARP continues to anchor the LCAO nearly 40 years later.

Older Americans and their representatives in Washington ended the decade of the 1970s in better shape than they had begun: with more income security, more political clout, and a bigger slice of the federal budget. Political observers noticed the aging population and the "graying of the federal budget,"[55] and suggested that the proverbial budgetary dilemma between "guns versus butter" might be recast as "guns versus canes."[56] As spiking oil prices and stagflation wreaked havoc on the economy, the bipartisan consensus around maintaining and expanding old-age entitlements began to erode. To the stereotype of the elderly as the "deserving poor" was added a new one: that of the "greedy geezer." Even as AARP's influence grew, it met increased resistance.

By the early 1980s, observers characterized the elderly lobby as a well-organized and powerful force that policy makers were reluctant to resist.[57] When President Ronald Reagan proposed Social Security benefit reductions in 1981—the first time benefits would be cut since the program's inception—Washington felt the full fury of retirees and near-retirees who perceived the threat to their benefits.[58] The same year AARP replaced Colonial Penn with Prudential as its health insurance underwriter. Aging policy activists interviewed in the mid-1980s said that AARP's politics shifted to the left after the break with Colonial Penn and the decline in Leonard Davis's influence over organizational policy.[59] Still officially nonpartisan, AARP leapt into action with other senior organizations to lobby against benefit cuts. As a result, the president withdrew the proposal and appointed the National Commission on Social Security (widely known as the Greenspan Commission) to study and recommend reforms that would make the program financially sustainable.

One of AARP's most potent weapons in the fight was its large and growing membership base, which by 1982 numbered over 14 million, far more than all of the other senior membership groups combined. Thousands of state and local chapters boosted AARP's visibility and lobbying strength in the states and helped mobilize the grassroots. Leonard Davis's pioneering direct-mail techniques for selling insurance now were used to mobilize members politically. "We have all the names on a computer," the group's assistant legislative counsel told *National Journal* in 1981. "We can communicate with these people by phone, mail or wire to get them to generate mail to get things we do like and stop things we don't like."[60] Further energizing the grassroots were voter education programs and political forums launched in the mid-1980s. Andrea Campbell's political participation study found AARP members more likely than nonmembers to contact elected officials generally, and to contact them about Social Security specifically.[61] The barrage of mail and phone calls helped persuade Congress to reject President Reagan's proposed benefit cuts.

Over the next two decades, AARP's membership, lobbying staff, and public visibility grew at an accelerated pace. Membership nearly tripled during the 1980s, hitting 33 million in 1990 and making AARP the country's largest nonreligious membership organization while dwarfing all other senior groups. The association had stepped up recruitment efforts with an ever-expanding array of membership benefits, taking advantage of the aging population, and had dropped the eligibility age from 55 to 50 in 1984. Also in the mid-1980s, AARP broadened and diversified its outreach by establishing women's initiative and minority affairs as two of its "four areas of immediate concern" along with health care and worker equity.[62]

AARP's presence on Capitol Hill grew along with its membership base. Paid staff doubled to 1,200 during the 1980s, including over 100 legislative staff. Its political advocacy became increasingly sophisticated and well informed with the creation of the Public Policy Institute, AARP's own think tank, in 1985. Now well armed with information and policy analysis, AARP developed a reputation in Washington as a professional and responsible lobby, hailed by legislators of both parties for its rational approach and willingness to negotiate.[63] By the end of the 1980s, AARP had its own zip code; *Modern Maturity* had the largest circulation of all the nation's magazines; a network of state offices and over 3,000 local chapters hosted meetings and mobilized tens of thousands of volunteers; the annual budget had reached a quarter of a billion dollars; and AARP had penetrated the national consciousness.[64]

AARP's fame continued to rise through the 1990s as its membership held steady at around 33 million. Now unquestionably a Washington powerhouse, it topped *Fortune* Magazine's list of most powerful lobbying organizations three years in a row at the end of the nineties.[65] Charles Morris's 1997 book was titled *The AARP: America's Most Powerful Lobby and the Clash of Generations*.[66] Increasingly sought after as a coalition partner, AARP helped anchor not only horizontal alliances with other senior groups, most prominently the Leadership Council of Aging Organizations, but also vertical alliances like Generations United, formed in 1986 in support of old-age, children's, and intergenerational advocacy.[67]

Symbolizing the group's success was the move in 1991 to its new headquarters, so opulent that AARP critic Dale Van Atta dubbed it the "Taj Mahal."[68] Morris describes a 10-story "striking building, a massive riff on classical themes in handsome sand-colored brick and preformed concrete . . . centered on a giant column and arch treatment over a courtyard and promenade (with) a crenellated tower on one end," a "bold, almost flamboyant design," a "strident power-statement," although it stretched a full block along a "down-at-the-heels commercial strip."[69] But the neighborhood has since shaken off the shabbiness and become a booming district of arts and entertainment, restaurants, and trendy stores. "We were lucky," Media Relations Director James Dau told me when I arrived in the summer of 2015; "someone had great foresight" in moving the headquarters to what was now a prestigious area of escalating property values.[70]

AARP entered the final decade of the twentieth century in triumph, having eclipsed the other senior organizations in numbers and Washington influence, and joined the ranks of the most powerful political organizations in the nation. Its business enterprises and product tie-ins created a wide array of membership benefits and earned hundreds of millions of dollars for political advocacy. Its longevity, large staff, policy expertise, and massive membership base made it the most effective defender of old-age benefits including Social Security and Medicare. Further, in a political system increasingly dominated by wealthy campaign donors, AARP had amassed political influence without creating a PAC to contribute to candidates and fund campaigns. Still disproportionately white and middle- to upper-middle class, its membership nevertheless was so economically, socially, and politically diverse that the organization could credibly claim to represent the broad population of older Americans.[71]

Challenges and Controversy in the Late Twentieth Century

As the AARP empire grew in both size and stature, so did the challenges facing both the organization and its older constituency. "Compassionate ageism," the notion that older people are needy and frail as well as deserving of government largesse after a lifetime of hard work, began to give way to the stereotype of the affluent, jet-setting retiree. The stagflation of the late 1970s, followed by the ascendance of President Ronald Reagan and the budgetary retrenchment of the 1980s, turned social welfare spending into more of a zero-sum game. Further, projections showed the Social Security trust fund surplus slipping into deficit within a few decades as the baby-boom generation reached retirement age.[72] In that context, the general consensus in support of Social Security and other old-age and retiree benefits began to crumble.

Ironically this is when AARP's reputation as a Washington powerhouse kicked in. As long as there was a general bipartisan consensus to maintain or even increase old-age benefits, AARP's advocacy consisted primarily of defending an easily-defended status quo. But serious challenges to that status quo arose in the early 1980s with the election of President Ronald Reagan, who proposed cuts in Social Security benefits early in his first term as part of an overall plan to reduce the federal budget, and with the rise of the movement for "generational equity."[73]

Proponents of generational equity argued that older people draw far more than their share of government largesse at the expense of children and younger adults. Americans for Generational Equity (AGE), founded in 1985, was the first political organization focused on purportedly overly generous old-age benefits. "Our organization is set up to hold AARP accountable to its 22 million members," founder Paul Hewitt said. "The largest and most powerful social lobby in our country is organized not on the basis of rich versus poor, but to benefit a single generation—the elderly—at the expense of all others."[74]

AARP also faced opposition, within the aging-based interest-group community, from a trio of conservative groups that arose in the late 1980s and early 1990s: the Seniors Coalition, United Seniors Association (now called USA Next), and the 60 Plus Association. Founded with the help of conservative direct-mail expert Richard Viguerie, they billed themselves as "conservative alternatives" to AARP and lobbied for limited government and free-market entitlement reforms. They have since been joined by a variety of other right-wing senior groups with heavy corporate funding, such as the American Seniors Association and the Association of Mature American Citizens.

Like the advocates for generational equity, the conservative senior groups continue to lobby for partial or full privatization of Social Security and Medicare, in direct and open opposition to AARP. Thus, while earlier conflicts among organizations representing older Americans were relatively minor disagreements among allies, the addition of newer, more conservative groups has led to an ideological polarization among senior advocates that mirrors the increasing partisan polarization in U.S. politics generally.[75]

Conservative opposition to AARP arose within Congress as well, as Republican-led investigations zeroed in on AARP in the 1990s and again in the early twenty-first century. One catalyst for the investigations was AARP's sheer size and wealth. The magnitude of its business operations—the product endorsements and royalties that provide more of AARP's income than membership dues—attracted the attention of the Internal Revenue Service, which audited its tax-exempt status in light of its earnings. Without conceding any wrongdoing, AARP nevertheless voluntarily settled with the IRS and agreed to pay $135 million in lieu of taxes for the years 1985–1994, and settled again for $52 million in 1999. In addition, the association paid the U.S. Postal Service $2.8 million in 1994 for mailing its product and service advertisements at non-profit postage rates. As part of the IRS settlement, AARP formally established its taxable, for-profit subsidiary—AARP Services Inc. (ASI)—in 1999, as a separate entity from the primary 501(c)(4) nonprofit advocacy and member services organization and its affiliated 501(c)(3) charitable unit, the AARP Foundation. This separation not only clarifies AARP's tax liability; it also helps preserve the credibility of its public service and policy advocacy, which are supported by the revenue earned at ASI.[76]

Nonetheless, AARP's critics contend that the separation is largely a sham, and that its business interests drive its politics, helping to create markets for its products. Republican-driven congressional hearings in 1995 and again in 2011 questioned AARP's tax-exempt status, especially since it accepts government grants, and endeavored to show connections between the policies pushed by AARP's lobbying activities—health care reform, for example—and its profitable product partnerships and endorsements, especially the supplemental health insurance plans. Supporters counter that AARP's policy advocacy is unaffected by the business side, and at any rate thousands of tax-exempt nonprofits across the ideological spectrum receive grants, sell products, and lobby government. The Republican-led congressional investigations, they said, were driven mostly by AARP's struggle against conservative efforts to slash or privatize Social Security and Medicare. In fact Democrats, too, questioned the motives of AARP's advocacy when it helped pass the Republican-favored Medicare Modernization Act in 2003.[77] AARP's size and policy influence had made it a target.

Not that AARP was batting a thousand in the policy arena. The group's endorsement was crucial to the passage of the Medicare Catastrophic Coverage Act in 1988, but then Congress repealed the MCCA the following year, after widespread protests by older people angry about the tax on higher-income beneficiaries.[78] Another setback followed with AARP's support for President Bill Clinton's failed health care reform effort in the early 1990s. And its multidecade advocacy for government-sponsored long-term services and supports, despite a serious struggle spearheaded in Congress in the 1980s by longtime senior advocate Rep. Claude Pepper of Florida, has gone virtually nowhere.

The challenges faced by AARP in the last two decades of the twentieth century—the declining consensus among policy makers around Social Security and Medicare, rising opposition from the conservative and generational equity movements, the policy-advocacy hits and misses—do not mean that AARP's influence was declining. On the contrary, AARP was frequently hailed—or panned, by critics—as one of the most powerful lobby groups in Washington throughout the 1990s. Perhaps ironically, the challenges made AARP's influence all the more visible and relevant. Age-based entitlement programs consuming most of the federal domestic budget helped create an age-conscious constituency, and with their benefits threatened, advocacy on their behalf became increasingly salient. By 2000, AARP, with 34 million members, thousands of local chapters and state offices, and a half-billion-dollar budget, had become their largest, wealthiest, and most visible advocate by far.

Twenty-First Century: Baby Boomers and Beyond

As the twenty-first century dawned, AARP was poised to grow even larger. The leading edge of the Post-World War II baby boom was approaching 60, and each year millions more boomers were age-eligible for AARP, but most were not yet retired. In 1999, the group had changed its name to just its initials (pronounced one letter at a time, though the single-syllable pronunciation "arp" is common as well). With the name change, AARP moved to broaden its appeal while highlighting the widely recognized AARP brand. Well established in Washington and increasingly active in the state capitals, AARP's growing influence matched its growth in size.

Challenges remained. The *New York Times* noted in 2001 that membership growth had slowed significantly over the past decade after nearly tripling during the 1980s. AARP, it said, was facing an identity crisis of sorts, struggling to maintain cohesiveness and relevance for a membership diverse in age, employment status, and political views. Bold political stances risked alienating members. Avoiding them, however, risked eroding AARP's influence on Capitol Hill.[79]

Attracting members from the highly individualistic and disparate boomer generation was essential to organizational expansion. John Rother, AARP's lead policy specialist and political strategist from 1984 until 2011, and a boomer himself, pushed the group to connect with boomer independence and individualism. Offer choices, recognize difference and diversity, maintain ideological flexibility in seeking policy options to the fifty-plus population, and present opportunities to indulge oneself and to change the world: AARP's multifaceted quality, ironically, could be a source of cohesion for the giant boomer generation.[80]

Brand enhancement became priority number one in the transition from Executive Director Horace Deets (1988–2001) to his successor Bill Novelli (2001–2009). When Deets stepped down, Novelli's extensive experience in marketing and social entrepreneurship made him the board's choice: "We were looking for someone with experience in branding and marketing," said Board President James Parkel. "Aggressive advocacy wasn't on our list."[81]

Under Novelli's leadership, AARP intensified its marketing efforts, escalating its use of television advertisements and burnishing its image with a bolder new logo sporting the motto, "AARP: The power to make it better"—a motto appealing to boomers' self-reliance and social-movement-oriented ambitions. *Modern Maturity*, already the nation's largest-circulation magazine for over a decade, had gone through something of an awkward transition in 1999 when a second magazine, *My Generation*, was added for boomer-generation members. In 2002, the new *AARP The Magazine* replaced both of them, with three slightly different versions mailed to members in different age groups, all updated to appeal more to hipness than to oldness. Like the organization's name itself, the new magazine title broadened the focus beyond "retired persons" and benefited from near-universal recognition of the famous initials. Online and Spanish versions reflected the group's modernization and increasing appeal to racial and ethnic diversity.[82]

Novelli reorganized and hired to make AARP more professional and businesslike—to its detractors, too corporate,[83] and to its supporters, more efficient and more productive. Annual dues increased to $12.50 and then, in 2009, to $16. New business ventures joined the old, royalties from insurance and other products more than quintupled, and revenues surged to over $1billion. State offices had opened in nearly half the states plus Puerto Rico and the Virgin Islands before Deets stepped down; under Novelli, offices extended to all 50 states, placed under tighter control by the national office, and AARP expanded its presence abroad as well by creating ties with senior organizations in other countries. The board of directors was professionalized. Previously chosen by delegates elected by members at the annual convention, now they were winnowed by a nominating committee and voted on by the current board. The annual megaconventions from 2001 to 2015, "Life @50+," now became star-studded social and entertainment extravaganzas, where thousands of members mingled and partied while browsing products and services and engaging in advocacy. At the conferences and in other aspects of member engagement, popular culture—music, sports, "Movies for Grown-Ups"—serves as a touchstone for uniting a demographically and politically diverse membership—a membership that peaked at over 40 million in 2008.[84]

Political advocacy expanded along with brand enhancement and membership recruitment. Lobbying staff and spending increased as AARP remained one of the highest-spending lobbying organizations in Washington throughout the first decade of the 2000s. Grassroots lobbying, stimulated through television and print advertising, mailings and publications sent to members, and millions of volunteer activists—even a small percentage of 38 million members makes quite an army—remained an active strategy as well. AARP's advocacy was widely credited—or blamed, depending on one's stance—as crucial to the passage of the Republican-supported Medicare Modernization Act of 2003, which added prescription drug coverage to Medicare (though without the price controls pushed mostly by Democrats) and established a private-insurance option to traditional Medicare known as Medicare Advantage. It was crucial again to the passage of the Democrat-supported Affordable Care Act, or "Obamacare," in 2010. AARP was also instrumental in preventing President George W. Bush's plan to partially privatize Social Security and has played a major role in ongoing federal budget negotiations, working to keep Social Security and Medicare benefit cuts off the table.

The dilemma, as Frederick Lynch put it in his study of AARP and the baby boom generation, is the "tension between this consumer services brand and a more aggressive 'warrior brand,'"[85] or navigating between the array of products, information, and services that bring in the members by the tens of millions, and the political stances that divide those millions along partisan and ideological lines. This tension is not unique to the twenty-first century; AARP has grappled with it from the start, as Ethel Percy Andrus sought to provide much-needed service and advocacy, and Leonard Davis sought to make money. It is a dilemma faced by any large multipurpose organization whose missions both complement and conflict with each other. But however schizophrenic, AARP's multiple pursuits also work to its advantage, as revenues from its business ventures enable it to maintain a high level of membership services and political advocacy while keeping the dues low.

Businessman A. Barry Rand, AARP's first African American executive director, succeeded Novelli in 2009, in the midst of another challenging period marked by losses in both finances and membership. The stock market crash and Great Recession of 2008 led to staff and program cutbacks, as well as a drop in membership the following year. Also contributing to membership loss was AARP's active support for the controversial Affordable Care Act.[86] Since peaking at 40 million in 2008, membership has hovered around 37 or 38 million, even as the population ages and the number of age-eligible Americans continues to grow. Still, its size dwarfs that of all other aging-based groups, and it remains one of the largest and wealthiest membership organizations in the nation.

Membership growth remained a major priority for AARP under the five-year leadership of Barry Rand and his successor in 2014, Jo Ann Jenkins, who previously had served as the group's chief operating officer and had led its charitable affiliate, the AARP Foundation. Taking over in the midst of the recession during President Barack Obama's first year in office, Rand led AARP to continue advocating for health insurance reform, not only supporting the ACA but also shaping it so that, for example, it would close the gap in Medicare prescription drug coverage commonly known as the "doughnut hole." As ACA opponents conjured inaccurate but frightening images of ACA-endorsed "death panels" and raised the specter of cuts to Medicare, AARP launched a multimillion dollar information campaign that Rand said was "the largest education effort our organization has ever undertaken."[87]

Asked about his long-term vision for AARP, Rand emphasized the "need to stay focused on our relevancy with consumers and the changes in technology" as well as "strategies to increase our diversity."[88] Jo Ann Jenkins, named AARP's first African American woman CEO in 2014, leads the continuing effort to make AARP relevant and useful to individual members, and to make aging a process to be embraced—not the butt of jokes like the dreaded letter every American receives upon turning 50, inviting them to join AARP. "Disrupting aging"—rejecting the negative stereotypes, focusing on opportunities rather than limitations that arise with advancing age—is her major theme, reflected in the title of her 2016 book *Disrupt Aging*.[89] AARP's website, with wide-ranging and interactive features for exploring options in later life including career and retirement, health and wellness, relationships, travel, and adventure, reflects the theme as well. The new 2014 logo replaces "The power to make it better" with "Real Possibilities"—not only an appeal to members' individual needs and aspirations but also, by happy coincidence, a motto coinciding with the last two letters of AARP.[90]

Building a widespread sense of satisfaction, loyalty, and unity of purpose continues to clash with AARP's political advocacy in an era of increasing partisan and ideological polarization. Defending Social Security and Medicare as crucial to older Americans' health and income security is no longer easy, despite the programs' enduring popularity among

Americans of all ages. These two programs consume a third of the federal budget and will consume even more as the population ages and medical inflation pushes health care costs ever higher. The federal government bounces from one budget crisis to another, largely unable to find common ground as conservatives push benefit cuts and propose partial or full program privatization, while liberals resist benefit cuts and even call for benefit enhancements.

AARP is a politically moderate organization in a polarized political system. Its members are roughly one-third Democrat, one-third Republican, and one-third independent.[91] Many members, mostly liberal, were angry and some quit when AARP supported President Bush's Medicare prescription drug coverage plan in 2003; many more, mostly conservative, were angry and some quit when AARP lobbied for President Obama's health insurance reform. Top lobbyist Rother's suggestion in 2011, that AARP could be open to Social Security benefit reductions in order to maintain the program's long-term solvency, made headlines and sent shock waves through the aging-advocacy community, alienating some of AARP's long-time allies.[92] AARP then publicly backed off, insisting that the budget not be balanced on the backs of the elderly. At the same time, its diversity and emphasis on membership growth makes any aggressive policy stance problematic.

AARP sought to make Social Security a major issue in the 2016 presidential election by launching the multimillion-dollar "Take a Stand" initiative, including television ads and public forums encouraging candidates to detail their plans. But it drew criticism, especially from more liberal advocates, for failing to take a stand itself, neither ranking candidates' responses nor listing its own preferred reforms.[93] Thus critics across the ideological spectrum denounce AARP for being too liberal, for being too conservative, for being too partisan, and for being overly cautious and noncommittal. Its opponents charge, further, that its combination of for-pofit business, nonprofit service, and political advocacy constitutes a conflict of interests.

Still, "AARP is an undeniably important and successful advocacy organization in American politics," notes interest group scholar Matt Grossmann,[94] as it continues to rank among the top political organizations in terms of money, size, longevity, prominence, activity, and involvement. When policy and media elites seek information about aging policy, endorsement of proposals, or representation of older Americans' views, they turn most often, by far, to AARP.

The revered Ethel Percy Andrus was a pioneer in social entrepreneurship, combining commercial success with political and social advocacy all aimed at enhancing the well-being of the aging. Having passed away when AARP's membership was barely one million, she might be amazed at the size and influence her creation had achieved. But she would recognize the hybrid nature of the organization, still unusual in its scale and scope, combining a vast and profitable business enterprise with the political and social mission of improving the lives of older Americans, based on her slogan, "what we do, we do for all."[95]

The chapters that follow will explore, more in depth, the growing membership base and chapter activities; political activities and influence; and the relationship among the business, service, charitable, and advocacy aspects of AARP.

CHAPTER THREE

AARP and Its Members: Maintaining America's Largest Interest Group

On August 29, 2005, Hurricane Katrina slammed into the Gulf Coast east of New Orleans, devastating the coastal area from southeast Louisiana to the Florida panhandle. New Orleanians emerged from their homes after the storm passed, finding minimal damage to the city. "We dodged a bullet," neighbors told each other with great relief. Several hours later, however, levees protecting the city and holding back the storm surge breached in several places, and the water rushed in, flooding 80 percent of the city, which sat in fetid water for weeks before it could be pumped out. Most of the city's housing stock was damaged or destroyed, their neighborhoods laid to waste. One of the hardest hit neighborhoods was Hollygrove. It was here, in Hollygrove, that AARP's Livable Communities program sprang into action.

The Hollygrove Livable Communities Project represents one aspect of AARP's membership service and community involvement, and it is highly acclaimed. Other aspects of AARP's membership growth and engagement are more controversial, especially when they involve politics and product promotion. This chapter examines the membership growth that made AARP famous, the wide array of selective membership benefits that led to that growth, the mobilization and representation of its members and of older Americans in general, and the organization's reach into states and communities nationwide.

The Hollygrove Livable Communities Project

Hollygrove is a working-class neighborhood at the western edge of New Orleans. Ninety-five percent of its 7,000 pre-Katrina residents were African

American, and 15 percent were over the age of 65. One of the neighborhood anchors was the two-story senior center, built in the 1920s, that provided programs and activities for older residents of Hollygrove and the surrounding area. New Orleans is a musical city, and Hollygrove boasts such famous natives as rhythm-and-blues singer Johnny Adams and multiplatinum rapper Lil Wayne. Even before the storm, however, the once-vibrant area had deteriorated with the loss of high-wage industrial jobs, white flight to the suburbs and subsequent defunding of public schools, and rising rates of violent crime related to the drug trade. Nevertheless, residents retained a strong sense of connection to home and neighborhood, anchored by networks of family and friends.[1]

Post-Katrina flood waters filled virtually all of Hollygrove's structures with several feet of water; furniture, appliances, all of people's worldly possessions floated from room to room and settled in a muddy, ruined mess. Many residents had tried to ride out the storm; the city's lower-income and older residents often lacked the mobility and resources to evacuate. Those who survived swam to safety or were rescued by boat or helicopter. On their return, neighborhood residents were determined to restore their lives and homes. Their efforts were well underway, but challenges were great and funding was short when AARP launched the Hollygrove Livable Communities Project there in 2007, two years after the storm.

AARP Louisiana started the Hollygrove Livable Communities Project as part of the national organization's drive to promote age-friendliness at the local level. For the last few decades, AARP had gradually increased its presence in the states and localities, focusing on people in their communities.[2] The goal of AARP Livable Communities is to increase community safety and security, walkability and public transportation, nearby stores and services, affordable housing, and other age-friendly features, enabling older people to "age in place" while raising AARP's profile. They also facilitate cross-partisan and intergenerational coalition building, since these are features that increase livability for residents of all ages.[3] Nowhere was the need for livability greater than in the ghostly landscape of post-Katrina New Orleans.

AARP brought resources, organization, fund-raising expertise, and vision to enhance and accelerate the neighborhood's development, according to leaders of the rebuilding effort. Hollygrove-based community development organization Trinity Christian Community (TCC) had been working at the forefront of that effort, along with the Carrollton-Hollygrove Community Development Corporation (CHCDC), which TCC helped to launch. Together with a coalition of groups, and volunteers recruited through AmeriCorps, TCC and CHCDC helped residents rebuild their homes, revitalize the neighborhood, and push back against the drug trade and crime that was beginning to encroach once again.[4] Leaders of both the TCC and the CHCDC were effusive in their praise of AARP. "They made a huge difference," said Paul Baricos, CHCDC's founder.[5] "They knocked ten years off the work cycle," said then–executive director of TCC Kevin Brown.[6]

Once AARP decided to get involved in 2007, then-Louisiana State Director Nancy McPherson (now California's state director) sought a neighborhood that could most use AARP's help "to add value to what was already going on . . . AARP wants to help places build their own capacities by strengthening what is already there," she said.[7] With a large number of older residents who were among the first to return to Hollygrove after the flood, and with struggling volunteer efforts well underway, Hollygrove fit the bill. "We had to sell them on our neighborhood," said TCC's Brown.[8] "They chose us," said CHCDC's Baricos.[9] "We were boots on the ground getting the job done," added Brown; "Nancy [McPherson] came in with a vision for the future."[10] That future took the community beyond hammer-and-nails rebuilding, to making the area safer and more sustainable for aging in place.

Important to AARP's intervention was helping residents to become their own advocates, identify their own goals, and work together to accomplish them. AARP established its first Livable Communities Academy in Hollygrove, partnering with Louisiana State University for an eight-week intensive course completed by 27 residents. "It made a big difference," said a 55-year-old long-time Hollygrove resident. "A lot of New Orleans neighborhoods are deadlocked by warring factions. The academy taught us how to work together. It gave us a base to build on."[11]

Residents working with the Livable Communities Project identified four key issue areas—transportation and mobility, health and caregiving, economic development, and public safety—and formed teams to establish plans and activities to address each area. Academy graduates worked with TCC, CHCDC, and other local groups to carry out their plans. Their accomplishments included an all-ages walking group, the Soul Steppers, for maintaining health, friendships, and safety in numbers; a new shelter at the bus stop; a directory of local businesses; green spaces and sidewalks; placement of crime cameras; the closure of a neighborhood bar that had become a dangerous hangout; and the Hollygrove Market and Farm, a community garden that now provides fresh produce for customers across the city. Most impressive to many residents, especially the youth, Kevin Brown said, was the visit from famous sportscaster James Brown, an AARP

Community Ambassador. This was no quick in-and-out for a photo opportunity, Kevin Brown noted; James Brown spent significant time in the neighborhood talking with residents about their postdisaster recovery.[12] For many older residents, the project's shining accomplishment, after much organized pressure on public officials, was the opening in 2015 of the Carrollton Hollygrove Senior Center, a $3.4 million state-of-the-art multipurpose facility, on the site of the old senior center that had long served as a center of community life.[13]

Five years after Katrina, Hollygrove's population was up to two-thirds of the pre-Katrina count, with an even higher proportion of residents over age 65 than before (16 percent), while the proportion of city residents aged 65 and over had dropped slightly.[14] AARP opened its first Community Resource Center in Hollygrove, with two paid staff and AARP member volunteers offering such standard AARP services as driver safety classes and income tax aid. Thanks to AARP, Brown and Baricos both enthused, Hollygrove residents not only rebuilt their homes; their neighborhood became a model of recovery and revitalization, shaking off a reputation for crime and decay, organizing and energizing its residents, and coming back even better than before.[15]

The best leaders are nearly invisible, leading community members to feel they did everything themselves, noted TCC's Brown, invoking Chinese philosopher Lao Tzu. That, he said, was the nature of AARP's involvement in Hollygrove.[16] It also embodies Ethel Andrus' emphasis on self-help and service to others.

AARP had been planning to hold its annual megaconference, "Life@50+," in New Orleans in 2005, but had to cancel in the wake of Katrina. Seven years later, in 2012, 20,000 people descended on the city for three days of "voluntourism," adding a public service component to Life@50+'s mix of information, exposition, and entertainment—all aspects of AARP's membership recruitment, retention, and service.[17]

Growing and Maintaining a Membership of Tens of Millions

The nation's 50+ population is an extremely diverse lot, socially, culturally, economically, even generationally. How can one organization unite some 38 million people with so many different points of view? The short answer, given by AARP itself and based on their member surveys, is that people join for the products and discounts, and renew for the advocacy and social missions, as well as the information and publications.[18] Organization leaders also cite their political advocacy as a draw for many members, but that advocacy has long been a double-edged sword for

AARP's relationship with its members. Such a large and diverse membership is unlikely to unite around any clear political position, while overly cautious stances can disappoint members hoping for strong advocacy. And so it is the membership benefits, coupled with AARP's marketing expertise—including those dreaded invitation letters that seem to find every 50-year-old in the country—that keep them coming, and staying, in the tens of millions.

It is not unusual, of course, for membership organizations to offer incentives for people to join—calendars, t-shirts, coffee mugs, keychains—and even to provide "gifts" like address labels and note cards to entice people to sign up or send donations. But AARP's wide array of membership incentives is both famous and long-lived. It started with founder Ethel Percy Andrus' determination to fulfill a need that the free market failed to provide: namely, health insurance for older Americans. Leonard Davis recognized the profit-making potential for Colonial Penn and provided the innovative mass marketing. Andrus is still revered and frequently quoted at AARP, while Davis remains invisible there since the scandal of the 1970s, but their shared legacy endures in AARP's expansive member services and product discounts.

Membership incentives help political organizations avoid the "free-rider problem": people who benefit from a group's policy achievements without sacrificing their own time and resources to participate. A rational individual, Mancur Olson suggested, has no incentive to participate if he or she can receive the benefits of collective action without paying the costs. Thus, interest group exchange theorists emphasize the importance of group leadership offering selective incentives, available only to group members, in order to gain members and membership support.[19] They identify three types of membership incentives: material incentives, or tangible benefits like product discounts; solidary incentives, or opportunities for socializing with like-minded people; and purposive incentives, or the satisfaction of supporting a good cause. AARP offers all three, though it is the wide array of selective material benefits that sets it apart from other groups and makes it the largest membership group on the U.S. political scene.

Interest group scholars offer numerous explanations for the origin and maintenance of political organizations, not all of which involve selective incentives for individual members. Some groups, like trade and professional associations and labor unions, may urge or even require membership for employment, licensing, or professional credibility. Many groups are not composed of individual members but rather institutional members such as firms or nonprofits. Many groups are started and maintained through funding by patrons—foundations, corporations, government agencies, or wealthy individuals—and many of those are composed only of staff, with virtually no membership. Many groups do offer selective incentives and have memberships numbering in the thousands or even millions. But none among the thousands of organizations that work to influence U.S. public policy match AARP's assortment of material benefits drawing in members by the tens of millions.[20]

"It Pays for Itself": Insurance, Discounts, and Other Material Incentives

Members of AARP, for annual dues of $16 per person or per couple, gain access to a variety of material benefits. Those listed here are representative of the whole array, but a comprehensive list would both consume too much space and be subject to change over time. A comprehensive and current list of benefits is available on AARP's website.[21]

The health insurance products are the best known and most lucrative for AARP. Of course, older Americans no longer have to turn to AARP in order to obtain health insurance. After Ethel Andrus and Leonard Davis took the initiative, other companies finally understood that seniors comprise a profitable insurance market. Now the market is healthy and the competition fierce. But about seven million people have AARP-branded health insurance, mostly Medicare Supplement (Medigap) and/or Medicare Part D (prescription drug) plans, and Medicare Advantage plans are also available.[22] All three are underwritten by UnitedHealthcare, the country's largest health insurer. AARP is happy to sell the plans to anyone—members and nonmembers alike.

Members can receive discounts on a variety of other health care and health insurance products offered by different companies, including vision and dental care, hearing aids, prescription drugs, long-term care, and even pet health insurance. Discounts on life, property, vehicle, and small business insurance plans are also available. Financial services include savings and investment plans, identity theft protection, and a cash-back credit card.

Travel benefits include discounts on airfare; train fare; hotels; auto rentals; cruises, tours and vacation planning; and lodging at national and state parks. Product and retail discounts include auto parts and repair as well as roadside assistance plans, selected grocery and drug stores, gifts and apparel, tickets and entertainment, home services, and several chain restaurants from fast food to higher-end chains. Discounted electronics, such as mobile phones, tablets, and wireless service plans, as well as electronic readers and e-books and audiobooks, are often geared toward older users, with features such as easily readable displays, simplified operations, and built-in tech support.

AARP's for-profit subsidiary, AARP Services, Inc., or ASI, manages the business end and the royalties collected for endorsing products. The companies that provide the discounts to AARP members benefit from both the large numbers of customers who are AARP members and from the cachet derived from AARP's endorsement, which serves much like the "Good Housekeeping Seal of Approval" for consumers.[23] In turn, the profits AARP earns from sales and royalties are plowed back into the nonprofit divisions—AARP's membership services and advocacy, and the charitable activities of the AARP Foundation—and help keep membership dues low. In addition, the huge potential customer base that comes with AARP's endorsements encourages producers to provide better, more useful products for consumers over 50.[24]

How valuable are all these products and discounts to AARP members? An informal canvassing of personal acquaintances in AARP reveals mixed reactions. "The discounts do me no good; I don't eat at chain restaurants," says one. "I saved a ton of money on my Retin-A prescription that insurance doesn't cover," said another; "already it's paid for itself several times over." Examples of both types abound. Clearly there is much from which to pick and choose, and some individuals find more to choose from than others.

A more comprehensive investigation, in the mid-1990s, into the value of AARP-sponsored and endorsed products, in particular the insurance and financial products, found them to be generally good deals. "Overall," Charles R. Morris concluded, "the member offerings are a respectable show and represent dramatic progress from the disgraceful profit-mongering of AARP's first two decades"—that is, the era when Leonard Davis largely controlled AARP to the benefit of Colonial Penn.[25] A more recent analysis of insurance and financial products in 2008 found some AARP-sponsored products to be among the lowest-cost on the market, while others were no better than average in price or value.[26] Different customers have different needs, making across-the-board comparisons difficult. But both studies concluded that in general, older, less healthy, and less wealthy customers are especially likely to find better deals through AARP than on the open market, for example, because of lower initial investment requirements for mutual funds or greater ease for higher-risk applicants to obtain life insurance. Further, a CBS Moneywatch four-part series in 2009 gave positive reviews to AARP's mutual funds, life insurance and annuities, and auto, property, and health insurance.[27] Senior discounts, meanwhile, are widely available outside of AARP, though mostly at ages considerably over 50. In this sense, it is the younger members who are more likely to get discounts not otherwise available. "We exercise very stringent quality control on products for which we receive royalties," said CEO Jo Ann Jenkins. They are "not necessarily the cheapest, but the best."[28]

Movies for Grownups, launched in 2001, reflects the group's efforts to encourage Hollywood to make more movies appealing to an older demographic, after AARP focus groups demonstrated frustration that so many movies are made for teenage boys. Film reviews and recommendations, special previews, and the lavish annual Movies for Grownups Awards ceremony not only shift the film industry's attention toward viewers over 50, but also provide more jobs for older actors, writers, and others involved in film production.[29]

AARP branding depends on trust, and a series of Harris Polls conducted between 2007 and 2012 found AARP to be consistently among the most trusted large organizations "inside the Beltway" of Washington, D.C.[30]

Publications, Information and Services: More Material Incentives

AARP's publications, information, and services also serve as material incentives. *AARP The Magazine* has by far the largest circulation of any magazine—nearly 24 million—exceeding the combined circulation of the next three largest (*Costco Connection, Better Homes and Gardens*, and *Reader's Digest*).[31] *Modern Maturity*, its predecessor launched by Ethel Andrus and Leonard Davis, was the nation's largest-circulation magazine by the late 1980s, and AARP's magazine has topped the list ever since. The bimonthly magazine, free with the $16 AARP membership and thus considerably less expensive than the average popular magazine, is a big membership draw, both in print and online.[32] Its pages are full of articles and snippets of advice, practical information, entertainment and celebrity news, leisure and travel tips, and more. With paid advertising as well as ads for AARP's sponsored products, it is also a major revenue source; in fact Andrus and Davis used the first issue to promote the health insurance policies that Davis sold through Colonial Penn.[33]

The aging of the baby boom presented growth opportunity, and to attract them, AARP added a second magazine in 2000, *My Generation*, for members born between 1946 and 1964. *My Generation* aimed to replace *Modern Maturity*'s rather frumpy and old-fashioned reputation with something young and hip, but it didn't take; it confused both members and advertisers. AARP's member survey found that members identified more with the AARP brand than with either magazine title, and so it combined both magazines into one and changed the name to *AARP The Magazine* in 2002.[34] It is published in three editions, one for members in their 50s, one for those in their 60s, and one for those aged 70 and over. In a recent issue (June/July 2015), the younger-targeted editions include tips on how to "nail a splashy cannonball," play injury-free beach volleyball, and make "fireworks" for the grandkids with a bottle of soda and a sleeve of Mentos; the older edition substitutes an article exposing myths about hearing loss. Advertisements in the younger edition lean more toward fashion and travel; those in the 70+ edition focus more on home safety features like stairlifts, grab bars, and medical alert systems. But the differences are few; the three editions are mostly the same. A Spanish-language magazine, *AARP VIVA Su Segunda Juventud*, launched in 2010, is no longer in print, but the website is available in Spanish.

In addition to the magazine, members also receive the *AARP Bulletin* ten times a year, a tabloid-sized newsletter more geared toward serious news and political information, along with still more tips on everything from personal finances to personal relationships. Like *Modern Maturity*, the *Bulletin* dates back to AARP's earliest years.

Members have access to books and pamphlets, on-site and online courses, workshops, webinars, and other resources for learning about everything from personal finances and budgeting to recipes and dating. Modern technology, auto purchasing and maintenance, home maintenance and adaptation for independent living, avoiding fraud and scams, seeking work and preparing for job interviews, maintaining physical health as well as memory and brain health, retirement planning, and the long-popular driver safety courses taken by half a million people every year: all these and more are topics of available information. Members also use print and online resources to navigate complex government programs and benefits: when and how to sign up for Medicare, how to weigh the options regarding when to file for Social Security, how to find available programs and their eligibility requirements, and how to avoid the pitfalls. While the nature and value of information has changed with the advent of the Internet—anyone now can look up anything—the print and online publications offer guidelines and helpful hints that are not necessarily actively sought, but that are useful to know. Many materials are accessible to anyone; others require AARP membership. Web resources and broadcast programming are offered in Spanish as well.

Life Reimagined, launched in 2013, provided an interactive website, supplemented with some offline seminars and print materials, through which members could explore options for improving and expanding their personal well-being, jobs, and relationships. Life Reimagined accords with trends toward greater longevity, an evolving and less stable job market, and postretirement work for reasons of financial security as well as self-actualization—the desire to remain active and perhaps even change course and set new goals. Users could follow customizable roadmaps, guided by questionnaires and activities helping them to reflect broadly on their goals and dreams, or more specifically on employment options, health and wellness, dating and relationships, and other areas in which they might wish to make changes in their lives. Life Reimagined had over a million users within months, but was discontinued in 2017 for review and possible reconstruction—an example of AARP's continuous adjustments to its array of products and services in an effort to maximize its appeal to members and potential members. Future generations of older Americans who have used computers all their lives will be more likely to embrace digital technology for exploring ways of changing or enhancing their own lives.

The AARP Foundation, AARP's charitable affiliate, offers programs and services targeting lower-income people over 50, whether or not they are AARP members, including free tax preparation, budget and financial advice, employment training and support, a home-foreclosure avoidance program, legal advocacy against discrimination and fraud, and raising awareness and funds to fight food insecurity among older adults.

One may ask: Is there any aspect of life after 50 that AARP does *not* address? Protesters with The Final Exit Network at AARP's 2014 and 2015 national conventions contended that AARP does not sufficiently address end-of-life issues such as assisted suicide, charging that AARP had refused to rent the group exhibitor space. AARP had indeed refused, stating that "we are unable to approve right-to-die societies and other like organizations as exhibitors" until it had delineated clear guidelines on those issues.[35] One article speculated that Final Exit's message did not fit the upbeat, fun-filled spirit of AARP's conferences;[36] another editorial praised AARP for barring exhibits by an organization that teaches people how to kill themselves.[37] But the search engine on AARP's own website does retrieve articles discussing end-of-life issues such as advanced directives, euthanasia, and assisted suicide.

Community, Entertainment, Voluntarism, Advocacy: Solidary and Purposive Incentives

Opportunities for social and civic engagement can entice people to join and participate in membership associations, and AARP does offer them. Membership surveys show that the material incentives are the biggest draw in recruiting new members to AARP. But the social change mission and political advocacy also help attract and, even more, retain members.[38] AARP has a network of separately incorporated local chapters where members gather mostly to socialize, and state offices with paid staff who work with volunteers in political advocacy and community service. Fewer than 5 percent of AARP members are chapter members, and about 10 percent tend to be active volunteers with the association—depending on how "volunteers" are defined. Politically, about five million members participate sporadically in contacting elected officials; about 17,000 are "active volunteers who suit up and visit the legislatures" on a regular basis.[39] Each single percentage of AARP's membership adds up to nearly 400,000 members; a small percentage of volunteers easily adds up to millions.

AARP's expansion of state and local activity has evolved over its five decades of existence. Within a decade of its 1958 founding, under the leadership of Executive Director Bernard Nash, it had over a million members and a staff of over five hundred, and had established adult education and driver improvement programs in some localities. It consulted with church programs serving the elderly, and sponsored group tours in the United States and abroad—important to Ethel Andrus's desire to promote social bonding and expanding horizons well into old age. By the mid-1980s, AARP had some 5,000 chapters and had begun consciously expanding its presence at the state and local levels.[40] The number of local chapters dwindled in the twenty-first century as widespread Internet usage and social media facilitated virtual interaction without the need to meet face-to-face; today's local chapters number around 1,300. But the state field offices now cover all 50 states plus Washington, D.C., Puerto Rico, and the Virgin Islands. They mobilize volunteers in a variety of activities, from lobbying state government officials to working in local service projects. The AARP Foundation Tax-Aide, established in 1968, is one of the largest service projects; 35,000 volunteers in over five thousand locations help more than two and a half million taxpayers with their tax returns annually. Two thousand volunteers with the Experience Corps tutor 35,000 elementary school students in literacy. Volunteers also help staff AARP Community Resource Centers and information centers in a growing number of cities around the country.

National conventions and Block Parties provide another outlet for socializing. The organization has held national conferences almost from the beginning—since 1961—but initially they were more for business purposes: delegate meetings to elect leaders and set policy. Over the years, as increasing numbers of nondelegate members showed up, the conventions became extravaganzas of entertainment and adventure. AARP's annual Life@50+ National Event and Expo featured forums, panels, and exhibits with information on political and social issues and advocacy, as well as information on products and services available through AARP and numerous corporate sponsors.

The Life@50+ megaconferences began in 2001, in part to attract more members from the aging baby boom generation. "The organizers of

AARP's annual 'Life@50+' conferences realize that the best route to boomers' wallets, hearts, and minds is through the music and popular culture of their youth," notes Frederick Lynch in *One Nation under AARP*, which focuses on the boomers as they reach AARP age.[41] For 15 years, through 2015, the Life@50+ conferences were huge celebrity-studded events in major cities throughout the country, drawing thousands out for a good time. Attendees heard political and social commentary from the likes of Dan Rather, Anita Hill, Erica Jong, and Maya Angelou; got health and beauty tips from stars such as Martina Navratilova and Raquel Welch; rocked out to performers like Elton John, José Feliciano, Paul Simon, and Chaka Khan. Attendance peaked at 27,400 in 2008, the year of AARP's fiftieth anniversary celebration, in Washington, D.C. While drawing only a tiny fraction of AARP's membership, the conferences were huge enough to delight host cities' tourism and business communities. In the aftermath of the Great Recession of 2008, travel became less affordable for many people. In addition, the Internet enabled people to experience much of what was offered—performances, speeches, panels, and presentations by celebrities and subject-matter experts—without having to be physically present. The final Life@50+ conference, in Miami in 2015, drew about 15,000 attendees.[42]

AARP Block Parties—local and regional events—replaced the national conferences beginning in 2016. "We can engage with more people," said Jason Weinstein, vice president of event strategy and services, "if we take our events to other people's events."[43] And so AARP sets up exhibits and activities at festivals and other large gatherings around the country—Odunde Festival in Philadelphia, Essence Fest in New Orleans, the National Book Festival in Washington, D.C., and the Sturgis Motorcycle Rally in South Dakota, to name a few—multigenerational events with large numbers of people over 50. At Fiesta San Antonio, members led Tejano dancing; at the Jacksonville Jazz Festival, there was line dancing and karaoke. Often there are celebrity meet-and-greets with speakers and performers from the events. "Authenticity," Weinstein emphasized; "we show up with something really authentic"—and better attention-grabbers for AARP than handing out pamphlets and flyers.[44]

Compared with the national conferences, the Block Parties are "bite-sized rather than a full meal," allowing AARP to engage more efficiently with over 100,000 members and prospective members around the country. Further, the events lend themselves to multigenerational engagement, highlighting AARP's intergenerational appeal—for example, entertaining children with 3-D printers and virtual reality headsets while chatting with their parents and grandparents about the benefits of joining AARP.[45]

In sum, the social connections and the support for AARP's political and social mission play a part in recruiting members, and even more in retaining members. But the major draw is still the impressive array of selective material benefits—originating with the health insurance coverage that had largely been denied to older Americans until AARP made it accessible—that is unique to AARP in its scope and variety.

Surges and Plateaus in Membership Growth

AARP's selective incentives largely explain its prodigious growth. The products and discounts attract members, and the wealth of information on politics and lifestyle issues, in print and online, does much to retain them. This is what organization leaders have concluded based on years of survey and focus-group research on members and prospective members. But selective membership benefits do not tell the whole story; in particular, they do not explain the surges and plateaus and, recently, even slight dips in membership over time. Nor do they explain why AARP's membership as a percentage of eligible persons peaked in the late 1980s and early 1990s at slightly over half of the age-eligible population, and then declined to about one-third of those eligible in 2014, as shown in Table 3.1.[46] Still, AARP remains far and away the largest of the several organizations representing older Americans and, aside from the Catholic Church and the American Automobile Association, the largest membership organization of any kind.[47]

Table 3.1 AARP Membership Size and Percentage of the Age-Eligible Population, 1959–2016

Year	Number in Thousands (Estimated)	% of Age-Eligible Population	Year	Number in Thousands (Estimated)	% of Age-Eligible Population
1959	5	<1	1988	29,700	47.4
1960	30	<1	1989	32,160	51.0
1961	38	<1	1990	33,025	51.2
1962	43	<1	1991	33,302	51.7
1963	49	<1	1992	33,756	51.7
1964	74	<1	1993	33,177	50.2
1965	73	<1	1994	32,176	47.8
1966	1,000	2.8	1995	33,086	48.4

(Continued)

Table 3.1 Continued

Year	Number in Thousands (Estimated)	% of Age-Eligible Population	Year	Number in Thousands (Estimated)	% of Age-Eligible Population
1967	1,100	3.0	1996	32,578	47.1
1968	1,190	3.2	1997	32,445	45.6
1969	1,370	3.6	1998	32,698	45.0
1970	1,630	4.2	1999	33,249	44.7
1971	2,210	5.6	2000	34,456	44.8
1972	3,130	7.8	2001	35,231	44.6
1973	4,500	10.1	2002	34,793	43.0
1974	5,810	13.9	2003	35,664	43.1
1975	7,100	16.6	2004	35,404	41.7
1976	8,200	18.8	2005	36,308	41.7
1977	9,450	21.2	2006	37,717	42.2
1978	10,470	23.0	2007	39,402	43.0
1979	11,300	24.3	2008	40,092	42.7
1980	11,700	24.6	2009	37,730	39.3
1981	12,970	27.0	2010	36,921	37.3
1982	14,200	29.1	2011	37,024	36.3
1983	15,750	26.0	2012	37,610	36.0
1984	18,070	29.5	2013	37,810	35.5
1985	20,880	34.0	2014	36,918	33.9
1986	24,300	39.3	2015	37,689	34.0
1987	28,000	45.0	2016	38,200	33.8

Notes: AARP's age eligibility was lowered from 55 to 50 in 1984. Membership numbers do not include the National Retired Teachers Association (NRTA), for which AARP does not have complete data; with NRTA, total membership in 1960 was about 130,000; in 1970, 1.9 million; in 1975, 7.5 million; thereafter a negligible difference, and the two merged officially in 1982. 2016 membership and population estimates are preliminary.

Sources: For membership numbers, including NRTA estimates, AARP Office of Media Relations. For population data, 1959–1979, U.S. Census Bureau, "Population Estimates: National Estimates by Age, Sex, Race: 1900–1979" (PE-11), www.census.gov/popest/data/national/asrh/pre-1980/PE-11.html; for 1980–2011, U.S. Census Bureau, U.S. Statistical Abstracts, www.census.gov/library/publications/time-series/statistical_abstracts.html; for 2012–2016, U.S. Census Bureau, American Fact Finder, factfinder.census.gov/faces/nav/jsf/pages/index.xhtml.

Marketing, of course, is key; effective marketing, arguably, is every bit as important as the value of what is being sold, whether it is toothpaste, a hit movie, a candidate for elective office, or an organization membership. Unlocking the secrets of successful marketing is extremely difficult, as every advertising executive and every campaign consultant knows. But name recognition, or brand familiarity, does encourage sales.[48] The AARP name is nearly universally recognized; surveys show that 98 percent of Americans know the brand.[49] It is often the subject of cartoons and comedians' gentle ribbing, often in the news when aging-related policies are debated, often in television commercials and in people's magazine racks or coffee tables, in social media, and in the millions of e-mails and direct-mail ads that find their way into the mailboxes of Americans 50 and over.

Receiving the invitation to join AARP—that letter that seems to find everyone on the verge of turning 50—has become a universal rite of passage and source of humor. The jokes incorporate all the stereotypes of aging that AARP works to confront and challenge.[50] But they demonstrate widespread familiarity with the brand; AARP has permeated the national consciousness.

How does AARP find all the 50-year-olds? "It's no big secret; there is no magic," said Lynn Mento, the senior vice president for membership and member engagement for several years until 2015.[51] "We've mapped every fifty-plus household in America," said Cheryl Matheis, who was an executive at AARP for nearly three decades.[52] The organization buys lists of people by age from various companies that service direct marketers; the lists come from multiple data sources including drivers' registrations, voter registration lists, credit card data, product warranties, and sweepstakes forms. Mento adds that AARP works hard to cross-check and corroborate the age information in the lists it acquires, not only to find all the 50-year-olds but also to make sure no one receives the letter by mistake; "we don't want to age them prematurely."[53] It is not magic, but it is, Morris notes, "an awesome, and expensive, operation that few other organizations could duplicate."[54]

Leonard Davis had been a pioneer in the use of commercialized direct mail, so the organization's direct-mail marketing dates back to the introduction of health insurance for members of the National Retired Teachers Association, expanding to the general public aged 55 years and over when AARP was founded in 1958. From there it grew exponentially. By the time Medicare began covering all Americans aged 65 and over in 1965, AARP had introduced more benefits that kept people enrolling, including life insurance, low-cost European tours, and discount pharmaceuticals and hearing aids. Benefits continued to expand and so did the membership.

By 1970, AARP had a membership of over a million and a half—4.3 percent of age-eligible Americans—and a staff of several hundred. Half a decade later the membership exceeded seven million. At the end of the decade, in 1980, fully a quarter of Americans 55 and over—11,700,000—belonged to AARP. Thus, the association had grown by an average of a million members a year throughout the 1970s, even as the quality of Colonial Penn's AARP-branded products was being questioned. When Ethel Andrus and Leonard Davis first offered to sell health insurance to older Americans through AARP, they were the only game in town. But Davis's company, Colonial Penn, did not remain competitive after Andrus died in 1967. By the mid-1970s, investigations by a U.S. Senate subcommittee, by *Money* magazine, and by the California insurance commission showed AARP's health and life insurance customers were getting relatively bad deals. With poor premium-to-benefit ratios, the policies paid out relatively little in benefits for what they cost. Leonard Davis's control over the organization had proved enormously profitable for him at the expense of members who purchased AARP insurance. The *60 Minutes* exposé in 1978 brought the scandal to a wider public.[55]

Once past the controversy, AARP had something of a renaissance. Although Executive Director Cyril Brickfield had been a member of Leonard Davis's inner circle—serving as AARP's executive director in the late 1960s, then as the association's legislative counsel from 1970 to 1977, then again as executive director from 1977 to 1987—he was determined to revive AARP's reputation and oversee its continued expansion, and he succeeded. Davis "didn't walk, he was shoved—and by his very own lawyers, acting with Cy Brickfield."[56] Prudential replaced Colonial Penn as AARP's health insurance provider in 1981. As some insurance policy holders remained with Colonial Penn, AARP needed a quick infusion of cash to get back on sound financial footing. In addition to shoring up the quality of the association's sponsored products and building up the suite of membership benefits, the group lowered the member eligibility age from 55 to 50 and stepped up its direct-mail recruitment and advertising.[57] Membership continued to expand, both in sheer numbers and in the proportion of the eligible population that joined. The number of members nearly tripled during the 1980s, to 33 million. One quarter of the eligible population had signed on by 1980; over half of the 50+ population belonged to AARP by the end of the decade.

Internal dynamics alone do not explain AARP's exceptional growth. The political climate of the 1970s and 1980s encouraged older people's political mobilization, as they first enjoyed expanded government benefits, and then saw those benefits threatened.[58] In addition, that period witnessed an extraordinary proliferation of political organizations headquartered in Washington, in part due to the newly widespread availability of computerized direct mail. AARP had a jump on most others in the use of direct-mail marketing, thanks to Leonard Davis's salesmanship in the organization's early years.[59]

A series of policies targeting old-age poverty and age discrimination between World War II and the late 1970s—in particular, the creation and expansion of Social Security, including cost-of-living adjustments, and the creation of Medicare and Medicaid—defined older Americans as a beneficiary group; their chronological age now had particular political relevance.[60] Sixty-five, as the age of eligibility for Medicare and full Social Security benefits, had become the clearest dividing line between "old" and "not old." But age is more fluid than that, and many people in late middle age find themselves contemplating retirement and other issues that become increasingly salient with advancing age. So Americans 50 years of age and over became a community—a highly diverse and contentious community, but with a common stake in government.

Older people now were more secure, but that enhanced security came at a cost that opponents said was too high. By the late 1970s, scholars, journalists, and other political observers were drawing attention to the "graying of the federal budget," the large and growing proportion of federal dollars being spent on old-age benefits,[61] and were characterizing older people as a powerful special interest group that kept their benefits "off limits to federal budget cutters."[62] Soon enough, the sympathy for seniors that had motivated public opinion and policy prior to 1980 showed signs of developing into resentment toward perceived affluence and privilege. "Americans are living longer and enjoying it more—but who will foot the bill?" asks a 1988 *Time* cover story, "Grays on the Go."[63] "Greedy geezers," snarled the cover of the *New Republic* in the same year.[64] "The tyranny of America's old" is "forcing the nation to short change the young," warned *Fortune* magazine in 1992.[65] Stagflation in the 1970s, budget-cutting and zero-sum politics in the 1980s pitting groups against each other, population aging, and projected shortfalls in the Social Security trust fund all contributed to images of older people as disproportionately wealthy and politically powerful, draining resources from the young.[66] President Ronald Reagan's proposed cuts to Social Security benefits, early in his first term in 1981, ultimately did not pass, but they signaled a new era of competition and contention over aging policy. These serious threats to old-age benefits emerged as AARP was severing ties with Leonard Davis and Colonial Penn, followed by a renewed surge in membership and in Washington respectability.[67]

These events occurred in the midst of the post-1960s "advocacy explosion" in Washington, D.C.[68] which enhanced AARP's ability to attract members while also increasing the number of interest groups competing for older people's support. Americans have long had a fondness for joining associations, as Alexis de Tocqueville famously observed during his visit in the early nineteenth century.[69] Tocqueville's admiration for the open and democratic environment so conducive to forming associations echoed the views of James Madison, the primary author of the U.S. Constitution. Multiple diverse, competing, and overlapping interest groups ensure myriad influences on policy, guarding against majority tyranny and despotism while enhancing the quality of democracy.[70] A major surge in interest-group proliferation followed the social movements of the 1960s; movements morphed into organizations, stimulating further organization of competing interests. Interest group organization and counter-organization was augmented by increased funding opportunities from patrons—including foundations, wealthy donors, and government itself—as well as by technological advancements in the use of computers to target masses of potential supporters.[71]

In many ways these developments greatly improved the ability of a wider variety of interests to influence public policy. But according to Robert Putnam in his book *Bowling Alone*, they also led to individual isolation, and less personal interaction at the community level. The result, he said, was a weakened civil society, characterized by the decline of parent–teacher organizations, fraternal groups, service clubs, bowling leagues, and other groups in which people gathered on a regular basis.[72] They were replaced by national-level mass-membership organizations, headquartered in Washington, which Putnam labeled tertiary organizations to distinguish them from the more locally-oriented secondary organizations. AARP, he said, is a "dramatic example" of tertiary organization, in which, "for the vast majority of their members, the only act of membership consists in writing a check for dues or perhaps occasionally reading a newsletter. Few ever attend any meetings of such organizations," so that their "ties, in short, are to common symbols, common leaders, and perhaps common ideals, but not to one another."[73]

Horace Deets, who rose from within to become executive director in 1987, took exception to the characterization of AARP as a tertiary organization.[74] True, the membership is far-flung. But, Deets emphasized in an interview, one of AARP's pursuits is to help members find ways to volunteer and remain active in their communities: "We find that there's a tremendous willingness on the part of our members to get involved when they find something they they're interested in."[75] Meanwhile, AARP also lobbies government for policies to improve the lives of people who are 50+, engages in charitable activities through the AARP Foundation, and earns enough money from royalties, advertising revenue, investments, and dues, that it need not depend on outside grants. AARP's multidimensionality does not mean that its members are uninvolved, Deets emphasized. Indeed, one of Ethel Andrus's primary goals was to assist older people in remaining active and reaching their full potential during their later working years and beyond retirement.

By the mid-1980s, beginning under Brickfield and continuing with Deets at the helm, AARP was taking further steps to extend its reach, especially to racial and ethnic minorities and to lower-income older people. In the face of challenges to the political status of older Americans, AARP moved to erase its image as a group for upper-crust "greedy geezers." Even as Social Security expansion and Medicare had increased the economic well-being of older people generally, many were still living near or below the poverty line. Particularly vulnerable are older women and members of minority groups, who are living alone, and who are very old. The association extended its lobbying efforts to issues of concern to lower-income older people, and announced the targeting of health care, women's interests, worker equity, and minority affairs as the four areas of immediate concern. AARP was not alone. Aging-based political organizations in general, like the National Council of Senior Citizens, the National Committee to Preserve Social Security and Medicare, and the Gray Panthers, worked to present a more inclusive, diverse, and multicultural public image, both to expand their membership appeal and to counter the image of older Americans as predominantly affluent, white, privileged, and powerful. For AARP in particular, it was a makeover of its previous image as a group catering largely to upper-middle-class professionals.[76]

Coalition building, both with other senior organizations and intergenerationally, is another strategy for both expanding the organization's reach and countering the selfish-special-interest image. Political coalitions, both ad hoc and formal, temporary and long-lived, are extremely common in the fragmented, group-oriented U.S. political system.[77] In 1978, AARP and 30 other senior advocacy and service organizations formed the Leadership Council of Aging Organizations (LCAO); by 2015, it had grown to over 70 organizations with AARP as the powerful anchor. Nearly a decade later, AARP was instrumental in the formation of Generations United (GU), a coalition of groups representing children and the elderly, for the purpose of supporting social welfare programs benefiting all ages and emphasizing mutual support across generations; today about

50 groups are GU members. Often dependent on working with other groups in the 1960s and early 1970s if it hoped to have any policy influence, by the 1980s AARP was itself highly sought after as a coalition partner, and it could afford to be selective. But confronted with the backlash against increased federal spending on aging-related programs, it emphasized organization alliances that would reduce the image of narrow self-interest and refute the greedy geezer stereotype.[78]

A third strategy for broadening its appeal in the 1980s, in addition to diversifying its outreach and building coalitions, was a growing emphasis on establishing a presence in states and communities. The effort accelerated in the late 1990s until there were offices in every state by the early 2000s, with paid staff helping to mobilize the grass roots in lobbying and volunteerism, and to exercise influence on state as well as national policy. Voter education programs, through mass mailings and publications, forums, and debates, also aimed to increase grassroots involvement. "So much of what is done that affects the audience we serve is either funded, regulated or delivered at the state level," Deets told the *New York Times*. "If you're going to be effective in serving your members' needs, you have to be a player at the state level."[79]

The decade of the 1980s, in sum, was a decade of exponential growth as well as permeation into the national consciousness. In 1980, one quarter of the eligible population (still 55 and over until 1984) belonged to AARP. From 1989 through 1993, over half of Americans aged 50 years and older belonged to AARP, peaking at 51.7 percent in 1991–1992 with over 33 million members. No other membership organization outside the Catholic Church approached the size of AARP.

Massive size also has its drawbacks for AARP as a political organization. In the late 1980s, AARP learned that lobbying on controversial issues can be dangerous for a group so enormous and politically diverse, even as the group's political clout was expanding. The association had lobbied hard for the Medicare Catastrophic Coverage Act, which became law in 1988. It was the largest expansion of Medicare since the program's inception, and it covered huge bills for major illnesses that were too costly to be covered under Medicare previously. Support for enhancing Medicare coverage seemed like a no-brainer for the elderly. But the additional coverage was to be paid for by beneficiaries themselves, through a surtax and Medicare premium increases. Although the costs would be borne mostly by higher-income seniors, older people across the income scale objected strenuously to being taxed for their benefits—so strenuously, that widespread protests led Congress to repeal the law less than a year after it was passed. Executive Director Deets estimated that 12,000–14,000 members resigned in protest—a tiny fraction of the 30 million membership, but enough to jolt the leadership into a period of political restraint and risk avoidance.[80]

Membership through the 1990s held steady at around 33 million, though it dipped to 45 percent of the 50+ population toward the end of that decade. AARP leaders were preparing for the mid-decade milestone that would present both a great opportunity and a great challenge: the fiftieth birthday of the leading edge of the baby boom.

AARP Pursues the Baby Boomers

Baby boomers are those 78 million Americans born between 1946 and 1964, into the post-World War II period of prosperity after the world warriors came home. They are often likened to a pig in a python, a big bulge moving gradually down the length of a snake after being swallowed, expanding the market for baby supplies, crowding into classrooms, overrunning college campuses and swelling the workforce, and ultimately overwhelming retirement and health care systems. They began turning 50 in 1996, began turning 65 in 2011, and were all AARP-aged by 2014. Thus AARP saw great potential for growth, while recognizing that this would be a generation difficult to lure into organization membership—and indeed it has been, as has the leading edge of Generation X right behind it.

Frederick Lynch examines the baby boom generation in his 2011 book, *One Nation under AARP: The Fight over Medicare, Social Security, and America's Future*.[81] The questions initially guiding his research concerned the boomers' aging and retirement. How would they fare, he wondered, given numerous demographic, economic, and political challenges? "The emerging central focus upon AARP in the book and its title" writes Lynch, "grew out of my realization, during the research process, that 'all roads led to AARP' . . . It is true, as I have often said, that 'Nobody knows boomers like AARP.'"[82] Through this knowledge, AARP leaders recognized that boomers could be a membership gold mine due to the cohort's sheer size, but also that they are hard to reel in as card-carrying members of AARP or any other group.

At first blush it might seem that boomers would be easy to organize for a cause. They were born into a relatively safe and prosperous era and raised on a healthy dose of optimism and we-can-change-the-world idealism. They witnessed, or participated in, social movements from civil rights to feminism to environmentalism to antiwar and antidraft protests. But the generation is extremely diverse and highly individualistic, often dubbed the "me generation." Social changes divided and polarized them;

growing up with television often isolated them from community involvement; crowded classrooms and a competitive workforce induced a rugged individualism and a self-serving quest for personal fulfillment. Coming of age during Vietnam and Watergate, many boomers became distrustful of institutions and disengaged from politics.[83] Michael Delli Carpini found the decline in political engagement since the 1960s—including lower voter turnout and campaign participation, less interest in politics, and declining trust in government—has affected the generations preceding and following the boomers as well.[84]

One of AARP's own reports on the baby boom generation, focusing on how to mobilize them as volunteers, also suggests that appealing to boomers' individualism and self-fulfillment is most effective. They are less likely than older cohorts to be driven by "a sense of duty, obligation, or religious commitment."[85] The report also emphasizes the diversity of persons in that generation, noting that effective appeals to boomer volunteerism "will be as diverse as the boomer cohort itself and the communities in which they reside."[86]

Regardless of how different or similar boomers are to other generations, at least one thing has been clear for some time: many in the boomer generation are financially ill-prepared for retirement. Their numbers jeopardize the future solvency of old-age entitlement programs.[87] Proponents of partially or even fully privatizing or dismantling those programs publicly highlight, or even exaggerate, the grim future of Social Security and Medicare, hoping to weaken public support. Meanwhile, declining availability of defined-benefit private pensions—guaranteeing retirement income for life—and their replacement with defined-contribution plans increases the risk of financial insecurity in old age.[88]

Some boomers are considerably more vulnerable than others. The array of programs ensuring a certain amount of income security and access to health care in old age and retirement does not reduce economic inequality among older Americans relative to younger cohorts. Instead, economic inequalities accumulate throughout the life cycle so that inequality actually reaches its peak in old age, as differences in asset, pension, and other resource levels outweigh the equalizing effects of government benefits. Social Security retirement benefits may even further aggravate economic inequality, as lower-income workers are more likely to take early retirement and, thus, reduced monthly payments.[89] Older people living in or near poverty are disproportionately female, unmarried, minorities, and/or disabled.[90]

Boomers are highly diverse and divided along socioeconomic, religious, racial, and ethnic lines, and divided along political lines as well.

Appealing to large numbers of politically divided and highly individualistic baby boomers to unite around aging-related issues and interests—when they resist thinking of themselves as "old" in the first place—was never going to be a walk in the park. AARP's membership numbers, stalled throughout the 1990s at around 33 million even as the older population continued to grow, demonstrated that difficulty.

John Rother—AARP's major policy strategist from 1984 until he left to become CEO of the National Coalition for Health Care in 2011—recognized the paradoxical opportunity and challenge in growing the membership by reaching out to the boomers. "Boomers want options and choices," Rother, a boomer himself, told Lynch. "They're optimistic, self-reliant, and self-indulgent."[91] Image makeovers to appeal to boomers began during Horace Deets' tenure as executive director. The name change in 1999, from the American Association of Retired Persons to simply AARP, was both more accurate—nearly half the members were not retired—and more attractive to boomers, who not only were not retired for the most part, but also were not eager to be reminded that they were headed toward old age. The short-lived magazine *My Generation*, referencing a 1960s hit song by The Who, also was a gesture to the baby boom generation. But market research showed that the AARP brand was now so widely identifiable that both *My Generation* and *Modern Maturity* were scrapped for *AARP The Magazine*, while the name change to AARP remained solid.

Membership began expanding again after AARP hired "marketing maestro" Bill Novelli in 2001.[92] The son of a Pennsylvania steelworker, Novelli, began a successful marketing career selling detergents and toothpaste, children's cereals and pet foods, at major marketing firms including one that he cofounded, Porter-Novelli. Working on a PBS account led him to develop an interest and pioneering expertise in social marketing, using marketing techniques to achieve positive social change. Previous successful campaigns included promoting CARE to combat global poverty, recruiting experts in various fields for the Peace Corps, and raising awareness of the dangers of underage smoking for the Campaign for Tobacco-Free Kids. At AARP, he worked to raise the group's profile in Washington and nationwide, and to encourage members to engage in social change through volunteerism and political activity.[93]

Novelli reorganized AARP more like a business, with more centralized, top-down control and more professionalized board of directors, executive team, and staff, and changed his title from executive director to CEO. Dues were increased to $16 in 2006; the logo was modernized with strong block letters and the "Real Possibilities" tag line in 2007 (to look "less like a government agency");[94] and membership, products, and services were expanded and marketed more aggressively. Novelli promoted Rother, already the public face of AARP and one of the best-known experts in aging and health policy in Washington. They expanded on the group's efforts to attract boomers, appealing to their individuality as well as to their resistance to the notion that growing "old" means growing sedentary. Some criticized Novelli's changes for being too corporate; others criticized them for an overly broad intergenerational, multicultural, international agenda that precluded a more focused identity and message; still others complained that too much centralized control dampened the energy and enthusiasm of volunteers.[95] But the organization grew steadily, reaching over 40 million in 2008.

Hopes of expanding further to 50 million and more were dashed with the Great Recession of 2008. After reaching 40 million, membership dipped and then hovered around 38 million by 2015—down to just over a third of the 50+ population. AARP is still, by far, "the biggest kid on the block," Rother notes,[96] big enough to be in a class by itself, big enough to make policy makers pay attention, and many millions larger than any other seniors group, or any other interest group of any type. Still, organization leaders continue to explore the reasons why AARP declined in numbers after decades of mostly sustained growth, and to figure out how they can maintain a membership in the tens of millions.

AARP officials list several reasons for the loss of two to three million members since 2008. First and foremost is the Great Recession of 2008 and the sputtering economic recovery since then, which not only made it harder for some people to pay the association dues but also forced the association itself to cut back on recruitment and retention activities. Annual dues increased from $12.50 to $16 in 2009, still low, but for some likely a stretch in the wake of recession.[97]

A small number of members have left in protest of AARP's controversial political positions, as had happened during the Medicare Catastrophic Coverage fiasco in the late 1980s. AARP supported the law that created Medicare Part D prescription drug coverage in 2003, a law heavily favored by congressional Republicans and opposed by Democrats in part because it did not include cost controls. As a result, AARP estimated that between 45,000 and 120,000 mostly left-leaning members left the association.[98] Even more controversial was the Affordable Care Act, known as Obamacare, which passed in 2010 and led to the loss of some 300,000 members by AARP's estimation.[99] While other aging-based groups, both liberal and conservative, are available for people to join, AARP leaders see scant evidence that those much smaller groups gain members at AARP's expense;

"we welcome their participation" in the political process, said Legislative Policy Director David Certner.[100]

AARP's politically diverse membership base—about one-third of the members are Democrats, another third are Republicans, and a third are partisan independents—creates a dilemma for the organization, one that Lynch characterizes as "the battle of the brands: consumer trust versus policy warrior."[101] Having alienated and lost some members after supporting the ill-fated Medicare Catastrophic Coverage Act in 1988, AARP, with Horace Deets at the helm, had taken a cautious approach to political issues, hoping to broaden its appeal across generations—from boomers still in the peak years of their working lives to older retirees, parents to great-grandparents—and across the ideological spectrum, by avoiding controversy.[102] Novelli was determined to revive what he called the "warrior brand" while also enhancing and aggressively marketing member products and services. Balancing and integrating both "brands" requires significant resources for education and damage control when some members object to controversial political actions, opens the group to conflict-of-interest charges, and poses the danger of an organizational identity crisis.[103] In the end, AARP does lose some members to controversy, but the Great Recession was a more serious challenge to membership recruitment and retention.

Generational, societal, and technological changes add to the challenges of maintaining mass membership organizations. Baby boomers tend to be more autonomous and less engaged in public affairs than previous generations, and less inclined to join organizations. Nor do succeeding generations appear any more likely to be joiners as they reach age 50 and beyond. Americans of "Generation X," those born between 1965 and 1980, began turning 50 in 2015; behind them are the "Millennials," born between 1981 and 1996. Both younger generations have been found to be even less likely than boomers to join civic organizations or express interest in politics; they are no less likely to engage in volunteer work, but their community involvement tends to be sporadic.[104]

The very meaning of "membership" is changing, furthermore, in the digital age. The traditional card-carrying membership is gradually transforming into something more fluid. "We no longer need organizations to start a petition, create media content, or find like-minded individuals," notes interest group scholar David Karpf.[105] The Internet has revolutionized the dissemination of information; a few keystrokes and clicks lead to answers that once required extensive research, or inquiries through more formal organizational channels. There is no need to contact AARP for information on when to file for Social Security or how to avoid a stroke;

just Google. But digital technologies may do more to enhance each member's engagement with organizations than to reduce their relevance. Bruce Bimber, Andrew Flanagin, and Cynthia Stohl surveyed and interviewed members of AARP, as well as MoveOn and the American Legion, about their digital-media use and their organizational involvement. What they found is that members can now more easily establish their own individual participatory styles, in interacting both with each other and with the organization. Members have more flexibility to decide how to make the organization useful to themselves, and how to support the organization's advocacy and social mission.[106]

"Disrupting Aging" in the Twenty-First Century

AARP's relationship with its members, and with the 50+ population more generally, reflects both changes in technology and changes in the nature of aging and retirement in the United States. These changes lead to a more personalized relationship between each member and the organization. CEO Jo Ann Jenkins, who ascended to that position in 2014, emphasizes this personalization in the context of an increasingly diverse older population—diverse not only in terms of demographic and socioeconomic characteristics, but also in terms of experiences in later life. AARP, she says, is more than ever about "disrupting aging," erasing stereotypes attached to any given age group, and thus expanding the vision of what one can do at any given age.[107]

Retirement, as a life stage and as a goal, has gone through significant transformations over the past century. A. Barry Rand, Novelli's successor as AARP's CEO from 2009 to 2014, writes that AARP was founded at a time when retirement was becoming a pleasant and sought-after goal, a time for leisure, travel, more time with family and friends, and other enjoyments. The creation and later expansion of Social Security, the increasing availability of private pension income, and the creation of Medicare, offered sufficient income and health security to growing numbers of older people to make retirement feasible. More recently, says Rand, the postretirement period has become less one of leisure than one of new beginnings, a career change, volunteerism, the pursuit of new hobbies or interests, and other "Real Possibilities" (as promised in the tag line of the new AARP logo), attributable to better health and greater longevity. "The first aging revolution was about freedom from work. The second one is about freedom to do something different."[108]

Jenkins and chief of staff Kevin Donnellan stress the same theme in explaining what they want to provide for AARP members: more opportunities to decide for themselves what they want out of the organization. They seek to make AARP relevant for retirees and mid-career workers alike by providing a wider variety of options. "We're working on personalizing the AARP experience, at personal and community levels," Jenkins said. "People don't want to be told what to do or think any more. They want individual choices, and the information and tools for making those choices." Jenkins dismisses the cliché that "50 is the new 30." Instead, "50 is the new 50."[109] "Own your age—and resist ageism," she told the audience at the final Life@50+ convention in Miami. This includes not only defying ageist stereotypes, but also making the environment more age-friendly, by demanding more of the public and private sectors. "We often blame our limitations on the fact that we're getting older. But in reality, it may simply be that our environment doesn't fit us anymore, or the product isn't designed to fit our needs."[110]

AARP's extended presence in states and localities around the country is part of this effort. The Livable Communities program is one way for AARP to increase its relevance in people's everyday lives and promote the brand. Features that make communities more livable include walkability and accessible transportation, basic services and stores in close proximity, affordable housing adaptable to all levels of ability and disability, centers where people can socialize, and public safety features including everything from sidewalks to protection from crime.[111] It also includes projects like the rebuilding of New Orleans' Hollygrove neighborhood after Hurricane Katrina. AARP's Livable Communities website includes a long list of resources and how-to's for individuals, groups of volunteers, and political advocates in communities across the country.

Life Reimagined, launched shortly before Jenkins succeeded Rand in 2014, represented another move toward flexible, personalized membership. The self-guided system offered resources for exploring new options in work, relationships, finance, health, and general well-being. With trends toward greater longevity, advances in health care, and shifting career paths, people's life trajectories often experience transitions when they used to start winding down. As Emilio Pardo, president of Life Reimagined and former chief brand officer for AARP, explained, "You start asking yourself, 'What is this all about? What's next?' . . . What we saw is the emergence of a new life phase that comes sometime before what is traditional retirement and what you want it to be. You throw in the fact that Boomers are going through this, and this is a huge shift in the society."[112] "The new word for retirement is 'work,'" a time for the things we've always wanted to do, from volunteering and entrepreneurship to travel and adventure, said senior vice president of brand integration Barbara Shipley.[113] Within months of the digital platform going live, Life Reimagined had over one million registered users, but it was taken offline in 2017 for review and possible overhaul.[114]

Individualizing AARP's offerings for personal benefit is not new. Directors Deets, Novelli, Rand, and Jenkins all urged people, in various ways, to take personal responsibility for their own aging. Technology makes it increasingly possible; the aging of the personal-fulfillment-oriented baby boom and subsequent generations makes it all the more relevant. But the emphasis on expanding horizons and finding personal fulfillment through helping others dates back to founder Ethel Percy Andrus.

AARP's message, in publications, online, and at conferences and other events, is relentlessly positive about aging. The message is one of empowerment, owning one's age, finding one's passion, grabbing opportunities to give one's life purpose and meaning, having fun, celebrating life. There is little to criticize here. But as Lynch notes, this positive image, the "devotion to their founder's altruistic, happy mantra of 'what we do, we do for all,'" can conflict with the association's "warrior brand," the advocacy function of pointing to the problems that many older people face, and demanding solutions to them.[115] The emphasis in AARP's digital and print publications is on positive change, parlaying one's skills and experience into new directions for personal fulfillment and service to others. It is a message that resonates especially for AARP members, who tend to enjoy higher income, education, and occupational status levels than the general 50+ population.

For many people, however, "mid-life crisis" is not a playful term; it is truly a crisis. The trend toward earlier retirement after the creation and expansion of Social Security began to reverse around the mid-1980s, in some cases because people have chosen to take advantage of greater longevity and better health, and continue working. But to some extent, the reversal is due to the need to continue to working, as a result of the decline in defined-benefit pensions, the increase in defined-contribution plans that shift the risk and responsibility for sufficient retirement income from employers to employees, and the recessions of the early 2000s and 2008 that reduced many people's retirement nest eggs. This is especially true for men. Older women's labor force participation has increased in part because of increasing opportunities as a result of the feminist movement that began in the 1960s, but also in part because of declining real wages that have made it harder for single-income families to earn sufficient income to live well and retire with financial security.[116] Many of the oldest old remain vulnerable, and many baby boomers face both income insecurity in retirement and reduced opportunities to continue working, especially after the Great Recession.[117] The dilemma for AARP lies in maintaining the positive, happy image while advocating for greater income and health security for vulnerable older people.

The issues of caregiving and long-term care present a similar dilemma: how to support individual family caregivers without reinforcing the idea that caregiving is solely an individual's—usually woman's—responsibility. Caregiving has become a major topic of concern in AARP's outreach, both in print and online, and for good reason: A study by AARP's Public Policy Institute finds that more than 40 million Americans provide 37 billion hours of unpaid care to adult family members and friends who are unable to handle daily activities on their own. These unpaid caregivers provide over 75 percent of caregiving services in the United States, contributing the equivalent of $470 billion to the nation's economy.[118] Further, those who do get paid for caregiving support in institutions or people's homes are among the lowest paid workers in the country's labor force—and, again, are mostly women.[119] It is important, Jenkins said, "for caregivers to know they are not alone, that they are part of a community" and that help is available.[120] To that end, AARP offers various, frequently promoted, resources for caregivers, including links to local support services, and tips and advice from the association through its online advice-sharing service. Further, Nancy LeaMond, the chief advocacy and engagement officer, expresses the hope that building a constituency for caregiving support among their members will help with advocacy for better government support down the road, despite the difficulty of gaining support for costly new benefits today.[121]

Surely caregivers can use the support. But at the same time, as Nancy Hooyman and Judith Gonyea suggest, such individualistic assistance as counseling, advice, and support groups serves to maintain the unpaid, informal labor force in caregiving.[122] The pressure is largely on women, as the "patchwork" of individual supports provided by a fragmented system of elder care "reinforces care labor as a woman's uncompensated, special task and helps her 'adjust' to her role."[123] Sandra Tanenbaum points to *Juggling Work and Caregiving*, authored by AARP's own family and caregiving expert Amy Goyer, as a prime example.[124] Goyer acknowledges that paid work and unpaid caregiving are so difficult to "juggle" that job and income security must often be sacrificed, a sacrifice especially hard on low-income, minority, and female caregivers. "She is unequivocal about which should take priority, using herself as an example. She urges caregivers to 'choose positivity.'"[125] The message is both encouraging and frustrating for the overwhelmed juggler, and therein lies the dilemma.

AARP is not insensitive to the vulnerability of the aging, especially those who live in poverty, who are disabled, and who have faced a life of discrimination based on race, ethnicity, religion, gender, or sexuality. Jenkins herself, the second woman (after Harriet Miller in the mid-1970s) and second African American (after Barry Rand) to serve as AARP CEO, first joined AARP in 2010 as president of the AARP Foundation, after more than 25 years of leadership and management in the public and nonprofit sectors. Asked about her priorities for AARP, she stressed not only the importance of "disrupting aging" but also the importance of meeting the needs of an increasingly diverse older population, and especially the needs of those who are most vulnerable and struggling.[126] Dilemma or not, AARP's mission is to represent the needs and interests of an extremely diverse 50+ population.

Mobilization, Participation, and Representation

"AARP is a group of people bound together only by a common love of travel discounts," former U.S. senator Alan Simpson is fond of saying.[127] Simpson is one of AARP's leading critics. Journalist Dale Van Atta, another critic, echoes the concern: "other than being over 50 and sharing a common desire for AARP discounts, nothing knits together the politically and generationally diverse dues-pay membership," and so "AARP has no business doing unauthorized lobbying for its membership. Its chimerical lobby wholeheartedly represents only what a few paid staff leaders decide is best for all older Americans."[128] Not only is it impossible to represent people with so many disparate views, it is deceptive to lobby government on their behalf, Van Atta continues. AARP's size, however, is a major source of its influence, and representation without influence is arguably useless.

Representation, said Hannah Pitkin, foremost authority on the subject, is "a making present of something absent—but not making it literally present. It must be made present indirectly, through an intermediary; it must be made present in some sense, while nevertheless remaining literally absent."[129] Some direction from the constituency, or membership, is important to representation, but so is effective advocacy for policies that meet the constituency's needs.[130] Furthermore, the constituency is both the membership and the 50+ population more generally. Thus, while it is important to assess an interest group's representative function, there is no single metric for doing so because representation is a complex and multidimensional concept.

Voluntary associations of individual members comprise only a small fraction, about 12 percent, of organizations in the American interest group universe. Given the general overrepresentation of the advantaged and well-connected in that universe, the few membership associations of individuals that do exist play an important role in "advocating on behalf of public goods, identity groups, and those with limited resources."[131] AARP's members are rather well-heeled relative to the American population as a whole and relative to the general 50+ population. Over half have incomes over $60,000, with 14 percent bringing in at least $125,000; over a quarter of the members have a net worth of over half a million dollars; over half have completed college and 20 percent hold graduate degrees.[132] AARP's defense of Social Security and Medicare, supported by majorities at all income levels and keeping more Americans out of poverty than any other government programs, makes it "a conduit through which the influence of less-well-off Americans flows."[133] The AARP Foundation, furthermore, focuses primarily on the needs of the more vulnerable older populations. These are essential aspects of what Dara Strolovitch calls "affirmative advocacy," interest group strategies to prioritize the interests of marginalized subgroups within their own constituencies, and to counter groups' tendency to pay more attention to their more privileged members.[134] AARP, in sum, plays an important representational role within the American political system, which tends to be biased toward the interests of those who are already advantaged.

Membership input remains an important aspect of interest group representation. Since most of AARP's 38 million members join for the selective incentives, leaders and staff are relatively unconstrained by members' policy preferences in making decisions about issue priorities and lobbying strategies.[135] Further, a 2001 change in the bylaws removed the election of members of the board of directors from national convention delegates and put it in the hands of the board itself; after that change, the Life@50+ convention became more strictly an entertainment and marketing extravaganza. Since then, some volunteers and staffers in the states have complained about the loss of autonomy as decision making became overly centralized in the national office.[136] All this fits a larger trend toward what Theda Skocpol calls "diminished democracy"—a trend toward increasing domination of interest group decision making by professionals at the expense of citizen participation.[137]

Former CEO Novelli counters that the current method of selecting members of the board of directors is no less democratic than the old way, in which some 35,000 members voted on a slate of candidates at the national convention.[138] The board of directors is a 17-member all-volunteer board that approves all of the association's policies, programs, activities, and services. The board also selects the executive officers, as in most large voluntary associations.[139] AARP's president and president-elect are board members who serve as principal volunteer spokespersons. New board members are screened and selected by the board itself for leadership abilities, knowledge and expertise, and commitment to AARP's goals. Novelli recruited board members with an eye toward both greater professionalism and greater racial, ethnic, and gender diversity. Lynch highlights AARP's expanding diversity mission, not only in the selection of the board but also more broadly in its marketing and outreach.[140] In the early twenty-first-century culture wars, AARP's multicultural outreach, extending to support for LGBT rights and marriage equality years before the U.S. Supreme Court struck down laws prohibiting same-sex marriage, attracts criticism from cultural conservatives.[141] That diversity mission may signify an evolution from its early reputation as the relatively conservative upper-crust group among seniors organizations, but it also reflects Ethel Percy Andrus's own efforts to break down racial and cultural barriers as an educator in the mid-twentieth century.[142]

Member input into organizational decision making is more important than ever, AARP leaders have long insisted. Some volunteers and staff members in the states disagree that decision making has become overly centralized, pointing to the frequent member surveys, conference calls, forums, and discussion groups through which the association gathers members' views.[143] Association officials cite the two-way communication between executives and staff and the membership. The association plays an important educational role, they emphasize, informing members in their publications, website, and mass mailings and e-mails about the important issues—for example, the benefits in the controversial Affordable Care Act of 2010 (Obamacare) for Medicare beneficiaries as well as those not yet eligible for Medicare.[144] The association also mobilizes members to get involved, especially since the mid-1980s when it stepped up its voter education programs, debates, and candidate forums, maintaining that the grassroots are real, not "Astroturf"—that is, that members are engaged, not simply contacting policy makers with prewritten postcards or e-mails provided by the organization.[145]

Democracy involves both constituency engagement from the bottom up and leadership from the top down; what is the ideal balance? Other contradictions afflict the association's relationship with its members as well. The membership is nearly evenly divided among Republicans, Democrats, and partisan independents; how can they all be represented in a political system that is quite polarized along partisan lines? About one-third of the members are under 65, and in fact much of AARP's advocacy and coalition building is intergenerational; after all, everyone aspires to reach old age, given the alternative, and older people have younger family members and loved ones. But does that make AARP's agenda too broad, to the extent that, as Lynch suggests, it might as well be the "American Association of Persons"?[146] The membership is somewhat higher in socio-economic status than the 50+ population generally, but its advocacy, in addition to the Foundation activities, often focuses on the needs of the most vulnerable elderly; does this affirmative advocacy enhance the democratic nature of the organization or skew it away from its dues-paying membership? For that matter, AARP benefits both by emphasizing the needs of low-income, minority, disabled, and otherwise disadvantaged older people in lobbying government and fighting the "greedy geezer" image, and also by celebrating the affluence and purchasing power of the older demographic for marketing purposes, and encouraging older people to be self-sufficient and individually responsible. Neither stereotype adequately fits the diverse older population, of course. Ethel Andrus herself was moved to establish an organization that could help vulnerable seniors like the retired teacher she found living in a chicken coop, even as she actively promoted independence and active engagement in old age. But to what extent can AARP be all things to all people without stumbling over contradictions?

Democracy in organizations is fraught with such dilemmas, and AARP is no exception. In many ways, the dilemmas are all the more acute in an association of 38 million generationally and politically diverse members, even as its membership is one of its great political strengths. In the following chapters, we explore these dilemmas further in examining the political priorities, strategies, and influence of AARP in the American political system.

CHAPTER FOUR

A Pragmatic Voice and a Powerful Ally

In 1965, Congress passed the nation's first major public health insurance programs, Medicare and Medicaid, with an overwhelming majority. In 2010, Congress passed another major health insurance overhaul, the Patient Protection and Affordable Care Act, commonly known as the ACA or Obamacare, by a narrow margin. Both legislative battles featured broad ideological conflict over the role of government in health care, as well as numerous compromises over specific provisions in crafting the final versions of the bills. But in the end, the Medicare and Medicaid bill passed with overwhelming support from Democratic legislators, who enjoyed a large majority in Congress, and support from about half of congressional Republicans. The ACA, on the other hand, passed without one single Republican vote in support, in a Congress narrowly divided between the two parties. The partisan division exhibited in the struggle over the ACA is part of a larger trend toward increasing partisan polarization during the decades separating the passage of these two landmark reforms to the American health care system.

AARP and the larger political system have both evolved, though not necessarily in tandem. At the time Medicare was enacted, AARP was still more of a service organization than a political organization; now it is one of the largest and most influential political players in Washington, and even in the states. An organization with a politically diverse membership, it plays a moderating role in an increasingly divided polity. As such, it is both a sought-after coalition partner and a target of criticism from all sides.

Some deride AARP as a narrow special interest group protecting and expanding old-age benefits at the expense of the young; others say it is too broad and cannot adequately represent its politically diverse membership. Some claim that AARP works to protect the relatively affluent and privileged "greedy geezers,"[1] while others suggest that it is overly focused on issues of importance to the poor and the disadvantaged rather than issues of importance to its own relatively upscale members. Some complain that AARP is too strident in its advocacy; others that it is too cautious and reserved. Some say the group is too liberal; others that it is too conservative. AARP is a "wholly owned subsidiary of the Democratic party," complained Republican senator Trent Lott in 2002. "AARP—what does it stand for? Always Advocating for the Republican Party," wrote Democratic Congressman Pete Stark in a letter to House Democrats the following year. AARP has the two quotes framed and proudly displayed inside its opulent Washington headquarters.[2]

Officially nonpartisan, AARP generally is characterized as moderately liberal or slightly left of center.[3] Its political focus on income security and health security—in particular, defending Social Security and Medicare—may put it in the crosshairs of free-market proponents of privatization, but is hardly a radical stance when both programs remain overwhelmingly popular with the general public. Its positions on social and cultural issues place it somewhat left of center as well, with its commitment to racial and ethnic diversity, nondiscrimination on the basis of sexuality and gender identity, multiculturalism, and internationalism—a broadly inclusive agenda in everything from its magazine articles and social events to the selection of its board of directors.[4] It is not a radical agenda for the early twenty-first century, but neither does it sit well with cultural conservatives who have criticized the association's support for gay and lesbian rights,[5] and its moderate stance on gun control.[6] Yet its centrism opens it to criticism from the left as well. Its size and prominence make it a popular target.

This chapter takes a closer look at AARP's political positions over the years, as well as its alliances and its critics, in the context of the politics of aging and in the context of the political environment overall. AARP today, I argue, is a moderate, pragmatic force in an increasingly polarized political system.

Political Polarization in Twenty-First Century America

Political polarization, on the rise in the United States during the last few decades, leads to a multitude of problems. The national government is wracked with division and dysfunction. The public is disillusioned with policymakers' failure to address economic stagnation, a ballooning national debt, increasing inequality, climate change and environmental degradation, moral decline, international conflict, and the constant threat of terrorism. Ideological extremism divides the parties, with a widening gulf between them, and moderates have nearly disappeared from Congress; the ability to compromise has given way to gridlock and stalemate.[7]

The political parties were not so polarized in the mid-twentieth century during AARP's early years. Both parties in Congress had liberal and conservative factions and a large number of moderates. Bipartisan coalition building and compromise were more the norm than the exception. The problem then, many political scientists argued, was that the parties were not sufficiently different from each other to offer voters a clear choice between alternative visions of the role of government. In 1950, the American Political Science Association task force called for more unified programmatic political parties.[8] But the U.S. constitutional system of separation of powers and checks and balances is not well suited to ideologically polarized parties. The possibility of divided government, the Senate filibuster, the Congress composed of representatives from highly diverse single-member House districts and states all facilitate influence from a wide variety of interests and depend on bipartisan negotiation and compromise to get anything done.[9]

The growing ideological polarization of the parties can be traced to a variety of causes mostly dating back to the 1970s and 1980s. Southern partisan realignment, in the wake of the Civil Rights Movement and the politicization of the religious Right, ultimately led to the near-disappearance of white Southern moderate Democrats and the rise of conservative Republicans in their place, while moderate Northeastern Republicans also became a disappearing breed. Economic and cultural issues have grown more aligned with each other, and less bipartisan, since 1980. Congressional districts have become more ideologically homogeneous, making extremist candidates more competitive. Chronic budget deficits and an expanding national debt, especially since the 1980s (and with a brief exception in the late 1990s) reduce the incentives for the parties to work together by supporting each other's top priorities. The proliferation of ideological and single-issue interest groups has helped to pull the parties toward the extremes, a trend intensified by the expanding amount and importance of money in election campaigns. The 24-hour news cycle and electronic media make it all too easy for us to get our news only from ideologically congruent sources.[10] Hyperpartisanship and economic inequality feed off each other as the widening gulf between the wealth and nonwealthy enhances partisan differences, which in turn make it more difficult for Congress to approve policies that would reduce inequality.[11] Not only are the congressional parties more polarized than ever, but the general public is increasingly divided, and hostile to the opposition parties, as well.[12]

Congressional polarization has been largely asymmetrical, according to Thomas Mann and Norman Ornstein's analysis: The Republican Party has moved much further to the right than the Democratic Party has moved left.[13] The partisan asymmetry is at least partly attributable to the Republican party's greater commitment to conservative ideology, in contrast to the Democratic party's policy-oriented appeal to the social groups in its supporting coalition.[14] Republicans' increasingly extreme free-market orientation and hostility to government domestic spending and taxing, coupled with the aging of the American population and high medical inflation driving up the costs of Medicare, Medicaid, and Social Security, have brought those issues to the center of partisan debate in the early twenty-first century.[15] President George W. Bush's drive to partially privatize Social Security in 2005 and congressional Republican leader Paul Ryan's proposal to largely privatize Medicare through premium supports in 2011 provide two examples.

As the 2012 Republican vice presidential nominee, Ryan was booed at the AARP national convention weeks before the election, as he discussed his plan and criticized President Obama's signature health care reform, the Affordable Care Act. "[The booing] was unfortunate," said media relations director James Dau,[16] although AARP opposed Ryan's proposal. That incident in turn drew a sharp rebuke from *The Wall Street Journal* while praising Ryan for relaying "some hard truths" about "the Democratic Party's entitlement agenda" that the AARP audience did not want to hear.[17] In an interview with the *National Journal* afterward, long-time policy director John Rother, who had recently left AARP for the CEO position at the National Coalition for Health Care, bemoaned the difficulty of working with both parties in search of common ground. "It's a reflection of the polarization of all things related to health care," Rother said. "And it's also a commentary just on the disappearance of the middle ground in the political debate."[18] This is the context in which AARP operates in the early twenty-first century, and it is very different from the political environment of AARP's early years.

Early Years: AARP and the Rise of the Gray Lobby

When Ethel Percy Andrus founded the National Retired Teachers Association in 1947, and AARP in 1958, well over a third of Americans aged over 65 lived below the poverty line. As a retired educator volunteering with the California Retired Teachers Association, Andrus was shocked to see how many retired teachers lacked adequate pension income and access to affordable health care. By then, the Social Security Act of 1935 had created a program of old age insurance, kicking off a nearly 50-year period of "compassionate ageism,"[19] which ran from the New Deal period through the Great Society and War on Poverty of the 1960s and 1970s. Political support for aging-based programs and benefits was based on an ageist stereotype of older people as poor, frail, and dependent. Most older people were indeed destitute prior to the creation of the Social Security system, and on the eve of the 1960s Great Society antipoverty efforts, the poverty rate for Americans aged 65 and over was still double that for younger people. New Deal and Great Society programs addressed poverty in general, and even Social Security and Medicare cover survivors' insurance and disability benefits for younger persons. But the social insurance programs, targeting primarily older and retired people, lifted many more people out of poverty than the generally more meager, means-tested programs for younger adults and children. Thus, the poverty rate dropped more quickly for people aged 65 and over, dipping below that of the population as a whole by the early 1980s.

Support for expanded old-age benefits was based not only on a sympathetic stereotype of poverty and frailty but also on the notion of deservingness and the promotion of work and productivity: Older people had worked and sacrificed all their lives, and therefore deserved comfort and support in their later years. The two largest social welfare programs by far, Social Security and Medicare, are structured to respond both to public compassion for the aged, and to the public's admiration for hard work and self-reliance. Supporters promote Social Security as a program to which individuals contribute, save, and earn benefits as a return on their investment, even though in reality it is today's workers who pay the payroll taxes that support today's beneficiaries.[20] Supporters of Medicare point out that most people of working age who have health insurance get it as a job-related benefit, and so retirees after years of work have earned the continuation of coverage in their later years. In addition, Medicare and Medicaid, the latter of which covers nursing home and home health care for many older people, were enacted as a compromise: liberal proponents of public health insurance for people of all ages at least got coverage for older and low-income people, while conservative proponents of a private, market-based health care system prevented passage of a more universal program of health care coverage.[21]

Andrus rejected the frail-and-dependent stereotype of older people. Instead, one's later years should be a time of independence, dignity, and purpose. She worked tirelessly to dispel the theory of disengagement—that old age is a time of gradual withdrawal from the activities and social networks of younger years.[22] Older people, she insisted, need meaning and purpose to their lives just as do younger people, and are just as productive as their younger peers. Having other sources of income including family money herself, she was certain that with adequate resources and without the barriers of age discrimination and ageist stereotyping, people have much to contribute to society no matter what their age. AARP, she hoped, would help to provide the tools and resources to enable older people to achieve self-reliance.[23]

AARP's activities in those years were more service-oriented than political, and focused on private sector solutions to old-age income and health insecurity. Most famously, Andrus sought a private company that would offer to sell health insurance to older people and retirees, leading to the partnership with Leonard Davis's company Colonial Penn, and she set up a mail-order discount prescription drug service as well. AARP, in her vision, would extend the opportunities for discovery and enjoyment of life; thus she pioneered group travel for seniors, and negotiated senior discounts for travel- and leisure-related businesses including restaurants, hotels, and automobile rental. She also encouraged people to continue working beyond the traditional age of retirement, and actively lobbied government to prohibit mandatory retirement. Finally, and perhaps most importantly, she encouraged older people to get involved in helping others; thus her motto, which is still a motto of AARP today: "To serve, not to be served."[24]

AARP's initial focus on the vitality and service contributions of its older constituency confronts the ageism in "compassionate ageism." Surely Andrus was not lacking in compassion. Indeed, the impetus for founding the NRTA and then AARP was the poverty-stricken retired teacher whom Andrus found living in a chicken coop, unable to stretch her meager retirement income far enough to take care of her own health and basic needs. At the same time, the availability of private-market health insurance and travel opportunities would not mean much to the most severely disadvantaged elderly. Corralling the collective purchasing power of older people in order to make health care and leisure activities more affordable can be a great boon to middle-class older people, but the very poor would have a hard time taking advantage of those benefits. Creating opportunities to volunteer and to serve others is a worthy pursuit and can help meet the needs of the most disadvantaged, but falls short of government's more comprehensive reach to all those in need. Many older people benefited from Colonial Penn's offer to sell them health insurance at a time when no one else would do so. Arguably nobody benefited more than insurance entrepreneur Leonard Davis, who invested $50,000 in startup funds and ended up on the *Forbes* magazine list of the four hundred wealthiest Americans with an estimated fortune of $230 million after he and AARP parted ways.[25]

In the context of the broad liberal consensus of the 1960s and 1970s, and even into the early 1980s, AARP was generally considered to be a moderately conservative force in the politics of aging. This was attributed both to its relatively affluent base and to its ties to the insurance industry by way of Leonard Davis's dominance. "[AARP's] underlying perspective and social outlook have generally been closely linked to that of business enterprise, especially the insurance industry, with which the group has evolved a symbiotic relationship," said Henry Pratt in his 1976 book *The Gray Lobby*.[26] "The AARP member is viewed as a white-collar or professional Republican who may come from any part of the country," noted the prominent scholar of aging politics, Robert Binstock, contrasting the association with the other mass membership senior organization of the time, the National Council of Senior Citizens (NCSC), whose membership consisted primarily of retired union members, especially from the industrial Northeast.[27]

The National Council was organized in 1961 with support from the labor union movement and the Democratic Party, initially to help in the push for the passage of Medicare. Aging-based membership organizations were not yet a force in national politics, but organized labor was one of the primary forces credited with helping to get Medicare passed, after which the NCSC became an influential group in its own right. There is little evidence that AARP opposed Medicare passage, but neither was it an active advocate. Andrus, who died two years after Medicare's passage, had appeared before Congress in 1959 to back a voluntary health care plan, administered by a private board of trustees, and paid for through deductions from Social Security benefits. This plan supported both Andrus's preference for freedom of choice and Colonial Penn's preference for making money selling health insurance policies—money that helped fund AARP's service mission in addition to making Davis a wealthy man.[28]

The White House Conference on Aging (WHCOA) in 1971 was a major stimulus for the politicization of AARP, and the growing power of the gray lobby. The WHCOA is held about once a decade to make policy recommendations for the security and well-being of older Americans. The first was in 1961. For the second WHCOA, in 1971, the staff invited some four hundred organizations—including business, labor, professional, religious, consumer, and service groups—to participate. Only about ten of those groups were political organizations concerned primarily with aging policy, and only three of those were mass membership groups for the aging: AARP, NCSC, and the more narrowly focused National Association of Retired Federal Employees. The rest were professional, trade, and service provider organizations. Their participation in the 1971 WHCOA marked the emergence of a widely recognized and influential interest-group sector focused on older people and aging policy.[29]

AARP and NCSC were the major organizational representatives of the aging population in the lead-up to the 1971 conference. While the two groups shared the basic goals of improving older people's well-being and increasing the salience of aging-related issues on the national agenda, there were broad areas of disagreement reflecting the difference in their memberships. AARP wanted the conference to highlight the role of the private and nonprofit sectors, with government action as a last resort. NCSC, in contrast, pushed for a more active government in meeting the needs of the elderly. The issue of national health insurance illustrates their differences. In the years following the 1971 conference, Congress debated establishing a more comprehensive national health insurance program, a cause advocated most forcefully by Senator Edward Kennedy of Massachusetts. NCSC supported it wholeheartedly, but AARP preferred an alternative plan sponsored by Senator Abraham Ribicoff of Connecticut, providing catastrophic coverage only for very costly medical care.

Two other issues dividing the two groups related to working beyond the age of 65: mandatory retirement and the Social Security retirement test. To Ethel Andrus, mandatory retirement was a form of age discrimination, and she lobbied hard to have it abolished. It was a more salient issue for the mostly middle-class, white-collar professionals who dominated AARP's membership, as many were willing and able to continue working beyond traditional retirement age; it was less salient to the blue-collar workers of NCSC. Similarly, AARP opposed the Social Security retirement test, which deducts a portion of benefits for earnings over a certain amount, because those who wished to continue working beyond the age of 65 felt penalized and argued that the deductions reduced the incentive to continue working. NCSC supported reduced benefits for those who continued working so that there would be more money in the system to benefit full retirees, and because paying full benefits to those continuing to work would burden younger workers with higher payroll taxes.[30] Finally, both organizations supported the Social Security reforms of 1972 to increase benefits and peg them automatically to cost-of-living increases. But NCSC lobbied much more actively in their favor, while AARP was more willing to compromise, on the grounds that large benefit increases could prove inflationary.[31]

Policy disagreements between AARP and NCSC in the 1960s and 1970s reflected the more middle-class and professional composition of AARP's membership versus NCSC's blue-collar, labor-union orientation. But both groups, critics suggested, largely neglected the needs of the most severely disadvantaged elderly—disproportionately nonwhite, female, older, disabled—those whose earlier life circumstances or catastrophic health issues hindered their ability to save for retirement, or to earn much in the way of Social Security benefits, much less retire with lucrative private pensions. Between 1959 and 1978, the poverty rate for Americans 65 years and older had dropped from 35 to 14 percent—from well above the overall U.S. poverty rate to a few percentage points below. Proponents of the aging portrayed this as a great victory over old-age poverty, and it was. But once the proportion of older people living in poverty had been significantly reduced, efforts to redistribute income to the aged most in need lost momentum, and the rising political influence of aging-based membership groups worked mostly to defend the benefits they had already gained.[32] Further, some charged, using advanced age as the eligibility requirement for government programs and benefits can segregate and isolate the elderly, perpetuating and even exacerbating the class and income differences of earlier years in the life cycle. Service providers, industries, and bureaucracies serving the aged end up reaping the benefits while treating aging, not poverty, as a problem to be solved.[33]

By the early 1980s, nevertheless, aging had become a widely recognized basis for political identity and political organization. AARP was especially prominent as its membership had surged past all others at over 11 million. Aging-based mass membership groups now included several others besides AARP, NCSC, and the federal employees' group NARFE. The Gray Panthers, a radical social change organization founded in 1970 by charismatic 67-year-old activist Maggie Kuhn, united older and young adults around a wide variety of progressive issues such as nuclear disarmament and economic inequality.[34] The National Committee to Preserve Social Security and Medicare (NCPSSM) was founded in 1982, initially as a direct-mail grassroots-lobbying organization in reaction to proposed Social Security benefit cuts during President Ronald Reagan's first term, and it has since added a robust direct lobbying contingent as well. The Older Women's League (OWL), a grassroots organization founded in 1980, lobbies for gender equality in public- and private-sector employment and benefits as well as social services for older women. In 1979, the aging-based membership groups, along with over 50 organizations including trade and professional associations, academic and research associations, service provider groups, labor union retiree groups, and health care reform advocacy groups, formed the Leadership Council of Aging Organizations (LCAO). The only aging-based membership organization not in the LCAO was the conservative, free-market-oriented National Alliance of Senior Citizens (NASC), which never developed a strong presence in Washington but did serve as a precursor to conservative senior organizations founded in the 1990s. Aside from NASC, the other membership groups lay generally to the political left of AARP.[35]

AARP's relative pragmatism, and the influence of its relatively affluent membership, remained apparent in the debate of Social Security reform in the early 1980s. By 1980, after years of high inflation and poor economic growth, Social Security faced an immediate funding crisis; the trust fund was projected to run short of money needed to pay benefits within a few years if adjustments were not made. Further, once the immediate crisis was fixed, the funding of Social Security faced a larger threat 20 or 30 years down the road, as the baby boom generation reached retirement age. As legislative solutions were crafted, business, labor, and aging-based interest groups weighed in.

AARP was part of Save Our Security (SOS), a coalition of over 100 organizations—primarily labor unions and aging advocates—launched in 1979 to oppose benefit reductions. Paul Light's detailed account of the politics surrounding the 1983 Social Security Amendments, *Artful Work*, describes AARP as one of the loosest members in the loose coalition.[36] All members agreed to hold the line on benefit cuts, but disagreed on other elements of the delicate compromise negotiated to keep Social Security solvent. Organized labor objected to raising the retirement age; labor and NARFE opposed extending coverage to federal employees; and AARP resisted taxing Social Security benefits because the tax would disproportionately affect its higher-income members. AARP also broke with SOS by agreeing to a one-time three-month delay in cost-of-living adjustments (COLAs) while the coalition held firm against any COLA delays. Meanwhile, among the business lobbies, the National Federation of Independent Business, concerned about payroll tax increases, became the lone holdout. AARP and the National Federation then joined forces in an odd alliance against the legislation. In the end, AARP and the National Federation failed to agree on a single alternative proposal, and were defeated; the reform legislation ultimately passed and was signed into law. Light quotes one SOS leader as saying that AARP "made a mistake by going out so hard against this package. They've thrown in with the conservative groups and have hurt their reputation. They've always been criticized for being too conservative, and this proves it."[37]

AARP's position in the 1960s and 1970s as the moderately conservative group among the mostly liberal senior organizations was based on the group's well-to-do membership, and on Leonard Davis's control over operations for the benefit of his insurance company, Colonial Penn. But that position was now in transition, prompted by both internal and external changes. Internally, AARP parted ways with Leonard Davis in 1979 and replaced Colonial Penn with Prudential as its insurance provider in 1981. Now, right around the time that the 1983 Social Security Amendments were passed, AARP was intent on restoring its credibility and stepping up its political activity.[38] It had plenty of reason to do so. The era of compassionate ageism was winding down, as federal spending on programs and benefits for the elderly consumed more of the federal budget and policy makers began questioning whether older people were getting more than their share. Still politically pragmatic with its rapidly growing, politically diverse membership, AARP now faced a very different environment, with escalating challenges on the right. In the mid-1980s, these challenges were framed in the parlance of "generational equity."

Generational Equity versus Generational Interdependence

Older Americans enjoyed much greater prosperity and lower poverty rates by the early 1980s than they had 50 years before, or even ten years before. The creation and expansion of Social Security, and the enactment of Medicare, Medicaid, and Supplemental Security Income have significantly reduced income and health insecurity in old age. Substantial numbers of older people—10 percent of those aged 65 and over—still live in poverty and many more in near poverty, but since the early 1980s they are less likely than the general population (13.5%) and less than half as likely as children (21%), to do so.[39]

The social safety net for younger adults, including families with children, consists mostly of relatively meager means-tested programs; recipients must go through a complex and demeaning process of proving they are poor enough to be eligible for benefits. Some are entitlements: benefits that are guaranteed to persons who are eligible according to formulas set by law. But the largest social welfare program for families with dependent children, Temporary Assistance for Needy Families (TANF), is not an entitlement program; benefits are subject to annual appropriations from Congress, which may or may not be sufficient to cover everyone who is eligible. Social Security and Medicare, by contrast, are social insurance programs that are universal rather than means-tested, with more generous benefits. They still leave a larger percentage of older people in poverty than in most other wealthy countries. But they are much more effective in reducing poverty than the public assistance available to working-age adults and their families.[40]

Retirement has become, for most, a reality or a realistic aspiration rather than an impossible dream; private pensions are better protected; and those who do wish to continue working enjoy protections against mandatory retirement and age discrimination. Many Americans celebrate these achievements, and Social Security and Medicare both remain highly popular with the public. But in the late 1970s, proponents of entitlement reform, rather than celebrate the programs' success, began promoting a new old-age stereotype: that of the affluent, hedonistic retiree, consuming the lion's share of federal domestic spending at the expense of younger adults and children.

The politics of Social Security and Medicare was starting to become an ideological battlefield, despite the programs' popularity. Scholars and journalists began calling attention to the "graying of the federal budget"—the rapidly growing proportion spent on benefits for the elderly—as a result of population aging,[41] Social Security expansion, and rising costs of Medicare and Medicaid due to medical inflation outpacing overall inflation. Federal spending on old-age benefits reached about one-quarter of the budget by the late 1970s and increased to over 40 percent by 2015.[42] Stagflation, the oil crisis, a floundering economy, and the first projections of future deficits in the Social Security trust fund all weakened the broad liberal consensus, which had been bolstered by strong postwar economic growth. Meanwhile, old-age advocacy groups—the "gray lobby"—had become a recognized force in Washington politics, led by AARP. "The elderly are well organized and well represented," wrote Robert Samuelson in 1981, warning that politicians' reluctance to rein in spending on the elderly "has created pressure for more cutbacks in other areas—especially aid to state and local governments and programs for the disadvantaged."[43] The aged, suggested Binstock, had become a scapegoat,[44] as warnings about old-age greed and intergenerational conflict escalated through the 1980s and beyond.

"The tyranny of America's old," read a *Fortune* headline in 1992; "America is spending too much on its elderly and too little on its young."[45] "Greedy geezers" declared a cover of *The New Republic* in 1988,[46] over an unattractive caricature of angry-looking old folks on the march. The political power and hedonism of the elderly, Phillip Longman suggested in a 1985 *Atlantic* article, endangers "justice between generations"—and

AARP, he said, was largely to blame, by depicting older people as needy and deserving of government benefits on the one hand, while touting their affluence and purchasing power on the other hand in order to attract advertising revenue.[47] Other writers, including politicians, journalists, and scholars repeated the theme throughout the 1980s and 1990s: older people's political power threatens the current and future well-being of younger generations.[48]

The movement for "generational equity" found a formal voice with the founding of Americans for Generational Equity, or AGE, in 1985. AGE was followed by other groups advocating on behalf of younger generations—Third Millennium and Lead or Leave—all contending that today's young workers subsidize their elders' profligate lifestyle while little is left in the budget for children's programs. Once the baby-boom generation reaches retirement age—and they will all be over 65 by 2030—funding for Social Security and Medicare will be so quickly depleted that there will be little or none left for future generations. Thus, Social Security and Medicare must be reined in, and benefits cut, sooner rather than later. But the political power of old-age advocacy groups makes it politically untenable to do so. "The largest and most powerful social lobby in our country is organized not on the basis of rich versus poor, but to benefit a single generation—the elderly—at the expense of all others," said AGE cofounder and Executive Director Paul Hewitt in a 1986 interview.[49] Like Longman, Hewitt took AARP to task for using the diversity of the older population to its own advantage. AARP sells advertising by portraying its members as well-to-do, with "half the discretionary income in the United States, and this is borne out by the fact that they buy about 80% of all Cadillacs, and 80% of all foreign travel plans are geared to affluent senior citizens. When it suits (the association's) purpose, a different set of statistics can be presented" to highlight the vulnerability of many older persons, especially the very old, "particularly women whose husbands are deceased, whose benefits have been cut by one-third and their husband's pension benefits cut off entirely. But lumping these people with the newly retired who have a lot of assets . . . tends to obscure the differences between the groups among the elderly."[50]

Pro-market conservatives, hoping to build support across the board for smaller government in general, and privatization of Social Security in particular, thus used the generational equity theme to appeal to liberals as well as conservatives. The image of affluent, self-indulgent retirees living it up while millions of children languished in poverty might, they hoped, rally support for means-testing the universal social insurance programs targeting older people. By targeting only the truly needy, rather than supplementing the incomes of affluent seniors, the federal government would have enough money—without raising more taxes—to lift poor children out of poverty as well.[51]

Countering the generational equity frame is that of generational interdependence, or generational solidarity: the idea that different generations support each other rather than compete for resources. Social Security, Medicare, and other old-age benefits are shared across generations. Most directly, millions of children and younger adults receive survivors' benefits and disability benefits. In addition, public pensions and health care coverage enable older people to maintain their independence and self-reliance, reducing their dependence on their children who then retain more disposable income for themselves and their own children. Older family members, in turn, often help younger members with finances, child care, and other needs. In communities as well as in families, the fortunes of different generations are intertwined, not in conflict.[52]

"We have to tell the younger people that Social Security is not a fight between generations—it's a family affair," said AARP's Executive Director Cyril Brickfield in response to generational equity advocates.[53] "I don't think the proper response is to take from one vulnerable group—the nation's aging population—in order to give more to another vulnerable group," said AARP's legislative director John Rother.[54] Reinforcing the point, AARP joined the National Council on Aging, the Children's Defense Fund, and the Child Welfare League of America in founding Generations United, a coalition of over one hundred other organizations representing children, youth, and older adults, to promote intergenerational collaboration and refute the charge that social welfare spending is a zero-sum game between age groups.[55]

The movement for generational equity, its detractors note, stems not so much from concern about children's welfare as it does from support for policies that would boost private-sector business—for example, partially privatizing Social Security by introducing private retirement accounts that could exponentially boost investment bank profits.[56] Investment banker and former Secretary of Commerce Peter G. Peterson, who became AGE's research director, warned in a 1987 *Atlantic Monthly* article that the growth of the old-age welfare state was draining resources from children and younger adults, "with dire implications for our future productivity."[57] Generational equity proponents drew on the research of respected demographer Samuel H. Preston demonstrating rising poverty among children as the elderly's fortunes increased.[58] But AGE's funding came primarily from "Social Security and Medicare's prime private-sector competitors: banks, insurance companies, defense contractors, and health care corporations."[59]

Generational equity proponents offered little in the way of policy proposals to improve the well-being of children. In fact even as proponents of entitlement reform were scapegoating the elderly, conservative discourse in the 1980s increasingly characterized younger welfare recipients as lazy, dishonest, and undeserving. President Ronald Reagan helped popularize the image of the "welfare queen," bearing children out of wedlock, refusing to work, and collecting welfare checks through fraud and manipulation.[60] Thus opponents of social welfare spending in general found ways to scapegoat beneficiaries across the age spectrum. Empirical evidence generally does not support the notion of a zero-sum game between generations in which spending on one comes at the expense of the other. Instead, countries with well-developed old-age welfare states tend to spend more on children's benefits as well.[61] Further, the proposal to target only the needy with means-tested benefits for Americans of all ages would almost certainly result in reduced benefits across the board. While universal social insurance programs like Social Security and Medicare are bolstered by widespread public support, means-tested public assistance programs enjoy much less middle-class support and are thus politically easier to reduce or dismantle. Means-testing old-age and retirement programs therefore would be more likely to plunge large numbers of older people back into poverty, rather than lift young families with children out of it.[62]

Americans for Generational Equity and allied groups focused much of their criticism on AARP because AARP's size, visibility, and influence made it such a formidable foe. AARP stood adamantly opposed to AGE's contention that the elderly's gains come at the expense of younger generations, and that therefore old-age benefits should be reduced. Yet AARP's leadership was not as strident in its opposition as other seniors' groups. Rother acknowledged the need to consider future generations. "If we put all our money into present consumption and not enough into education, investment and research and development . . . [w]e are in effect stealing from the future," he said in 1986 at the height of the generational equity debate. "We are lowering the rate of economic growth for future generations. In that sense, I think the concept of a generational approach to public policy may have some validity."[63] Not that he was advocating a reduction in old-age benefits in order to shift resources to the young. "Our success has been pronounced in improving economic security for one of the most vulnerable parts of our population, the older population," he wrote in *Justice across Generations*, a collection of different viewpoints about generational justice published by AARP's Public Policy Institute. "I think it is quite ironic that for some of those persons raising the issue, the prescription is to turn our back on some of our achievements, rather than to share those achievements and share those lessons more broadly with other vulnerable persons."[64]

Intergenerational coalition building was good politics as well as good policy. Those future generations would someday reach the age of AARP eligibility themselves, starting with the baby boomers—Rother's own generation—who would begin turning 50 in 1996, just a decade away.

Long-Term Care and Catastrophic Coverage

AARP expanded rapidly in size, power, and visibility as the 1980s progressed. Now free from the control previously exerted by Leonard Davis and Colonial Penn, and having lowered the age of eligibility from 55 to 50, it appeared well placed to meet the challenge posed by the movement for generational equity. Yet divisions within the ranks of a highly diverse 50+ population, and even within the association's own membership, proved to be challenging enough. One key illustration of this challenge was the ill-fated Medicare Catastrophic Coverage Act (MCCA), passed by Congress in 1988 and repealed by Congress the following year. AARP struggled and compromised in order to get it passed, but in the end that struggle backfired on the leadership.

The MCCA was the first major expansion of Medicare in the program's history, designed to protect beneficiaries from the enormous costs of sudden illness and medical bankruptcy. Had it survived, MCCA's Medicare expansion would have covered astronomical acute-care medical expenses, prescription drugs, and some related expenses. An aging-friendly program expansion, it nevertheless divided the aging-based organizations, in part because it did not include long-term care coverage. Medicare's lack of coverage for long-term care, through home-based services or in nursing homes, is the major gap in the program's health care coverage. Medicaid does include long-term care coverage, but because Medicaid is means-tested, beneficiaries must divest themselves of income and assets in order to qualify. The MCCA filled a number of gaps in the Medicare program, but long-term services and supports were not among them.

AARP has long been an active advocate for coverage of long-term care. Together with the affordable health care advocacy group Villers Foundation (later named Families USA), AARP launched the Long-Term Care Campaign in 1987, mobilizing over one hundred other groups to promote social-insurance coverage of long-term services and support for chronic illness and disability. Congressional advocates led by Florida Congressman Claude Pepper pushed legislation to provide long-term home-care services, but the legislation never passed. AARP and other groups ultimately backed the MCCA even without long-term care coverage, on the grounds that some Medicare expansion was better than none. But the Gray Panthers and the National Committee to Preserve Social Security and Medicare (NCPSSM) wanted to hold out for the addition of long-term care coverage.[65]

The biggest obstacle to support for the MCCA, for most senior advocacy groups, was the financing mechanism. The new benefits were to be paid for solely by beneficiaries themselves, by way of a modest increase in Medicare premiums, plus a surtax on the wealthiest 40 percent of seniors, which rose with income to a maximum of $800 for the top 5 percent. This method of financing was unprecedented. At a time when Congress and the Reagan administration were in budget-cutting and tax-cutting mode, the MCCA's financing could be justified as a "user's fee," paying for new benefits without raising taxes. But old-age advocates were naturally concerned that seniors would object to paying the full cost of the new benefits. The flat premium increase, though modest, would be hard on lower-income seniors. For many AARP members, the big flaw was the progressive surtax, which hit upper-income seniors the hardest. Worse, nearly a quarter of beneficiaries, including some retirees, already received some of the same benefits through their employer-based insurance plans and were likely to object to paying more for what they already had. Nevertheless, AARP continued to support the MCCA, encouraging Congress to pass it and then touting the benefits after it passed. The prescription drug coverage was especially important to AARP leaders, and they also stressed the protection against catastrophic costs that often led to medical bankruptcy. AARP's own public opinion polls showed strong support for the legislation—at least before Congress passed it.[66]

Headline-making demonstrations broke out soon after the MCCA became law. Images of angry seniors wielding picket signs—most dramatically, blocking the car of House Ways and Means Committee Chair Dan Rostenkowski, yelling and pounding on the car windows—hit the news, and opposition continued to escalate. AARP officials continued to promote the MCCA's new benefits through mass mailings, videos, and personal contacts by trained volunteers. But the new benefits were phased in slowly, while premium and surtax collection began immediately. The legislation was complex and not easy to explain. Public anger was fueled further by mass mailings from groups opposed to the MCCA, especially from the National Committee to Preserve Social Security and Medicare, which apparently led many people to believe they would be paying the maximum surtax of $800 even though most beneficiaries would pay no surtax at all. The protests grew so fierce that Congress ended up repealing the legislation in 1989, just a year and a half after its passage.[67]

As support for the MCCA dropped among older Americans and opposition grew, "AARP stood virtually alone among senior-citizen interest groups in defending the legislation's benefits as worthwhile and necessary."[68] As the MCCA went down in flames, lawmakers questioned whether AARP had lost touch with its own constituency.[69] Many AARP members complained, especially the more well-to-do, and some 12 thousand to 14 thousand members resigned in protest—barely a dent in a membership of 30 million. But AARP took some sobering lessons from the MCCA affair. The most obvious lesson is that people are likely to balk at paying extra taxes or fees for benefits they already have; the broader lesson is that when benefits are widely dispersed but costs concentrated on a smaller group—higher-income beneficiaries in this case—the intensity of the smaller group's opposition is likely to overwhelm the more moderate support of potential beneficiaries.[70] In general, losses weigh more on people's minds than potential gains, and the psychological and political reaction against loss, or perceived loss, of money or benefits evokes strong protest.[71] AARP would encounter similar fury 20 years later when its support for health care reform evoked protests from members convinced that their Medicare benefits would be cut. In the case of the MCCA, the widespread support for Medicare expansion evident in AARP's public opinion surveys was overwhelmed by opposition to the surtax beneficiaries would have to pay—or thought they would have to pay—once the program was passed and implemented.

AARP leaders drew at least two more related conclusions from the MCCA protest and repeal: Be more cautious in taking specific positions on future legislation, and expand the ground game in the states by opening more state offices and strengthening the volunteer grassroots networks. "One thing we learned was that it wasn't sufficient to just do the policy analysis here in Washington," Rother told the *New York Times*. "You really had to lay the groundwork all across the country."[72] Rother recognized that lobbying is a two-way street, involving not only persuasion of policy makers, but also constituency education. Complex benefits such as those in the catastrophic coverage bill are hard to explain; simple negative messages too easily overwhelm the complicated explanations.[73]

Surprised by the strong reaction against a program that AARP officials believed to be beneficial to the large majority of seniors, the association became more cautious and deliberate in its policy advocacy for more than a decade following the MCCA repeal. The protests and resignations of thousands of its members drove home the fact that with membership growth came membership diversity. Its membership now covered a wide range of income levels, ideological proclivities, and partisan loyalties. Many members were at the peak of their careers while others had been retired for decades. Always officially bipartisan, now AARP strove more than ever to stay in the middle of the road, and to build slow but steady consensus before taking a firm stand on any issue.[74] The group became so cautious that some Washington policy makers felt it had lost some of its lobbying effectiveness.[75] Thus AARP's political influence was fraught with paradoxes that became all too clear in the wake of the MCCA catastrophe. The association represented older Americans, whose political power compelled Congress to vote overwhelmingly to repeal a law that it had passed overwhelmingly just the year before. Yet policy makers became skeptical of AARP's influence and ability to speak for them. AARP was universally considered to be one of the most influential lobbies in Washington—the 800-pound gorilla—in large part because of its size that dwarfed nearly every other political association. But its size and diversity made it all the more difficult to speak with a unified voice.

AARP's active yet cautious approach was evident in the fight over President Bill Clinton's health care reform proposal in 1993–1994, the Health Security Act. In the wake of the MCCA repeal, AARP and other senior organizations began lobbying seriously for national health care reform that would ensure health insurance coverage for Americans of all ages. Long-term care coverage and prescription drug coverage would have a greater chance of passing as part of a more comprehensive reform package. And comprehensive health insurance reform for people of all ages would have a better chance of passing if older people, who already were covered under Medicare, also benefited—by the inclusion of long-term care and prescription drug coverage. Thus, AARP made health care reform a priority in the early 1990s and supported President Clinton in that effort.[76]

The Clinton administration and congressional reform proponents were eager for AARP's support as the largest and most powerful of the aging-based groups. AARP in turn actively worked with them and pushed for inclusion of long-term care and drug coverage, although in the end the Health Security Act excluded comprehensive long-term care coverage, instead providing some home- and community-based services for the severely disabled. Unlike some aging-based groups like the Gray Panthers and the Older Women's League, which held out for a single-payer system rather than one that remained private-insurance-based, AARP was willing to make compromises. It was especially important to AARP officials that the legislation have bipartisan support in Congress, in order to facilitate outreach to their own bipartisan membership. Committed though it was to passage of health care reform, AARP dragged its feet in officially endorsing the Health Security Act. Its leaders believed that the reform package benefited Americans over the age of 50, including Medicare beneficiaries over the age of 65, overall. But they worried that the complexity of the legislation made it difficult to explain and gain broad consensual support from its members; that the cuts in future Medicare spending included in the bill would stimulate opposition; and that, in short, it might end up with another Catastrophic Coverage-type catastrophe on its hands. By the time AARP was ready to endorse, it was too late; the effort to get a bill through Congress collapsed.[77]

Following the collapse of the Health Security Act in 1994, the window of opportunity for comprehensive long-term care coverage essentially closed. Several years of yawning federal deficits and an expanding national debt, along with increasing conservatism in Washington under President Reagan and then, in 1994, the first Republican majority elected to both chambers of Congress in 40 years, left little room for budget-expanding social insurance programs. Further, Representative Claude Pepper, the strongest advocate in Congress for old-age benefits, in general and long-term care in particular, had died in office in 1989. Hopes were still alive for another AARP priority—adding prescription drug coverage to Medicare—but budgetary politics were becoming increasingly divisive and zero-sum, putting advocates for the aging on the defense. AARP remained a major player in Washington politics, with its membership of well over 30 million and its pragmatic willingness to work with policy makers of both parties. Meanwhile, the political world around it was becoming increasingly polarized.

Twenty-First Century: Bipartisanship in a Polarized Environment

Aging policy became one of the major partisan battlegrounds in the polarized policy environment of the late twentieth and early twenty-first centuries.[78] Both Social Security and Medicare continued to enjoy a high degree of public support, and so politicians of both parties avoid speaking in terms of cutting benefits or dismantling programs. Instead, they tout solutions that will "save" the programs, while tossing blame at partisan opponents for anything they can call "benefit reductions." But their solutions are very different. Liberal Democrats favor a strong governmental role in providing social welfare for collective security. Thus they generally support the current government-financed social insurance system that provides protection from income insecurity and the loss of health insurance upon retirement. This includes some redistribution of wealth to ensure at least a basic standard of living for the most vulnerable. Lower-income Social Security beneficiaries, for example, generally receive a higher proportion of their preretirement monthly income, although wealthier beneficiaries receive higher amounts. Any change to the current system favored by Democrats would generally involve increased benefits, financed by higher taxes. Conservative Republicans, in contrast, favor free-market reforms that would shift collective responsibility for retirement savings and health care to individuals. Although this increases individual risk without guaranteeing a decent standard of living, conservatives believe the market is more efficient than government, while the profit motive improves the quality of health care and other services. Thus they favor more sweeping reforms to Social Security and Medicare such as means-testing or partial privatization through the use of individual accounts—reforms that are more politically palatable branded as "entitlement reform" than as reductions to the two widely popular social insurance programs.[79]

Republicans, having gained a majority in both chambers of Congress in 1994 for the first time in 40 years, now were emboldened to slash domestic spending. Both parties were growing more unified within, as the number of moderates in Congress declined. Bipartisan opposition to cutting social welfare programs, still strong in the 1980s,[80] collapsed.

First to go was the major cash assistance program for alleviating children's poverty, Aid to Families with Dependent Children (AFDC). The 1996 Personal Responsibility and Work Opportunity Act converted the AFDC entitlement program into a block grant to states, reduced and capped the funding, added work requirements for the parents, and imposed a five-year lifetime limit on family benefits. Thus government expenditures on the new program, Temporary Assistance for Needy Families (TANF) declined rapidly, and the number of families served shrank by two-thirds, even as the national poverty rate rose in the wake of the Great Recession of 2008.[81] The passage of the 1996 welfare reform legislation demonstrated the relative ease with which a major public assistance program, targeting only low-income recipients, can be dramatically reduced and transformed, in the political climate of the late twentieth and early twenty-first centuries. It passed Congress on a largely party-line vote, essentially refuting the notion that congressional conservatives supported reduced old-age benefits in order to shift resources to children.

Conservative opponents of the welfare state had used the generational equity argument to convince the public that older people, far from the deserving needy, were the affluent greedy. But by the mid-1990s, they were couching their arguments less in terms of shifting resources to from the old to the young, and more in terms of reducing government spending and shifting resources to the private sector.[82] Americans for Generational Equity had faded from the scene by the early 1990s, and its research director Peter Peterson helped to found the nonpartisan Concord Coalition, emphasizing federal deficit and debt reduction. Warnings of future generational warfare over the budget continue to reverberate as a theme.[83] But AGE's primary objectives, like those of the Concord Coalition, were not about shifting governmental resources from the old to the young, but rather reducing federal domestic spending across the board.[84] Individuals would thus be offered more choice, but would also take on more personal responsibility, and more risk, for their own retirement savings and health insurance.[85] This would surely drive more elderly and disabled people into poverty, proponents of current programs argue, and future generations of older people would suffer for it. But conservative opponents argue that projected growth in entitlement programs will soon overwhelm the budget, while reducing federal spending and the national debt now will lay a foundation for economic growth beneficial to future generations.[86]

There is broad bipartisan agreement that some changes to the finance and benefit structures of Social Security and Medicare will be necessary in the coming decades in order to avoid shortfalls, and that the longer Congress waits to act, the more painful those changes are likely to be. The two programs combined had surpassed 40 percent of the federal budget by 2015 as baby boomers were reaching the age of 65—ten thousand boomers a day beginning in 2011 and continuing for another nineteen years. The Social Security Board of Trustees in 2015 projected that the Social Security trust fund reserves would be depleted in 2034, after which incoming tax revenue would only cover 75 percent of scheduled benefits through 2090—a wrenching decline in benefits if adjustments were not made by then.[87] Costs also continue to rise for Medicare and for Medicaid, which funds the bulk of nursing home and home health care, not only because of population aging but also because medical inflation continues to outpace that of the consumer price index, even after the passage of the Affordable Care Act in 2010.

The projected shortfalls put pressure on the federal government to reform old-age entitlements. But elected officials are reluctant to raise taxes on anyone, or to cut benefits and risk alienating older Americans. Not only does voter turnout rise with age,[88] but those boomers reaching age 65 at a rate of ten thousand a day constitute a very large cohort of older voters. There has been very little evidence over the years that older people vote differently from younger people, much less vote as a bloc.[89]

But there is also evidence that attitudes toward spending on Social Security affect older voters' choices more than those of younger voters.[90] Similarly, there is some evidence that publicity about Medicare cuts included in the Affordable Care Act of 2010 created something of an age-based schism in subsequent elections, with older voters moving toward the Republican party.[91] Loss aversion is a powerful psychological motivator, and politicians are aware of voters' sensitivity to risk and loss. Nor do Social Security and Medicare reductions appeal to middle-aged or younger voters, whose support for both programs remains stratospheric.[92]

Policy makers across the ideological spectrum speak in terms of preserving, saving, and enhancing Social Security and Medicare, and not in terms of reducing or eliminating them. Nevertheless, the policy approaches of the two parties are very different, as are their respective spins. Liberals and conservatives alike extol the virtues of self-reliance for older people. Liberals maintain that the social insurance programs pull millions of people out of poverty and enable seniors to retain their financial independence, freeing their children and grandchildren from financial and caregiving burdens as well. Conservatives assert that private retirement savings accounts and greater personal responsibility for health care costs are more conducive to independence and self-reliance.

Officials in both parties generally agree that changes are needed for long-term solvency of both Social Security and Medicare. But liberals contend that relatively minor, incremental adjustments will sustain the programs in their current form indefinitely. Their objective is to encourage confidence in the programs and support for making adjustments now, while there is still time to phase them in slowly and with minimal pain. Conservative opponents of social insurance warn of a looming crisis, accelerated by the aging of the baby boom generation in the midst of slow economic growth and a ballooning national debt. By undermining confidence in the programs' solvency, their objective is to convince the public that drastic reform is the only way to save them.[93] The Greenspan Commission had already extended Social Security's solvency through incremental adjustments in 1983, despite conservatives' charges that the system was then in crisis requiring more drastic measures.[94] But proponents of overhauling old-age entitlements, including means-testing benefits and mandating greater personal responsibility for retirement savings, contend that such incremental changes offer short-term relief without addressing the longer-term fiscal crisis that will hit future generations.[95]

AARP stands firmly on the liberal side of that debate, supporting the current structure of Social Security and Medicare. Its openness to incremental benefit changes for long-term solvency, and its willingness to accept bipartisan policy compromises, sometimes creates conflicts with groups like the labor-affiliated Alliance for Retired Americans (formerly the National Council of Senior Citizens),[96] the more strident National Committee to Preserve Social Security and Medicare, and the radical-activist Gray Panthers. But these organizations remain allies, members of the Leadership Council of Aging Organizations, and advocates of preserving old-age entitlements.

The relative consensus among old-age mass membership groups around government-financed benefits was broken in the late 1980s and early 1990s with the rise of three conservative groups: the 60 Plus Association, The Seniors Coalition, and United Seniors Association (now USA Next). Founded with the help of conservative direct-mail fund-raising pioneer Richard Viguerie, these three groups lobby for limited government, low taxes, and free-market reforms. Some political observers suggest that these groups are more active as fund-raisers than as political advocates.[97] But over the years they have been sporadically active in lobbying for conservative causes and in funding mostly Republican political campaigns. Much of their funding comes from corporate sources largely opposed to AARP on some of its major issues including health care reform and pharmaceutical price controls. Democratic Party consultants and consumer advocacy group Public Citizen reported that the 60 Plus Association and United Seniors Association received major funding from the pharmaceutical industry.[98] More recently, 60 Plus is reportedly one of a large network of nonprofits through which billionaire activists Charles and David Koch have contributed millions of dollars in support of conservative political candidates.[99]

Together with the Association of Mature American Citizens (AMAC), founded in 2007, and similar groups that crop up and sometimes disappear, the conservative senior member organizations often use AARP as their foil. Like 60 Plus, they promote themselves as "the conservative alternative to AARP."[100] "AARP: Association Against Retired Persons" reads a 60 Plus bumper sticker.[101] "For many years, there was only one senior organization. Now, you have a choice," says AMAC's website.[102] AARP may be more bipartisan and flexible than the other senior membership organizations to its left, but to the groups on its right, AARP's size and influence make it their favorite target.

AARP, then, finds itself roughly in the ideological center-left of the aging-policy issue network—the network of people and organizations inside and outside of government working to influence aging policy.[103] As Washington politics has become more polarized, the disparate assortment of competing and overlapping interest groups so typical of

American politics has become more clearly and closely aligned with the political parties.[104] Membership groups representing older Americans now cover the ideological spectrum from left to right, with AARP largely holding down the middle, though generally more in sync with the Democrats.[105] At the same time, the pluralistic system of cross-cutting groups has not disappeared into a one-dimensional conservative-versus-liberal battleground. Interest groups still form ad hoc alliances and coalitions around particular issues, usually with like-minded groups but often with "strange bedfellows," like AARP's brief alliance with the National Federation of Independent Business leading up to the 1983 Social Security reforms. "The Hill is more polarized than the sectors," noted Nancy LeaMond, AARP's chief advocacy and engagement officer, remarking on the difference between partisan standoffs in Congress and the more fluid relations among interest groups.[106]

AARP has been willing to take positions contrary to the narrow or expressed interests of its 50+ constituency, in order to build cross-generation coalitions, or to compromise on desired legislation. In the late 1990s, for example, AARP partnered with the Concord Coalition, its adversary on Social Security and Medicare privatization, to hold town hall meetings and find common ground on solutions for long-term program solvency.[107] This makes it unusual among political organizations, which tend to be more extreme than their constituents, rather than less so.[108] But the partisan and ideological diversity of AARP's membership—approximately one-third Democratic, one-third Republican, and one-third independent—gives the association some leeway in coalition building. At the same time, any controversial issue position runs the risk of angering one or another segment of its membership, thus urging caution. The diversity of its members' age and life situation—about a third its members are aged below 65—also complicates efforts to create membership solidarity. The upshot is that whenever AARP is embroiled in controversy it risks losing members, and sometimes has lost tens of thousands at a time, as happened in the wake of the passage and repeal of the Medicare Catastrophic Coverage Act in the late 1980s.

Medicare Modernization, Social Security Privatization, and Health Care Reform

Three twenty-first century controversies illustrate AARP's flexibility and willingness to work with both political parties, sometimes at the risk of angering many of its members: the passage of the Medicare Modernization Act of 2003, the aborted effort to partially privatize Social Security in 2005, and the passage of the Affordable Care Act, popularly known as Obamacare, in 2010. AARP's endorsement of the Medicare Modernization Act, pushed by Republican President George W. Bush, frustrated many of its more liberal and Democratic members. Its support of Democratic President Barack Obama's signature health care reform, in turn, alienated primarily conservatives and Republicans in the association.

The Medicare Modernization Act (MMA) of 2003 is best known for extending Medicare coverage to prescription drugs through Medicare Part D. As an expansion of benefits—in fact, the largest expansion of benefits since Medicare was passed in 1965—it would normally be more of a liberal proposition. But the MMA was originally proposed by the George W. Bush administration, supported by all but a few congressional Republicans, and opposed by all but a few congressional Democrats. One reason it drew so much conservative support and liberal opposition was because it failed to impose any price controls on pharmaceuticals; in fact the law prohibits government from negotiating cheaper drug prices. Conservatives also supported the large increase in subsidies to private insurance companies as an incentive to offer seniors managed health care plans to compete with traditional Medicare, through a program called Medicare Advantage. Finally, the MMA introduced a type of means-testing to Medicare for the first time, by increasing Medicare Part B premiums for higher-income beneficiaries. In sum, most Democrats viewed the legislation as doing more to benefit private industry than consumers, and moving toward the Republican Party's goal of privatizing Medicare.[109]

Bill Novelli, upon assuming the leadership of AARP two years earlier, had stated that adding prescription drugs to Medicare coverage was among the association's highest priorities. Novelli was determined that the association would retain its pragmatic, bipartisan approach but would now pursue a more aggressive advocacy role in Washington, after more than a decade of relative caution. The Medicare Catastrophic Coverage debacle had shown how risky it was to take bold positions on controversial issues when members are so ideologically diverse and divided. But too much restraint carries its own risks: some AARP members and policy makers alike had begun questioning AARP's political relevance, as, for example, when AARP timidly and belatedly expressed support for President Bill Clinton's health care reform.[110] "AARP has had a certain sense of complacency," Novelli said soon after taking over. "We need to do something about that. What we're going to do is keep pushing the envelope."[111] The lack of prescription drug coverage was the biggest gap in Medicare; pharmaceutical usage and prices had skyrocketed in the decades since its passage. Medicare was already wildly popular, and the additional benefit would be a boon to seniors across the ideological spectrum; "we know very well that our members really, really want this," said Novelli.[112]

But not everyone in the group approved. Many Democrats in Congress and within the association felt betrayed by AARP's alliance with congressional Republicans and the pharmaceutical industry. Other left-leaning senior organizations—the Alliance for Retired Americans, the National Committee, and the Gray Panthers—criticized AARP for supporting a bill that opened the door to Medicare privatization and that lacked price controls. Coverage was incomplete: a gap in coverage was derided as the "doughnut hole" because Part D covered prescription costs up to a limit, then beneficiaries had to cover the rest themselves until catastrophic coverage kicked in. Thus recipients with chronic conditions could be on the hook for thousands of dollars a year. Nor did the MMA legalize reimportation of cheaper drugs from other countries as many beneficiaries had hoped. Some critics charged that AARP had supported Part D private plans so that it could offer its own plan and profit from it. Others complained that AARP had gone corporate, allowing itself to be bullied or seduced by influential Republicans. Many of AARP's own volunteers at the state and local levels felt they had not been sufficiently consulted and vigorously opposed the MMA; the association, they said, was losing its grassroots appeal. Some 60 thousand members left the organization as a result, some burning their AARP cards in protest.[113] When President Bush signed the MMA, he thanked the conservative groups 60 Plus, the United Seniors Association, and The Seniors Coalition, as well as AARP for their help and support.[114]

AARP's alliance with Republicans on Medicare Modernization may have led to the loss of tens of thousands of members, but may also have strengthened its appeal with baby boomers. While Americans aged 65 and over are wary of any change to Medicare, boomers, still several years away in 2003 from starting to turn 65, were open to introducing some private competition into the program, AARP's research showed.[115] Boomers appreciate political independence, and "would find AARP more appealing" if they see the group "as independent and sophisticated," said aging politics specialist Robert Binstock.[116] Novelli and Rother both contend that AARP's pragmatic approach helped achieve the best deal possible from a Republican-majority Congress. "You can't practice modern healthcare without prescription drugs," Novelli said. "And yet they weren't covered under Medicare."[117] "Something had to be done," said Rother, "and we pushed for the possible rather than the pure."[118] "One wonders how many resignations there would have been if AARP had opposed a bill that provided prescription drug coverage under Medicare for the first time," note Schulz and Binstock. "It is quite possible that millions of members were at stake."[119]

Two years later, AARP repaired relations with Democrats and broke with President Bush in opposing the top domestic priority of the president's second term: partial privatization of Social Security. Bush had nurtured the idea for years, and now was ready to push for reform that would divert a portion of workers' payroll tax contributions into private, individually managed accounts, reducing the amount going into the traditional Social Security defined benefit plan. AARP pushed back with a vigorous lobbying effort and a five million dollar advertising campaign with the message that modest, incremental changes would sustain the system for generations; drastic reforms like private accounts would unnecessarily place too many future retirees at risk.[120] Still, the more left-leaning aging-based organizations were more adamant about preserving current structure and benefit levels while AARP signaled a more pragmatic openness to change.[121] Not surprisingly, the conservative senior organizations supported the president's proposal, and so once again AARP found itself in the center-left position among aging-based membership groups.

AARP's opposition to President Bush's Social Security reform proposals suited its members well. Membership continued to grow, reaching a peak of over 40 million in 2008 before the Great Recession led to a downturn of over two million the following year, in 2009. It was also in 2009 that AARP would take its most controversial action under Novelli's leadership: supporting President Barack Obama's health care reform package, which would pass Congress in 2010 as the Patient Protection and Affordable Care Act of 2010, better known as the ACA or Obamacare. The ACA included provisions that would benefit both Medicare beneficiaries—such as phasing out the doughnut hole for more complete prescription drug coverage—and younger AARP members—such as subsidies for individual health insurance, reduced out-of-pocket expenses for preventive care, and easier access to health insurance for those with pre-existing medical conditions. Nevertheless, opposition to the plan was widespread, and this time it was the more conservative members opposed to the policy of a Democratic president who were unhappy.

AARP built a coalition of strange bedfellows to promote health care reform. Divided We Fail, launched in 2007, included the Business Roundtable, the National Federation of Independent Business, and the Service Employees International Union. The loose coalition of business, labor, and consumer groups hoped to raise awareness and to place affordable, accessible, quality health care high on the public agenda. AARP's persistence in advertising and maintaining such widespread support across the ideological spectrum of powerful interest groups helped to shape and promote the reforms. It also enabled President Obama to make health care reform a top priority of his new administration, at a time when the Great Recession that his administration inherited might otherwise have knocked health care off the agenda. At the same time, the organization's alliance with conservative business groups likely impeded its support for a more comprehensive government-financed, single-payer health care system, disappointing the more liberal supporters of major reform.[122] But such a major transformation of the health care system was a "nonstarter," John Rother noted, with Americans generally wary of government, and support in Congress was almost nil.[123]

AARP's approach to health care reform was, as usual, pragmatic, cautiously expressing support publicly while lobbying for favored provisions, especially to close the doughnut hole in prescription drug coverage. The effort was successful: the gap in drug coverage was scheduled to be phased out by 2020. By the time the ACA passed Congress, AARP was fully behind it.[124] Divided We Fail had successfully pushed for reform, but began to divide and fail over the details of the legislation soon after Obama was sworn in. Organized labor wanted more universal coverage. Business wanted a private-insurance-based system without employer mandates to provide or pay for employees' insurance.[125] The National Federation of Independent Business ended up suing the federal government in one of the most formidable challenges to Obamacare's survival. The program survived, though not entirely intact. A narrow majority of the U.S. Supreme Court ruled in *NFIB v. Sebelius*,[126] in 2012, that the individual mandate to purchase health insurance or pay a fine was a constitutionally permissible use of the government's taxing authority, but that the federal government could not force the states to accept federal dollars in order to expand Medicaid.[127]

Despite AARP's endorsement of the ACA, older people opposed it more than any other age group. The reform was to be financed in part by reducing growth in Medicare spending, primarily by trimming subsidies to private Medicare Advantage plans, which cost more per beneficiary than traditional Medicare, and by gearing provider reimbursements more toward patient health outcomes and less toward fee-for-service. But reform opponents raised the specter of "Medicare cuts" leading older people to believe their benefits would be slashed.[128] A provision to expand Medicare coverage to voluntary consultations with a doctor to discuss end-of-life planning was labeled by opponents as "death panels," evoking images of "pulling the plug on granny."[129] Fact-check website PolitiFact voted the rhetoric about death panels as "the lie of the year."[130] A survey by the Kaiser Health Foundation found that half of seniors mistakenly thought their Medicare benefits would be cut, while most were unaware of such benefits as lower out-of-pocket costs for preventive services and prescription drugs.[131] While Americans were highly polarized along partisan lines in their attitudes toward the ACA, they were also divided along age lines, with support dropping sharply after the age of 65.[132]

Conservative opponents of the ACA, in sum, rallied opposition among the elderly by playing up antigovernment, anti-Obama, and death-panel themes. In essence, the ACA was a multigenerational health care reform, which included benefits for Americans between the ages of 50 and 65 as well as for those over 65 and on Medicare. But older Americans in communications and town hall meetings with public officials expressed anger at what they perceived as benefit cuts.[133] AARP launched a multimillion dollar educational campaign to explain the benefits of the bill, under the direction of CEO Barry Rand, who took over in 2009 as the ACA was still moving through Congress. "It's the largest education effort our organization has ever undertaken," said Rand, explaining that people like the benefits, yet remain wary of "Big Government": "Government hands off my Medicare," as the cliché goes. Ideological polarization, Rand said, has overwhelmed public discussion of what is actually in the law.[134]

The educational campaign continued years after the ACA's passage, in the face of relentless congressional Republican efforts to repeal it. It has not been easy. The health insurance reforms encompassed in the ACA are complex, not easily boiled down to sound bites or catch phrases. Opponents' evocation of "big government" and "death panels," on the other hand, resonate, especially among conservatives, but also, in a larger sense, among the aging. "I have never seen such disciplined opposition *after* passage" of a bill, said AARP's chief lobbyist LeaMond.[135] Republican House Speaker Paul Ryan still contended, in the wake of the 2016 national elections, that "because of Obamacare, Medicare is going broke"—falsely, according to *The Washington Post* Fact Checker.[136] The battle over health care reform continues, even after Republican plans to scale down the ACA in 2017 could not get through Congress despite multiple attempts. Sociologist Frederick Lynch credits AARP for "exercising much-needed leadership and long-term vision on one of the most vexing public policy issues of the twenty-first century. Few others did so."[137]

Tens of thousands, perhaps as many as 300,000, members left AARP in the wake of its advocacy for the ACA.[138] Other aging-based groups on AARP's left and especially on its right have criticized the association and perhaps have gained members at AARP's loss. The labor-affiliated

Alliance for Retired Americans signed up nearly 4,000 new members the month after AARP helped usher George W. Bush's Medicare Modernization Act through Congress.[139] Conservative for-profit groups, the American Seniors Association and the Association of Mature American Citizens, said they gained tens of thousands of members, many former AARP members, in the wake of the ACA passage.[140] Other observers find little evidence that rival groups are horning in on AARP's influence or—in the case of the conservative groups—mobilizing grassroots beyond "astroturfing" through direct mail.[141]

At any rate, the loss of hundreds of thousands of members barely makes a dent in a membership of nearly 40 million. AARP leaders acknowledge the dilemmas involved in representing a large, ideologically diverse membership. Membership loss on occasion has made the association skittish about taking bold stands, as happened after the Catastrophic Care catastrophe of the late 1980s. But there is no sign that any other organization will remotely begin to compete with AARP in size. Other senior organizations are not gaining at AARP's expense, said AARP's Legislative Policy Director David Certner. Instead, while AARP remains the "go-to organization" and the credible source of information for policy makers, the aging-based groups collectively keep aging issues visible and salient. "We welcome their participation," he said.[142]

Take a Stand: Social Security and the 2016 Election

Partisan battles over Social Security and Medicare heated up once again in the wake of the Great Recession, which began in late 2007 and was in full swing as President Barack Obama was sworn into office in January, 2009. By that time, gross domestic product (GDP) was falling at the rate of 5 percent, and the economy was shedding hundreds of thousands of jobs a month. As tax revenue declined and federal spending expanded to stimulate the economy and help people weather the crisis, the federal deficit swelled from $161 billion in 2007—just over 1 percent of the GDP—to a peak of $1.413 trillion in 2009—nearly 10 percent of the GDP. The rapidly expanding national debt drove President Obama and Congress into crisis mode. It also placed Social Security and Medicare, by now consuming over a third of the budget, in the sights of both Democrats and Republicans.

President Obama convened the National Commission on Fiscal Responsibility and Reform in 2010, to develop a policy blueprint for bringing the budget back into balance and the federal debt under control. The 18-member commission is informally known as Bowles-Simpson or

Simpson-Bowles, after its two cochairmen: Democrat Erskine Bowles, an investment banker and former White House Chief of Staff under President Bill Clinton, and Republican Alan Simpson, former senator from Wyoming and a prominent critic of AARP. Although never officially approved or enacted, Bowles-Simpson's recommended spending cuts and tax hikes continued to serve as a framework for discussion and debate among policy makers. Some of their suggested Social Security reforms included raising the retirement age, slowing benefit growth for higher-income workers, bringing all state and local employees into the system, adjusting the cost-of-living index downward, and increasing the payroll tax cap.[143]

AARP steadfastly opposed cutting benefits in order to balance the budget and reduce the debt. "AARP members care deeply about making sure that Social Security and Medicare are there for our kids and grandkids," Executive Vice President Nancy LeaMond stated in a 2010 press release before the Bowles-Simpson commission was even appointed. "We are committed to supporting balanced and responsible approaches to reducing the nation's debt, but we remain strongly opposed to a proposal that would target Social Security and Medicare as piggy banks for arbitrary debt reduction."[144] AARP joined in fighting benefits cuts along with the Strengthen Social Security coalition, an alliance of labor unions and progressive groups—including aging-based organizations ARA, NCPSSM and the Older Women's League as well as Generations United—created to counter Bowles-Simpson's recommendations and led by the advocacy group Social Security Works.[145]

Commission cochair Simpson struck back in his usual colorful way. In a letter to the executive director of the Older Women's League, who had expressed concern on HuffingtonPost.com about his "constant bashing of seniors," Simpson wrote, "yes, I've made some plenty smart cracks about people on Social Security who milk it to the last degree. . . . We've reached a point now where it's like a milk cow with 310 million tits!" Leaders of Social Security Works and several groups within the alliance called for him to resign from the commission. AARP stopped short of calling for Simpson's resignation, but AARP's Senior Vice President Drew Nannis excoriated the remark as "offensive for several reasons, particularly for belittling a bedrock program that is the foundation of family security for all generations," going on to say that Simpson's remarks "undermine the serious work of the commission and give us little confidence the commission can fairly look at important programs such as Social Security." Simpson wrote OWL a letter of apology.[146]

The Bowles-Simpson Social Security reform receiving the most attention, once President Obama offered to accept it in a deal with congressional

Republicans in 2012, was the downward adjustment to the cost-of-living index, known as the chained consumer price index, or chained CPI. The chained CPI would hold benefit increases slightly lower than the general rate of inflation by calculating the cost of living based on substitutions—for example, buying less expensive apples rather than more expensive oranges. AARP and other aging advocates like Social Security Works argued that the cumulative reduction in benefits would be hard on seniors, especially as they faced rising medical costs. "People are under the impression that it's kind of a small change. Given the money it's bringing in, it's actually a pretty significant change. It's a lot of money out of people's pockets directly. It's thousands of dollars," said AARP lobbyist David Certner.[147] President Obama dropped his support for the chained CPI in his budget negotiations with Congress when Republicans refused to accept tax increases as part of a compromise.

"Unfortunately," complained the Pete Peterson-funded Committee for a Responsible Federal Budget, "politics has gotten in the way . . . Benefit changes as sensible as measuring inflation more accurately have become an anathema to the AARP and to many on the left."[148]

At the same time, AARP's policy experts recognize the need for adjustments to assure Social Security's long-term solvency, especially as aging baby boomers swell the ranks of retirees. The association periodically publishes "pros and cons of options on the table in Washington," explaining the likely effects of a variety of benefit and tax adjustments.[149] AARP's John Rother, arguing against Social Security privatization in a 1995 *Time* magazine cover story titled "Social Insecurity," suggested that the program's future solvency would probably require some combination of benefit reductions and payroll tax increases.[150] He was repeating Social Security advocates' familiar argument that incremental adjustments over time will sustain the program far into the future. In doing so, Rother disputed the crisis rhetoric of privatization advocates, whose support for radical change informed the magazine's cover copy: "The Case for Killing Social Security."[151]

But when Rother told *The Wall Street Journal* 14 years later that AARP could accept modest benefits cuts in the future as part of a deal to maintain the program's solvency, the *Journal* portrayed it as a big change. "Key Seniors Association Pivots on Benefit Cut," read the headline; "AARP . . . is dropping its longstanding opposition to cutting Social Security benefits," said the first sentence.[152] "Shock waves rippled through Washington," [153] or so it seemed in the flurry of headlines that quickly followed: "AARP Wobbles on Social Security Benefit Cuts," said ABC News;[154] "AARP Flips Position," said Newsmax;[155] "AARP Slammed . . ." said NBC

News.[156] "Did AARP Really Sell Out Seniors on Social Security?" wondered CBS News.[157] Just as quickly, CEO Barry Rand sought to clarify that "contrary to the misleading characterization in a recent media story, AARP has not changed its position on Social Security."[158] Legislative Policy Director David Certner agreed, emphasizing the distinction between cutting benefits to help balance the federal budget—which AARP opposes—and adjusting benefits and taxes over time to keep the program solvent. "Our policy for decades has always been that we basically support a package that would include revenue enhancements and benefit adjustments to get Social Security to long-term solvency," said Certner. "That has been our policy stated over and over again for, I mean, literally it has to be two decades, now."[159] In fact, the original *Wall Street Journal* article made the same distinction, making note of AARP's opposition to cutting benefits for the sake of deficit reduction, its opposition to means-testing benefits, and its preference for relying more heavily on tax increases to fill the Social Security trust fund's financial hole.[160] "We have maintained for years—to our members, the media and elected officials—that long-term solvency is key to protecting and strengthening Social Security for all generations," said CEO Rand, expressing a position that does not conflict with AARP's campaign to keep Social Security benefits off the table in federal budget negotiations.[161]

Nevertheless, many of AARP's liberal allies "hammered" the association "for refusing to oppose any and all cuts to Social Security benefits."[162] Both of the Social Security experts who cofounded Social Security Works criticized AARP's willingness to negotiate on benefits. "It's terrible negotiation strategy to signal a willingness to compromise before negotiations are joined," said Eric Kingson.[163] "I think it gives cover to lots of politicians who would like to see cuts in the program. It is very dangerous," said Nancy Altman, who added that benefit cuts are not needed; solvency can be maintained by lifting the payroll tax cap alone.[164] Other aging-based groups in the Strengthen Social Security coalition were equally critical. "AARP is losing the confidence of seniors around the country," said Max Richtman of the National Committee to Preserve Social Security and Medicare.[165] The Alliance for Retired Americans' Executive Director Ed Coyle said the ARA might have to distance itself from AARP on Social Security; "AARP does not speak for all seniors."[166]

But Rother emphasized the need to be flexible in order to have a seat at the table and influence policy. "The ship was sailing. I wanted to be at the wheel when that happens," he told *The Wall Street Journal*.[167] Any solution to long-term solvency would have to be bipartisan in order to pass, and Republicans would not accept tax increases without benefit reductions as well. "The [Strengthen Social Security] coalition's role was to kind of anchor the left, and our role is going to be to actually get something done."[168] The point was repeated years later, when AARP's Certner again defended Rother for expressing the same position AARP had held for years. Policy makers contact other senior groups to make political points and show their support. But "AARP is still *the* credible source for information, the go-to organization for people on the Hill on aging issues. They come here when they really want to get something done."[169]

Rother himself left AARP soon after the kerfuffle over the *Wall Street Journal* article, to become president and CEO of the National Coalition for Health Care. The move, he said, was an opportunity he could not resist, and was unrelated to the controversy. Still, he had become a bit frustrated with the internal reaction at AARP. Concerned about the timing of the *Journal* article in the midst of congressional budget negotiations and conflict over whether to raise the debt ceiling, AARP asked Rother not to talk to reporters without permission and not to rock the boat.[170]

AARP and Rother's National Coalition on Health Care continue to cooperate on the twin goals of reining in health care costs without cutting Medicare and Medicaid benefits. "The big underlying problems are not the programs," Certner contends. "They are rising health care costs."[171] The year of the *Journal* article controversy was the same year that Representative Paul Ryan proposed privatizing Medicare by transforming it into a voucher program, through which beneficiaries would use premium supports from the government to shop for health insurance on the private market. Strongly opposed to that idea, AARP and the National Coalition on Health Care advocate retaining the current Medicare program and cutting costs in other ways, such as adjusting provider payments.[172] Still, as the ongoing battle over the Affordable Care Act demonstrates, older people are extremely sensitive to any suggestion of tampering with Medicare. "You want to be perceived as being a strong advocate, but at the same time your long-term interest is in solving a problem," said Rother in 2012. "The art, if you will, is to make sure that you are operating and messaging in such a way as to get the best possible result for your members within the context of solving the problem."[173]

One year before the 2016 presidential election, AARP launched the Take a Stand campaign, pushing candidates to explain their plans for the future of Social Security. Thousands of members attended campaign events to ask candidates about their plans; members received preprinted petitions addressed to members' congressional representatives asking them to "open a national conversation about the future of Social Security" and "lay out your plans." AARP's publications and Take a Stand website detailed candidate positions; television ads called on candidates to address the program's future shortfall. One ad showed a donkey and an elephant standing by a ringing telephone, with the voiceover saying: "You can't deal with something by just ignoring it. But that's how some presidential candidates seem to be dealing with Social Security. Americans work hard and pay into it. So our next president needs a real plan to keep it strong. Hey candidates: answer the call already."[174] "If our leaders don't act, Social Security benefits could be cut by nearly 25%," read the headline of a Take a Stand ad in the *AARP Bulletin* weeks before the election. "It's time to update Social Security for the 21st century so we can keep the promise for future generations," the ad continued.[175]

The problem, said AARP's more liberal critics, is that AARP itself would not take a stand. Instead, candidate responses were reported without any comments on the merits of their plans, whether or not those plans included benefit cuts. The public wants politicians "to take the *right* stand, not *a* stand," argued Social Security Works' Executive Director Alex Lawson.[176] Further, argued progressive Social Security advocates, the Take a Stand campaign echoes the crisis rhetoric of conservatives, undermining confidence in Social Security by making its financial future seem more dire than it actually is.[177] Indeed, election-year statements from the conservative aging-based groups did foretell an impending crisis. The 60 Plus Association warned that "we have been on a glide path to insolvency for a long time now. It is past time to end the finger pointing and election year rhetoric and avert the crisis ahead."[178] The Association of Mature American Citizens proposed conservative reforms such as means-testing benefits, raising the retirement age, and "incentives to save," in a posting headlined "AARP's Rival Has a Good Social Security Plan."[179]

The 2016 presidential election was bitterly divisive, between two generally unpopular candidates, Democrat Hillary Clinton and Republican Donald Trump, the ultimate winner. Nevertheless, it was not a battle between two orthodox partisan candidates. Clinton was the first woman ever to be nominated by a major party, but as former First Lady, former senator, and former secretary of state, she was entrenched in the Democratic Party establishment at a time of high antiestablishment sentiment among voters. Populist antiestablishment billionaire candidate Trump campaigned on several issue positions that deviated from those of the conservative free-market oriented Republican Party establishment. On Social Security, candidate Trump rejected House Speaker Paul Ryan's support for major entitlement reform, stating his opposition to any benefit cuts; on Medicare, he broke with free-market proponents in advocating for government negotiations with drug companies to lower the prices of prescription drugs.[180] AARP's Take a Stand summarized Clinton's stance toward Social Security as opposition to any benefit cuts; improved benefits for widows and for caregivers, to be paid for by raising the payroll tax cap and taxing other income; and opposition to middle-class tax increases. Trump's position was to "keep promises made through Social Security," heading off future threats to solvency by growing the economy, reforming taxes and trade agreements, and rooting out fraud, waste, and abuse.[181]

By the time the election season was rolling toward the first state caucuses and primaries, progressive groups like Social Security Works, and some of the more liberal members of Congress, were pushing not only to hold the line on Social Security benefit cuts, but even for across-the-board benefit expansion. The federal debt crisis that had spurred budget-reduction talks and Obama's willingness to embrace the chained CPI had diminished. Economic growth brought in more tax revenue, and spending on some of the economic stimulus programs in the wake of the Great Recession was winding down, reducing the deficit by two-thirds from its peak in 2009. Further, Social Security benefits were increasingly inadequate for many retirees. The metaphorical three-legged stool providing the basis for Americans' retirement—Social Security, private pensions, and personal savings—was slowly collapsing. Fewer employers offered traditional defined-benefit pensions, and real wages for many Americans were stagnant or declining. Social Security, the third leg of the stool, needed a boost to maintain retirees' basic income security.[182]

For those reasons—and likely to enhance Democratic fortunes in the upcoming election—President Obama, speaking in Indiana in June, 2016, announced his support for expanded benefits. The announcement "was nothing less than a sea change."[183] Now, all of the senior organizations that had allied with AARP in opposing benefit cuts, as well as a growing number of Democratic members of Congress, were pushing for expansion. Candidate Clinton advocated targeted expansion funded by tax increases on higher-income Americans, and candidate Trump pledged not to make any cuts. AARP's Take a Stand campaign, intent on focusing attention on long-term Social Security sustainability, now seemed overly cautious and noncommittal. The association had taken something of a beating by steadfastly supporting the Affordable Care Act; now its allies were disappointed in its failure to take a clear stand in favor of more generous benefits.[184]

More controversy erupted for AARP during the 2016 election year, this time drawing criticism from the left: the Center for Media and Democracy, a research and advocacy group, revealed that AARP had provided funding to the American Legislative Exchange Council (ALEC). ALEC is a nonprofit, corporate-funded organization of state legislators and private-sector advocates of free markets and limited government. Its members work together to draft model legislation that conservative legislators then introduce and try to pass in their own states.[185] Many of its top issues are directly contrary to AARP's political positions. ALEC has pushed legislation to reduce public pensions and to impose restrictions on voting without a special photo ID that increases the burden of voting for people with limited mobility. ALEC has also pushed states to refuse Medicaid expansion under the Affordable Care Act, which would help lower-income seniors pay for long-term care. It supports Social Security privatization, ACA repeal, and a Constitutional Balanced Budget Amendment that would endanger the current levels of support for Social Security, Medicare, and Medicaid. No wonder, then, that labor unions and liberal groups, including Social Security Works and the Alliance for Retired Americans, as well as many AARP members, pushed AARP to withdraw from ALEC.[186]

It took only a week, from the time of the revelation to the time AARP announced it was letting its ALEC membership expire. Responding to a flurry of complaints on its members' online forum—"This organization works to undermine the very beliefs that I thought AARP stood for," said one posting; "I have placed my trust in AARP for 16 years—but now I wonder if my trust has been misplaced," said another—AARP defended the fee paid to ALEC as an entrée to ALEC's annual meeting, where representatives could engage with hundreds of state legislators from around the country. "AARP's engagement with ALEC is **NOT** an endorsement of the organization's policies," the association's statement reassured its members. "Being non-partisan means interacting with organizations on *all* sides of key issues—not just those whose views are identical to your own."[187] But pressure from members and organizational allies led AARP to withdraw. That earned a rebuke in turn from conservative consultant and former ALEC contributor Jean Card, who chided AARP for being "bullied" by liberal groups into leaving ALEC, "retreating from a situation where everyone might not agree, and where ideas are discussed and debated."[188]

Avoiding partisanship during an intensely rancorous election in a highly partisan era is not easy. With 38 million ideologically diverse members, AARP is a very large target. As such, it takes shots from all sides.

Conclusion

AARP represents a politically diverse membership of 38 million—roughly evenly divided among Democrats, Republicans, and independents—and, more broadly, a politically diverse 50+ U.S. population of over 110 million. Its large membership lends it both political influence and credibility in representing the varied and wide-ranging interests of Americans aged 50 and older. But it also creates a number of political dilemmas for the association.

Any strong position on a controversial issue can easily alienate some members even as it gratifies others. AARP angered many of its more liberal members, for example, by supporting the Republican-sponsored Medicare Modernization Act of 2003, which added a prescription drug benefit to Medicare but failed to impose cost controls. Six years later, AARP angered many of its more conservative members by supporting the Patient Protection and Affordable Care Act, commonly known as Obamacare, which included a number of benefits for Medicare beneficiaries and increased access to affordable health insurance for Americans aged over 50 but not yet eligible for Medicare, but which opponents portrayed as a potential loss of benefits and protections. The association's advocacy for the Medicare Catastrophic Coverage Act in 1988, at the time the largest expansion of Medicare since the program's inception, backfired when many seniors strenuously objected to the law's tax hike, and Congress repealed it a year later.

The political diversity of its members, most of whom join for the discounts, practical information, and other membership benefits often compel AARP to take a more centrist, even cautious, approach to controversial aging-related issues. Political organizations generally must walk a fine line between taking principled stands on the one hand, and compromising those principles in order build winning coalitions and achieve real policy gains on the other hand.[189] It is an especially tricky balancing act for AARP. Strident advocacy can drive some members away. But an overly cautious approach has at other times opened the association to complaints that it is failing to exercise sufficient political influence on its members' behalf.

Economic inequality is one of the underlying sources of political diversity among the 50+ population. AARP members are relatively more affluent, educated, and older than the general 50+ population; two-thirds are 65 years and older, over half (57%) have a college degree, and over half (56%) have annual incomes of at least $60,000. The association's emphasis on "successful aging," portraying older people as active, productive, and independent, combats ageism while encouraging the private sector to develop and market products and services for the benefit of a lucrative aging market. But it also feeds into the "greedy geezer" image used by opposing groups to justify slashing and privatizing aging-based programs and benefits.[190] While conservative opponents advocate means-testing

Social Security and Medicare benefits in order to focus on the needs of the most disadvantaged elderly, AARP and other social insurance advocates argue that means-testing benefits ultimately leads to loss of public support, transforming universal programs into ones that are much more meager and stigmatized. Ironically, universal social insurance programs keep millions more people out of poverty than do programs targeting only the poor.

Tension also persists between the long-term outlook for future generations and the shorter-term outlook for the current generation of Americans aged 50 and older. AARP's defense of aging-based programs and benefits, especially Social Security, Medicare, and Medicaid—the major source of public funding for nursing home care—speaks to the interests of its current members, while drawing criticism from generational equity proponents who say that old-age benefits deflect resources from the young. But AARP also has a long-term interest in the young and middle-aged Americans who comprise its future membership base. Thus it actively engages in coalition building with children's and youth advocates, and maintains a pragmatic approach to negotiating for changes to Social Security, and to finding ways to cut health care costs, in order to ensure the long-term solvency of all three programs. This opens it to criticism from members and allies who are more focused on short-term benefits than on long-term sustainability. Many of AARP's natural allies in the interest group universe take umbrage at its pragmatism and willingness to compromise; many of its strange-bedfellow coalition partners (such as the National Federation of Independent Business) work with AARP on particular issues while opposing many of its broader goals. Among senior membership organizations, AARP is both a valuable coalition partner and—especially to those on the right—a major adversary.

AARP's agenda is overly broad at a time when Social Security and Medicare benefits are at great risk, suggests Frederick Lynch, who has studied AARP extensively. Its pragmatic, bipartisan advocacy is too cautious and ambivalent to be effective in today's polarized political environment. It emboldens the advocates of entitlement reform and privatization; "it is a grave error that will only encourage further concessions and demoralize activist members."[191] With Republicans controlling both chambers of Congress and the White House after the 2016 elections, the risks are even higher, and the polarization over entitlement reform even more intense. Even before the new government took over in 2017, congressional Republican leaders were offering plans once again to downsize and partially privatize Social Security, and to convert Medicare into a system of vouchers or premium supports.[192] Also on their agenda was the repeal of the Affordable Care Act, including the Medicaid expansion and the closing of the Medicare prescription drug coverage gap or "doughnut hole." Now, more than ever, Americans aged 50 and over need AARP's strong, strident, unbending advocacy.

Effective advocacy may also involve working with both sides of the aisle, though, especially when they have a hard time working with each other. Partisan and ideological polarization in Washington has made it difficult for policy makers to break the gridlock and find mutually acceptable solutions to the nation's problems. Can AARP's pragmatism help bridge the gap? CEO Jo Ann Jenkins expressed that hope in the wake of the divisive elections of 2016:

> Partisanship has reached such an uncivil extreme that it is dividing our nation and prohibiting leaders from both political parties from coming together to do the people's work. Far too often the politician's goal is not practical solutions, but political advantage. When policy is debated only in terms of political gains and defeats, the American people lose. Instead of solutions, we get stalemate. And, as this election showed, the American people are tired of it. . . . At AARP, we will do all we can to restore civility and trust to our political discourse. As a new administration and new Congress prepare to take office in Washington and new legislatures and governors prepare to lead their states, AARP is ready to work with them to help find practical solutions to the issues people 50 and over care about, and to do our part in creating an America as good as its promise.[193]

CHAPTER FIVE

AARP's Influence: 38 Million Members, Washington Insider Status, and No Campaign Dollars

AARP's influence in national policy is legendary. Starting out mostly as a service organization that provided health insurance to an older population often unable to buy it on the open market—and soon thereafter, a money-maker for its affiliated insurance company, Colonial Penn—AARP gradually became more political, especially after the break with Colonial Penn in 1981. By the late 1980s, AARP's political influence was widely acknowledged, praised by its friends and panned by its foes. Washington insiders and observers have called it "the major player in the 'gray lobby,'"[1] "America's most powerful lobby,"[2] and, more ominously, "the most dangerous lobby in America,"[3] and it is very often portrayed, well into the twenty-first century, as the "800-pound gorilla" in national politics.[4]

But not everyone stands in awe of AARP's influence. No one disputes that it is huge. But "big isn't necessarily better."[5] It is so large and politically diverse that organization leaders are sometimes cautious about taking bold political stands on specific issues. Its 38 million members are not so much unified politically as they are "bound together by a common love of airline discounts and automobile discounts and RV discounts," says frequent AARP critic and former U.S. senator Alan Simpson.[6] This makes its power more symbolic than the influence exerted by smaller groups of dedicated grassroots activists, Eric Laursen suggests.[7] Scholars of aging politics in the 1970s noted that AARP had not been involved in the creation of the major welfare-state programs offering income and health security to older Americans—Social Security, Medicare, and Medicaid—and that its influence was primarily defensive, supporting incremental policy adjustments at most.[8] Christopher Howard made much the same point 40 years later: Although AARP's size, resources, and Washington connections had grown exponentially in the ensuing decades, its power is "more apparent when it plays defense than offense," and at any rate it is defending programs that are already highly popular with Americans of all ages.[9] So, does AARP's political influence live up to the legend, or is it more of a myth?

American politics is too complex, and the avenues to power too numerous, to make sweeping generalizations about any one group. Those who assert that AARP is, or ever has been, either the most powerful or the most dangerous political organization in the country surely exaggerate. But its influence on a wide range of policies affecting the lives of older Americans, from public pensions to public health and more, is significant and undeniable. Its size, its wealth, its policy expertise, and its insider status with policy makers give it formidable clout; its reach extends to state-level as well as national-level politics. Mostly liberal or center-left in orientation, it nevertheless possesses an unusual ability to work across a wide swath of the ideological spectrum in a political environment that has become increasingly polarized. It is one of the few organizations representing consumers that can often hold its own in a political system dominated by producer groups, especially large corporations. All-powerful it is certainly not, but its clout remains the envy of many organized interests in Washington, and a boon to its constituents and allies. Furthermore, AARP exerts some influence on the private sector, demonstrating the potential profitability of understanding the needs and desires of the 50+ population, just as Ethel Percy Andrus persuaded Leonard Davis back in 1955 that there was a great unmet need, and money to be made, in selling health insurance to retirees.

Assessing Interest Group Influence

There is no magic formula for assessing an interest group's strength and influence within the complex and fragmented American political system. James Madison, the primary author of the U.S. Constitution, argued in *The Federalist* #10 that the competing and overlapping interests in a large, diverse republic would ensure that everyone had a voice with no one interest dominating the rest. The fragmentation of government written into the new Constitution—the three branches of government checking and balancing each other, and the division of sovereignty between nation and states under federalism—would facilitate access to government for a wide variety of interests.[10] French historian and diplomat Alexis de Tocqueville, observing American's propensity to form associations, concurred that the multiplicity of interest groups, combined with a deeply rooted political consensus in which "differences of opinion are mere differences of hue," helped keep the young nation peaceful and tyranny-free.[11] But what makes some groups better organized and more influential than others? Political scientists have spent over a century trying to answer those questions.

Pluralist theory envisions American politics much as Madison did: myriad overlapping groups, competing for policy influence, winning some and losing some, but no one winning all the time at the expense of the rest.[12] Reality flies in the face of this ideal, elite theorists contend, as wealthy interest groups, business groups in particular, have the resources and connections to prevail most of the time.[13] As E. E. Schattschneider wrote in 1960, "The flaw in the pluralist heaven is that the heavenly chorus sings with a strong upper-class accent."[14]

Volumes of case studies and some large-scale analyses of dozens of groups involved in hundreds of policy areas have reached this conclusion about which groups prevail: "It all depends."[15] Group influence is highly contingent, depending on the nature and scope of the issue at hand, the circumstances at the time, the policy makers' ideology and inclination, and much more. Researchers examining the complex factors that lead to interest group success in different contexts are guided by the framework of neopluralism.[16]

Organizational resources matter, neopluralists acknowledge, and AARP is in many ways resource-rich. Policy makers respond favorably to groups with resources like large memberships, voter mobilization efforts, and policy information that saves them time and sharpens their arguments in debate.[17] But the groups wealthiest in resources are not guaranteed winners. As Frank Baumgartner and his colleagues noted in their massive study of interest-group activity on 98 policy issues, "one needs also to consider the issues on which groups are working, who else is active on those issues, and the construction of like-minded coalitions on the issue."[18] Complex issue networks—people working inside and outside government on specific policy matters—include a variety of groups, some of which are allies, some of which are adversaries, and some of which agree on certain points while disagreeing on others. Through conflict and coalition, as policies make their way through passage and implementation, multidimensional issue spaces gradually filter down into more simplified "sides" that are either "for" or "against."[19] As partisan polarization has increased in recent decades, each opposing side is increasingly aligned with one party or the other. Attributing influence to any particular group in this complex process is a dubious proposition. Nevertheless, AARP does stand out.

AARP's Clout and Resources

"There is no group acting as a counterweight to the A.A.R.P.," wrote John Tierney in the *New York Times Magazine* in 1988, going on to explain that there were no comparable organizations representing Americans of other age groups or generations. "The closest thing to a voice for the baby boomers [who in 1988 had not yet reached 50 years of age] is . . . Americans for Generational Equity," which as Tierney noted was more of a think tank than a lobbying organization, and at any rate wished to avoid a reputation as "granny-bashers."[20]

But of course there were, and are, numerous groups acting as counterweights to AARP, depending on the issue and the surrounding circumstances. AARP is involved, sometimes simultaneously, in numerous overlapping issue networks, such as those dealing with public pensions, health care, poverty reduction, public transportation, housing, and age discrimination. Thus it has at various times opposed finance industry lobbyists on partial privatization of Social Security, health insurers on health insurance reform, and free-market conservative or libertarian groups on public assistance programs, to name a few. An allied group in one policy conflict can be an opponent in another. The National Federation of Independent Business (NFIB), for example, joined AARP, the Business Roundtable, and the Service Employees International Union in the "Divided We Fail" coalition to advocate for health care reform in 2007. A few years later, the NFIB was fighting the Affordable Care Act in Court (*NFIB v. Sebelius*, 2012),[21] while AARP was heavily promoting the benefits of the ACA.[22]

The difficulty of ranking and rating interest group influence has not deterred political observers from attempting to do it. Perhaps the best known ranking of U.S. political organizations is *Fortune* magazine's Power 25. Nearly every year between 1997 and 2001, *Fortune* surveyed Washington insiders—legislators, lobbyists, congressional staffers, and White House aides—asking them to rank the most powerful lobbying groups. For three years in a row, 1997 to 1999, AARP ranked first. In 2001 AARP ranked second to the increasingly dominant National Rifle Association (NRA).[23] The next three with the highest average rankings were the NFIB, the American Israel Public Affairs Committee (AIPAC), and the giant labor federation AFL-CIO.[24] More recently, in 2014, entertainment website Listosaur.com ranked AARP number four in its list of the "10 most powerful special interest groups in America," after the NRA, the U.S. Chamber of Commerce, and the American Medical Association.[25] Listosaur's ranking is based on "a number of factors, including membership numbers, finances and history."[26] Data-driven though these rankings are, they are still rather subjective, and the *Fortune* Power 25 is, as Baumgartner and his colleagues note, "a reputational measure, not a scientific indicator of influence."[27] But they do reveal widespread recognition of AARP as a major player in national policy.

Interest group influence may be more easily appraised when viewed within the issue networks in which they operate. Matt Grossmann's extension of neopluralism does just that. His theory of behavioral pluralism explains why some constituency groups—such as older Americans—become better represented and mobilized than others. His theory of institutional pluralism explains how certain organizations become the most prominent and active representatives of their constituency groups, and he examines AARP as a clear success story.[28] Grossmann gauges the political prominence and the political involvement of more than 1,600 advocacy groups in Washington across a wide range of issue networks. He measures an organization's prominence by the relative number of mentions in major print and televised news media. The measure of organizational involvement in national policy making includes congressional committee hearings, presidential announcements, administrative agency rulemaking, and federal court proceedings. Grossmann also gauges organizational mobilization by examining requests for public or member political action on their websites, requests to attend meetings or demonstrations, and participation in public events such as panel discussions and conferences. He measures organizational resources by examining groups' age, membership size, staff size and lobbying capacity, ties to political action committees and local chapters, and the breadth of their issue agendas. AARP placed "among the most successful 5 percent of advocacy organizations on every indicator of resources, activity, prominence, and involvement."[29] It is no wonder that AARP is so often cited as one of the most influential organizations in Washington, not just among aging advocates but within the entire interest group universe.

A closer look at AARP's political resources reveals that it is resource-rich indeed, especially compared with the 1,600 groups in his study—"all organizations with a presence in the Washington area that aspire to represent a section of the public broader than their own institution, staff, and membership," that is, excluding "companies, governments, and their associations."[30]

Age. Organizational longevity tends to increase a group's visibility and influence. AARP, founded in 1958, and its precursor, the National Retired Teachers Association, founded in 1947, are both at the older end of the middle 50 percent of the groups Grossmann examined. They are a decade or two older than the average, and two or three decades older than the median organization. While a few groups have been around for over a century, most date back only to the early 1980s.[31] AARP was not especially active politically in its early years, but by the early 1970s, it was up to nearly ten million members and was recognized, along with the National Council of Senior Citizens, as a major force within the emerging gray lobby.[32]

Money. With an operating budget of a billion and a half dollars, AARP can afford to throw its weight around. Nearly two-thirds (64%) of its revenue is derived from royalties—paid by providers of member benefits, especially insurance, for the use of AARP's name, logo, and mailing list—and from paid advertising in its publications. One-fifth of its revenue comes from membership dues, and the rest comes from grants, contributions, and program income.[33] The business earnings keep the membership dues low while enabling the association to be financially self-sustaining in its advocacy. Thus Frederick Lynch characterizes AARP as "an unusual, hybrid profit/nonprofit 'social entrepreneur' organization that sells reasonably priced financial and insurance products to older Americans and then plows the proceeds back into social services, policy advocacy, and an overall 'positive aging agenda.'"[34]

Membership Size. AARP's membership is its primary political resource. With its 38 million members dwarfing nearly all other mass-membership organizations, AARP employs the power of the grassroots in numerous ways, from the AARP/Vote campaign of the mid-1980s to the "Take a Stand" campaign, raising the profile of Social Security as an issue, during the 2016 elections. Its frequent member surveys show that most join for the discounts and other benefits, but renew largely for the advocacy and social mission, and for the raft of information that arrives in the association's print and online publications, mass mailings, e-mails, and social media.[35] Much of that information is of a practical nature, but much of it is political. Campaigns like 2012's "You've Earned a Say" encourage members, via town hall meetings, online surveys, and national advertising, to contact public officials and AARP leaders with their concerns. AARP voter guides and local candidate debates expose members to candidates' issue positions. One-quarter of voters nationwide are AARP members, according to AARP's Legislative Policy Director David Certner,[36] and their votes make a difference. In 2014, Nancy LeaMond, AARP's chief advocacy and engagement officer, noted that every U.S. senator but one (Mark Warner of Virginia) won the 50+ vote.[37]

AARP is the "undisputed king of membership organizations [having] perfected the benefits and services model of functional organizing," says Peter Murray in his in-depth study of over 50 civic organizations.[38] The vast array of products, services, publications, and information obtained for just $16 in annual dues attracts the outsized membership. The only nonreligious membership organization larger than AARP is the American Automobile Association (AAA), with over 55 million members. AAA attracts members with a variety of member services including emergency roadside service and product and travel discounts. It does lobby government, but on a relatively narrow range of roadway and traffic issues; its headquarters is in Florida, not Washington, D.C., and it is more a federation of regional clubs than a national advocacy group. Another large-scale membership organization is the National Rifle Association (NRA), with about four and a half million members—a membership much smaller than AARP's, but intensely engaged in local group and political activities. Although AARP members are not as active and engaged as those in the close-knit NRA community, many do respond to AARP's calls to action.[39] Many members who volunteer with AARP engage in political activity. LeaMond, who oversees public education campaigns, community engagement, and volunteerism, counts on some 17,000 active volunteers around the country who "suit up and visit the state legislatures," and another five million or so who engage on an occasional basis, for example, calling or writing to public officials.[40] As messaging consultant Rich Tau told Frederick Lynch, "AARP is powerful because of their sheer numbers. . . . Even if they mobilize 1 percent of their base, it generates impact and looks very impressive. . . . All it has to do is whisper."[41]

Lobbying is the secondary influence, say AARP's leaders; the direct lobbying "augments the voice of the constituency."[42] The all-volunteer board also serves to convey grassroots concerns to the organization's executive team; they are "pillars of the community" from "outside the Beltway."[43] Not everyone believes the membership has sufficient input; some volunteers and state-level staff felt that the general membership lost some of its influence when policy decision-making was centralized at the national level in the early 2000s.[44] Regardless, AARP's grassroots mobilization, combined with the association's policy expertise and inside-the-Beltway connections, sustains its prominence in aging-related policy discussions.

The two types of lobbying—direct lobbying and grassroots lobbying—complement and bolster each other. The most successful political membership organizations combine grassroots mobilization and direct lobbying in this way. Elected officials in particular respond to active, engaged constituencies and potential voter mobilization. But without effective direct lobbying, an organization's grassroots campaigns using preprinted postcards, one-click online messaging, or other canned responses are often perceived as phony grassroots, or "Astroturf." Conversely, when organization representatives provide credible information and cultivate good relations with public officials, those officials are more likely to perceive mass-membership actions as genuine grassroots rather than simply as Astroturf.[45] AARP's reputation as a lobbying powerhouse backed by its massive membership was well established in Washington policy circles by the mid-1980s.[46]

Staff Size and Lobbying Capacity. AARP's lobbying staff, like its membership, dwarfs that of most other political organizations representing public groups. In 2016, AARP had 36 lobbyists registered with Congress, 21 on AARP's own staff and another 15 external lobbyists hired from professional firms, and over half of them had previously worked in government.[47] The average advocacy organization in Grossmann's study has just two or three lobbyists on their staff and one or none hired from outside. Only a small minority of groups have large staffs of political advocates like AARP.[48] Hundreds more of AARP's 2,000+ employees work in policy research, advocacy, and outreach.

John Rother came to AARP in 1984 to lead its policy advocacy and research, as the association expanded its political activities after its break with Colonial Penn. For the next 27 years he was "the public face of AARP—an expert on health care and Social Security and the influential policy chief at the powerful lobby group."[49] "He's a real policy guru," said Bill Novelli, AARP's executive director from 2001 to 2009.[50] Rother was an eight-year veteran of Capitol Hill, serving first as chief counsel for labor and health to Senator Jacob Javits, and then as special counsel for the Senate Special Committee on Aging. AARP's political division doubled in size within a few years of Rother's arrival. It also established its own think tank in 1985, the AARP Public Policy Institute, for policy research, analysis, and development of proposals and strategy.

Genial, pragmatic, and extremely knowledgeable, Rother was instrumental in establishing AARP's reputation for credible and reliable advocacy. Policy makers and other Washington insiders praise the group's advocacy for being "politically pragmatic," "professional and very responsible," "highly principled," and understanding that "there has to be some give and take."[51] Charles Morris, referring to AARP as "America's most powerful lobby" in 1996, concedes that "although it is not fashionable to say so, AARP has gradually emerged as one of the more responsible of Washington lobbying organizations," in large part because it "has passed up the opportunity for winning cheap applause from its members in favor of the more difficult, but more responsible, position."[52] The reputation has stuck. Other aging-based groups may be contacted for political points, said Legislative Policy Director Certner in 2015, "but we are *the* credible source for information, the go-to organization for policy makers on aging issues. They come here when they really want to get something done."[53]

Money helps of course, and AARP has a lot to spend. The lion's share of AARP's expenditures goes into nonpolitical outreach, service, and communications, but it is also one of the top spenders on lobbying in Washington. Congress has kept records of lobbying activities and spending for public disclosure since 1998, as required by the Lobbying Disclosure Act of 1995. AARP spent just over $260 million between 1998 and 2016, making it the eighth highest spender overall. Dwarfing all other organizations is the U.S. Chamber of Commerce, which spent over a trillion dollars during those years and was the top spender in every year except for 1998, when it came in fourth after two tobacco companies and Bell Atlantic. Second in overall spending for 1998–2016 is the National Association of Realtors with nearly $373 million, followed by four health-industry groups (the American Medical Association, the American Hospital Association, the Pharmaceutical Research and Manufacturers of America, and Blue Cross Blue Shield) and General Electric. All other organizations in the top 20 besides AARP also represent sectors in business and industry. AARP is the only consumer group to appear in the top 20.[54]

AARP was the second highest spender on lobbying in 2003, 2005, and 2008. In 2003, AAPRP supported the Medicare Modernization Act, which added prescription drug coverage to Medicare for the first time. In 2005, AARP successfully helped defeat the effort toward partial privatization of Social Security. In 2008, the primary issues in AARP's advocacy were health care reform and budgetary issues, in the midst of that year's national elections and the Great Recession. Since 2008, AARP's spending on lobbying has dropped rather steadily from over $35 million to $8.7 million in 2016.[55]

AARP is not alone in declining spending; both lobbying expenditures and the number of registered lobbyists have dropped in Washington in recent years.[56] Just how much they are declining is something of an open question, and in fact publicly disclosed lobbying information might be taken with a grain of salt. The law's definition of "lobbyist" permits many people who influence policy for a living to avoid registering simply by giving themselves such titles as "policy consultant" or "strategic adviser." "It's porous as a sieve," one former White House aide said of the law.[57] But relatively speaking, AARP's lobbying expenditures have decreased; in 2016, AARP was number 49 in the list of top spenders. Still, in an influence industry dominated by business and industry, particularly those in health care, AARP stands out as a singular major player among consumer groups.

Local Chapters. "Fewer than one-fifth of advocacy groups have state or local chapters," Grossmann finds in his interest group survey.[58] AARP is one of the few that do. Only about 5 percent of AARP members are involved in one of the 1,300 local chapters, however, and even when the number of local AARP chapters peaked at around 6,000, only a tiny percentage of members were involved.[59] Chapter activity, at any rate, has always been primarily social rather than political. "Why not check out an AARP chapter near you!" suggests the AARP website, noting that "each one has its own personality and focus. Chapter activities can include meals, cultural outings and trips, and for many, community service is a major priority."[60] Most of AARP's volunteer mobilization, whether politically or service-oriented, is handled by professional staff at the national and state offices. Still, as the association has expanded its state office network since around the turn of the century, there has been some recognition that face-to-face interaction at the local level can be a resource for political information sharing and organizational visibility.[61]

Breadth of Issue Agenda. AARP's issue agenda is as broad as its membership is big. Only a few organizations that Grossmann examined take positions in more than a dozen issue areas; most organizational agendas include no more than two major issue areas.[62] AARP's annual report and "advocacy snapshot" for 2015 list dozens of issues at the national and state levels under the general headings of "health security," "financial resilience," and "personal fulfillment."[63] Health security includes issues such as Medicare benefit levels, family caregiver tax credits and other supports, Medicaid expansion in the states, and improvements to state health insurance exchanges. Financial resilience includes a slew of issues related to protecting and expanding social insurance and public assistance programs that affect Americans aged 50 and over, as well as fighting age discrimination, holding down utility costs, and more. Personal fulfillment includes everything from public transportation options to voter identification laws. Public disclosure of lobbying activities at the federal level shows the issue agenda to be more than words on paper; AARP's reported contacts with public officials cover issues ranging from health care, retirement, and taxes to telecommunications, civil rights, and veterans' affairs—17 of the Center for Responsive Politics' broad issue categories in 2015 alone.[64] The report shows numerous contacts not only with members of Congress but also with a wide range of bureaucratic agencies. Combined with the litigation unit, the association engages all three branches of government. As LeaMond notes, "advocacy doesn't stop when a bill is passed."[65]

Some political organizations with a narrow agenda may exert significant influence as niche groups, dominating in the area of their specialized expertise.[66] But an expansive issue agenda increases a group's prominence and visibility, enhancing the group's access to policy makers and its reputation as a credible source of information.[67]

No PAC or Candidate Endorsements. AARP does not endorse candidates or contribute to their campaigns. Candidate support is the one resource in Grossmann's study that AARP does not deploy—by choice. This has been a matter of internal discussion. General Counsel Cindy Lewin at one point suggested that AARP establish a political action committee (PAC), but "I was voted down," and then convinced that establishing a PAC was not the way to go.[68] Strategically, for AARP, candidate funding and endorsements could do more harm than good.

Conventional wisdom in Washington holds that money does buy influence. While there is little evidence that campaign contributions influence floor votes in Congress, evidence abounds that campaign money increases access, especially at the congressional committee level, where bills are most often altered or finalized, advanced or killed. Campaign money can increase the chances that an issue will get on the governmental agenda—or stay off.[69] But only about 10 percent of the public interest groups Grossmann examined had PACs. The primary source of campaign contributions, like the primary source of lobbying dollars, is business and corporate organizations.[70]

AARP leaders believe that maintaining their nonpartisan, pragmatic reputation makes their advocacy more effective. The money game in national elections is fraught with the appearance of favoritism and even corruption. Restrictions on campaign finance are full of loopholes that make it easy legally to exceed the monetary limits by supporting candidates "independently" of their campaigns, and to bypass public disclosure by contributing through tax-exempt social welfare organizations, designated as 501(c)(4)s in the federal tax code.[71] AARP is a 501(c)(4) organization itself, but unwilling to use the designation to make undisclosed campaign contributions: "501(c)(4)s that do that are giving that designation a bad name."[72] Individual employees do contribute to campaigns, overwhelmingly supporting Democrats. Of $250,215 in employee contributions between 1990 and 2016, 85 percent went to Democrats.[73] This is not surprising in an era of partisan polarization with Republicans far more likely than Democrats to support major entitlement reform that would reduce or partially privatize Social Security and Medicare benefits. But eschewing an organizational PAC helps maintain AARP's nonpartisan, pragmatic reputation.

Candidate endorsements could easily alienate large segments of AARP's politically diverse membership, which is roughly evenly divided among Democrats, Republicans, and independents. Thus, AARP publishes voter guides in print and online, posing questions to candidates and printing their responses; it holds candidate forums and debates; it encourages members to follow the candidates' views on issues like Social Security and Medicare. Critics charge that without taking a stand and endorsing candidates who most support AARP's agenda, the voter guides and forums do "little more than give glib politicians another platform."[74] But AARP still channels its political spending into advocacy, not into candidate campaigns, and it avoids candidate endorsements altogether.

AARP has become the most visible and influential organization representing older Americans, a position it has held at least since the late 1980s. But the magnitude of its political influence is tied to the political standing and the political fortunes of the 50+ constituency that it represents. AARP might appear to be at the pinnacle of its power when public support for the elderly and old-age benefits is widespread. But its influence is more consequential when there is political pressure to reduce those benefits, as there is in the early twenty-first century.

Older Americans as a Political Community

Nobody wants to look like a "granny-basher"—least of all in politics. As the primary institutional representative of older Americans, AARP has this advantage: it represents a generally sympathetic constituency. Public esteem for the elderly runs high, reinforced by generational bonds, and perhaps by the knowledge that, barring tragedy, we will all be there some day. But as political pressures mount to scale back the major programs benefiting older adults, AARP's job becomes harder. "My intuitive idea of power," said political theorist Robert A. Dahl in 1957, "is something like this: A has power over B to the extent that he can get B to do something that B would not otherwise do."[75] The flip side of power is the ability to preserve a favorable status quo by keeping any unfavorable change off the policy agenda.[76] AARP's political power, in either sense, rests not so much in how well older people are doing politically, but how successful it is in protecting and expanding old-age benefits against the pressures to reduce them.

The political situation of older Americans has evolved over the last several decades. After the expansionary period following World War II into the 1970s, political observers began calling attention to the growing proportion of the budget that was dedicated to older people. Gradually the "compassionate ageism" that had led to benefit expansion gave way to "scapegoating" the aged for selfishly dominating a big chunk of the federal budget,[77] and ultimately to partisan and ideological discord over size and structure of federal health and income security programs.

Robert Hudson and Judith Gonyea trace this evolving social construction of older Americans, drawing on Anne Schneider and Helen Ingram's typology of target populations.[78] Schneider and Ingram argued that the political popularity and generosity of programs benefiting each group are determined largely by the group type. The four types of target populations for public policy are based on two dimensions: first, the groups' political power, and second, the groups' legitimacy, or how they are perceived by political decision makers and stakeholders. Groups perceived as positive or sympathetic, but lacking in political power, are labeled "Dependents." Those perceived in a positive light and also politically powerful are labeled as "Advantaged." Groups that are strong politically but perceived negatively or unsympathetically are labeled "Contenders." Older Americans, Hudson and Gonyea suggest, were historically Dependents, moving gradually into the Advantaged category in the decades following World War II, and then becoming Contenders as challenges to old-age benefits began to escalate in the early 1980s. The elderly have never fit in the fourth category—"Deviants," or groups both perceived negatively or undeserving, and politically weak.

The era of older Americans as Dependents lasted well into the twentieth century. Compassion and respect for the elderly as a group made them the primary beneficiaries of the country's two largest periods of social welfare expansion: the New Deal of the 1930s and the Great Society/War on Poverty of the 1960s and 1970s. Old age often meant job loss, destitution, and dependence on family members or meager public relief, which worsened in the Great Depression as employment and earnings declined and savings were wiped out. The Social Security system created in 1935 provided limited relief, but it provided the foundation for expansion of benefits and coverage in subsequent decades, to breadwinners' surviving family members, to people with disabilities, and to the vast majority of workers. Poverty was still disproportionately high among the elderly on the eve of the 1960s Great Society and War on Poverty, but after the creation of Medicare and Medicaid, further expansion of Social Security benefits, and a number of other programs and benefits targeting primarily the aged, their poverty level fell below that of the general population and their income levels grew. This was the period that Binstock characterized as "compassionate ageism,"[79] based on the ageist belief that older people are helpless and frail. In fact the economic diversity of younger years persists into old age, but by the late 1970s, older Americans enjoyed much higher levels of health and income security than they had before. Private pensions were increasingly common as well. Retirement had become a realistic and desirable goal.[80]

Public sympathy for older people as Dependents did not just come from compassion; it came also from the popular notion of the aged, along with veterans, disabled persons, and others unemployed through no fault of their own, as the "deserving poor."[81] The contributory structure of Social Security gave it an aura of earned benefits after decades of hard work, sacrifice, and compulsory savings.[82] In 1965, the Medicare program extended health care coverage to older and disabled Americans without expanding single-payer coverage to the population as a whole.[83] Both social insurance programs, then, entailed compromises between liberals and conservatives, both extending a helping hand to the needy while encouraging individual self-reliance. In addition, numerous other programs created between the 1930s and the 1970s raised the standard of living for many seniors. Some proved especially beneficial to seniors without targeting them specifically—for example, the Supplemental Nutrition Assistance Program (formerly Food Stamps) and Medicaid, which covers most long-term care—while others targeted older people specifically, providing cash assistance to the poor, delivering an array of services, and prohibiting age discrimination in employment. Bipartisan support for old-age security was so strong during that period that politicians of both parties claimed credit for maintaining and expanding old-age entitlements and other benefits.[84]

Older Americans transitioned from the Dependents category to that of Advantaged as seniors became organized and mobilized. It was not so much the mobilization of older people that led to favorable policies; it was, instead, the other way around. Aging-related government programs and benefits defined older people as a beneficiary group. Diverse and divided as they are by party and ideology, by socioeconomic status, by gender and race and ethnicity and religion and values and lifestyles and more, older people now were united by a common political identity. Policy elites and reformers created the policies and expanded the benefits, and now older people had a major stake in government. Like so many other citizen groups, political scientist Jack Walker observed, political organizations representing older Americans were "one of the *consequences* of major new legislation, not one of the *causes* of its passage."[85]

AARP was founded prior to the Great Society wave of social welfare expansion, and by the mid-1970s was recognized as an integral part of the emerging gray lobby.[86] But critics maintained that it was more interested in business profit than in political advocacy, and early in its history, that may have been so. Until AARP severed ties with Leonard Davis and Colonial Penn in 1981, much of its membership promotions and political activities arguably served to expand Colonial Penn's business. After the break with Colonial Penn, AARP's business side became more of a support for its rapidly expanding membership outreach and political advocacy.[87] AARP's rise as a political power coincided with the mobilization of older Americans in support of the programs that now significantly enhanced their economic status and retirement prospects.

Seniors exemplify the positive effects of policy on participation. In 1950, when just 16 percent of persons aged 65 and over received Social Security benefits, older people were less politically involved than younger adults. As Social Security benefits and coverage expanded in the 1950s through the 1970s, so did seniors' political activity.[88] Voters aged 65 and over turned out at an increasing rate, while turnout declined among middle-aged and especially young voters. By the late 1980s, seniors were voting at a higher rate than even the middle-aged, and they continue to do so. Older people's political campaign activities and campaign contributions lagged behind all other age groups into the 1970s, but then rose dramatically, again as campaign activity among younger adults declined. Most dramatic was the rise in contacting members of Congress, which spiked among seniors in the early 1980s after President Reagan proposed Social Security benefit cuts.[89]

Older people's political involvement increased with the creation and expansion of Social Security, Andrea Campbell revealed, for a variety of reasons. The program has provided recipients with more money and more free time, facilitating their participation, in addition to giving them a stake in government. As benefits and coverage expanded, a growing number of retirees and their survivors receive significant chunks of their income from Social Security. Thus their interest in the program is "immediate, quantifiable, and tangible."[90] Tracking developments in Social Security policy against participation trends between 1973 and 1994, Campbell demonstrates how seniors' political activity—writing letters to Congress in particular—surged whenever those benefits were threatened.

Lower-income seniors, depending most heavily for income on Social Security, were especially likely to respond to threats to the program, even though political participation generally tends to rise with income.[91]

AARP members are even more likely than nonmembers to contact elected officials generally, and to contact them specifically about Social Security, even controlling for variables, like socioeconomic status and political interest, that also affect participation, Campbell found. The data she examines cannot reveal whether AARP mobilized members to write to Congress, or whether AARP members are more interested in politics to begin with, and more inclined to contact officials. But the association does stimulate members to contact officials through its publications, e-mails, website, and social media, in response to aging-related policy events. Thus it stands to reason that AARP's mobilization efforts increase the likelihood that a member will take action.[92] Indeed, by the mid-1980s, aging-based mass membership groups were famous on Capitol Hill for their success in flooding Congress with mail and phone calls.[93] And by then, the rapidly growing AARP had far surpassed the others in size.

Not all government benefit recipient groups are so easily mobilized politically. Public assistance programs, which are means-tested, tend to suppress rather than encourage political participation. Applying for such benefits tends to be a humiliating and disempowering affair, requiring proof of low income and serious need. Recipients often come away with depressed political efficacy, feeling that participation is useless because the government is unresponsive and demeaning. Already lacking the resources conducive to political activity, even after receiving benefits, which are relatively meager, recipients of public assistance programs are subject to negative stereotypes and low public esteem. In contrast, beneficiaries of social insurance programs like Social Security and Medicare are not subject to means tests; their interactions with government agencies are more positive and engaging; the public sees them as deserving, their benefits having been earned.[94]

The policy-participation cycle, then, does not always have salutary effects, but for older Americans, it has. Benefiting from social insurance programs that are not means-tested, seniors have become increasingly interested and attentive, as well as politically efficacious and engaged—factors that increase a group's political representation and mobilization even more than numbers, high socioeconomic status, or stridency of views.[95] AARP and other aging-based political organizations are both cause and consequence of government policies. They arose and became politicized along with the rise of the old-age welfare state; they continue to educate and mobilize their constituency while also lobbying to maintain and expand the programs benefiting older people. The widespread compassion and respect, the positive messages about their deservingness, the high degree of political mobilization, and the well-established organizational representation of older Americans are all hallmarks of being Advantaged.[96]

Gradually, however, older Americans have been transitioning from the Advantaged category to that of Contenders: groups that are politically powerful, but perceived by policy makers and the public as undeserving government beneficiaries, or at least as receiving more than their share. Even as the political stature of seniors and their political organizations grew, the willingness of voters and policy makers to protect their programs began to wane. The very success of entitlement programs in lifting so many out of poverty and increasing their income and health security has created pressures to rein them in. Population aging and rapid medical inflation have led to an ever-increasing portion of the federal budget directly benefiting the elderly. Anemic economic growth, persistent deficits and an expanding national debt create pressure to reduce federal spending even as entitlement obligations rise. Finally, increasing ideological polarization in recent decades between the two major parties has diminished the previous consensus in support of old-age benefits, and has even led to proposals for partial privatization of Social Security and Medicare.[97]

The seeds of this declining consensus were sown back in the late 1970s, when political observers noticed that aging-based benefits were consuming a large and growing portion of the federal budget, and policy elites' support for expanding or even maintaining benefits was starting to dissipate.[98] In the early 1980s, President Reagan offered the first serious proposal to cut Social Security benefits, and although he faced bipartisan opposition in Congress at first, driven by a flood of constituent letters and phone calls, new Social Security legislation in 1983 phased in benefit changes to keep the program solvent. The movement for generational equity in the mid-1980s helped spread the "greedy geezer" stereotype in the popular press. Negative images of selfish, affluent retirees have done little to sway public opinion, however. Social Security, Medicare, and old-age benefits in general have remained highly popular with Americans of all ages—so popular that conservative proponents of benefit reductions or program privatization still couch their proposed reforms in terms of "saving" the programs.[99] But the ascendance of the more conservative anti-tax wing of the Republican party, coupled with early twenty-first century economic and fiscal realities, ensure that pressures on old-age entitlement spending will intensify. In this conflictual environment, with older Americans as powerful but beleaguered Contenders, the political identities of people over 50 may become increasingly fractured. Any reforms that phase in benefit cuts through means testing or partial privatization would very likely exacerbate economic inequality among future generations of the aged, further dividing them along partisan, ideological, and class lines.[100]

By the time older Americans were transitioning from Advantaged to Contenders, AARP had emerged as the most prominent and widely recognized organization representing them.[101] With seniors as Contenders, representing their interests is both more difficult than representing them as Advantaged, and more consequential. AARP's policy influence must be gauged not only by what it "wins" in terms of protection and expansion of policies that benefit Americans aged 50 and over but also by how strident and powerful are the groups opposing it. Representing older Americans is, furthermore, increasingly complicated to the extent that older Americans are divided along partisan, ideological, and class lines. AARP's ability to represent its diverse membership without alienating its more affluent members or neglecting its more vulnerable constituency becomes a more difficult and delicate balance when seniors are Contenders than when they are Advantaged.

A Powerful Voice for the Vulnerable

AARP's stated commitment to the most vulnerable aged dates back to its founding, when Ethel Percy Andrus discovered one of her fellow retired educators living, destitute, in a chicken coop—the discovery, according to AARP lore, that moved her to organize retirees on a national level.[102] Nevertheless, Robert Binstock's examination of the handful of political organizations concerned primarily with aging-related issues in 1972, including AARP, concluded that their goals "are not of a kind suitable to redress the economic and social condition of the severely disadvantaged aged," despite the fact that 25 percent of persons sixty-five and over still lived in poverty.[103] In the 1980s, as AARP stepped up its advocacy in the wake of its break with Colonial Penn, it sought to modify its reputation as an advocate primarily for upper-middle-class professionals and executives, and reach out to disadvantaged and minority groups. Women's and minority affairs, along with health care and worker equity, were designated as the four top political priorities.[104] Although AARP members still tend to be more affluent than older Americans generally, the focus on more vulnerable populations is not the paradox it seems at first blush. The commitment to diversity in leadership and membership recruitment, Frederick Lynch notes, is "largely a reflection of the culture and ideology of the upper-middle and professional classes . . . This worldview is built upon . . . acceptance of globalization, mass immigration, multiculturalism, and the belief that the nation's economy, growing age/class/ethic schisms, and civic culture can be 'managed' in a bipartisan fashion."[105]

The policy focus on the most vulnerable older persons has been reinforced under the leadership of Jo Ann Jenkins, who declared that "low income is a passion of mine," emphasizing the need to work with, and for, the 50+ population at all levels of income.[106] That passion was evident during her three-year presidency of the AARP Foundation, the group's charitable arm, where AARP's Board Chair Carol Raphael said "she breathed tremendous energy and focus into the foundation."[107]

Jenkins, the first African American woman to serve as AARP's CEO, came from Mobile, Alabama, where her father worked as a merchant marine and her mother worked at home. Soon after graduating from Spring Hill College in Mobile, she began her career in the federal government, ultimately rising to the position of chief operating officer for the Library of Congress. While at the Library, she served for six years on the board of directors of AARP's business arm, AARP Services, Inc., joining the association as Foundation president in 2010, and then chief operating officer in 2013. Thus she had been involved in the various nonprofit and for-profit aspects of AARP by the time she was named CEO in 2014. Cheerful and energetic, she talks enthusiastically about "disrupting aging"—the title of her book—a positive, active, stereotype-bashing view of growing older.[108] Thus it is geared largely toward people with resources to take advantage of the information and advice. The royalties, though, support the AARP Foundation, where Jenkins' focus on hunger, housing, income insecurity, and isolation among the most vulnerable elderly remain the primary issues. She launched the Drive to End Hunger campaign while running the Foundation, to raise awareness about the millions of Americans aged 50 and over who are chronically food-insecure, for example, partnering with NASCAR and with Denny's restaurants for publicity and fund-raising drives.

Many people, especially on the Left, may nevertheless scoff at the notion of AARP as a major champion of the poor and disadvantaged. Its membership is relatively affluent; its politics is center-left, not radically redistributionist. Senior organizations like the Gray Panthers, the Alliance for Retired Americans, the National Committee to Preserve Social Security and Medicare, and Social Security Works are more focused on the most vulnerable aged, more strident in their demands to protect and expand social welfare programs for the needy and disadvantaged, and less bipartisan or more radical in their politics. During the 2016 national elections, those groups joined with over 300 other national and state organizations in the Strengthen Social Security coalition to push for expansion of Social Security benefits, while AARP's Take a Stand campaign highlighted the issue without taking any firm positions itself or joining the coalition.

Evaluated on the basis of influence as well as policy, though, AARP may be considered one of the strongest advocates for low-income Americans. Washington's powerful lobbying groups mostly represent business and professional interests, consequently representing policy preferences of the more affluent.[109] Examining public attitudes and policy responsiveness across four policy domains—economic and tax policy, foreign and national security policy, religion and morality, and social welfare—Martin Gilens found that public policy reflects the preferences of affluent citizens much more than those in the middle class and especially more than those who are poor.[110] But the relationship between income and responsiveness is weakest in the social welfare domain, in which lower-income persons find a powerful ally in AARP, especially on Social Security and Medicare. Although both programs enjoy widespread public support, middle-class and poor people are more likely than the wealthy to support benefit increases, and less likely to support any scheme that might reduce benefits, including partial privatization.[111] R. Allen Hays finds AARP to be one of the most frequent and prominent groups testifying before Congress on issues of particular interest to the poor, including housing subsidies, food and nutrition, and public assistance programs like Supplemental Security Income.[112] Larry Bartels, like Gilens, finds members of Congress to be most responsive to constituents who contact them, and higher-income people are more likely to contact their representatives.[113] But as Campbell noted, lower-income seniors are more likely to write to Congress when they feel their Social Security benefits are threatened, because they more often depend on Social Security for most of their income. And like Bartels, she finds that policy makers respond.[114] Gilens concludes that AARP, "as a mass-membership organization, might actually be considered a conduit through which the influence of less-well-off Americans flows."[115]

AARP, in sum, may be relatively moderate and centrist in its politics, but its large membership base and extraordinary resources make it a major player and a sought-after coalition partner in national politics. That influence is especially consequential in redistributive policies, or policies that transfer significant amounts of income or wealth from some people to others. Like many political organizations, AARP lobbies on issues big and small. Some are relatively low-key issues, like reauthorization of the Older Americans Act, which is important to state and local communities in providing services to lower-income older persons—meals, transportation, senior centers, caregiver support, job training, and other services for maintaining seniors' health and independence—but which is a low-budget program enjoying bipartisan support (although even its relatively low funding has not kept up with inflation and population aging, and faces potentially deep cuts under President Donald Trump's proposed budget).[116] There is something of a trade-off, as Rother notes, between the easier victories of the smaller-scale issues and the bigger issues, which are more salient to the membership but also more partisan and polarizing.[117] It is in the more controversial, big-budget redistributive policies where interest group influence is most significant, and most contested. The following section traces the development of AARP's political influence over the decades of its existence, illustrating some of its major victories and defeats.

AARP's Influence through the Decades

The 1960s. AARP's "advocacy goals look to both the private and public sectors," John Rother noted,[118] and indeed, Ethel Andrus' first major advocacy goal was persuading private insurance companies to take a chance on retirees. She had approached more than 40 insurance companies about selling group health insurance policies to members of the National Retired Teachers Association—AARP's precursor founded in 1947—and they all declined.[119] It was a missed opportunity comparable to publishers' initial refusals of J.K. Rowling's first *Harry Potter* novel, Decca Records' rejection of the Beatles, and Western Union's dismissal of Alexander Graham Bell's new gadget, the telephone.[120] Leonard Davis decided that insuring older people was a good risk, and he made hundreds of millions of dollars after expanding the market with the founding of AARP in 1958. In a youth-oriented culture, AARP still works to persuade companies that older people can be a lucrative market.

AARP's engagement with the public sector has expanded since its early days, of course. The image of 1960s-era AARP as an organization mostly concerned with service to the aged and with maximizing profit by selling insurance is not far off the mark. Ethel Andrus, the idealist, emphasized service; Leonard Davis, the businessman, emphasized profit. But AARP, including Andrus herself, did begin lobbying government, and laid the groundwork for its future political influence by building its membership base and amassing the fortune that would support its advocacy. The association focused primarily on "elaborating a large range of benefits," which advanced both Andrus's service goals and Davis's business objectives.[121] The combined membership of NRTA and AARP expanded from 130,000 to about 1.9 million between 1960 and 1970.[122]

Andrus herself spent much of her time on the road, lobbying in state and national capitals and promoting the interests and independence of older Americans at various conferences and forums. Even in the NRTA's early years she advocated for better public pensions and tax breaks for retired teachers.[123] But she was more intent on promoting independence and fighting ageism—for example, eliminating mandatory retirement and other barriers to late-life work and other activity—than on expanding government benefits. "A.A.R.P. holds no meetings to bewail the hardships of old age, nor to formulate pressure programs nor stress potential political strength of older folk, nor to urge government subsidy," she is quoted as saying in 1965—sometimes quoted by critics wishing to show how AARP has since run off the rails.[124] Yet she also understood the need; AARP, she wrote, "is not unmindful of those older persons who do need help from a governmental source and we have been diligent in our efforts to bring about improvements in these programs, but we know that most older persons are able to live independently and [with] dignity."[125]

Henry Pratt's detailed study of the gray lobby up to the mid-1970s shows that Andrus testified before Congress in the years prior to the 1965 passage of Medicare and Medicaid, advocating a more market-based "trusteeship" for providing health insurance to the elderly. Trustees would include representatives of health care industry, business, aging, and labor associations. Consistent with virtually all other scholarly accounts of Medicare politics, Pratt says that "NRTA-AARP was not on record as opposing the Medicare measure passed by Congress in 1965, but neither was it among the bill's active promoters."[126] Among senior organizations, it was the labor-affiliated National Council of Senior Citizens that vigorously supported the passage of Medicare and Medicaid.[127] Critics of AARP during the Colonial Penn years, as well as AARP's organizational allies in subsequent years, suggest that AARP feared that Medicare could eat into its health insurance profits.[128] "There is no suggestion that Andrus ever viewed AARP as primarily a business proposition," says Morris. "She does not appear to have gotten rich from the enterprise, and she always stressed its idealistic mission as a self-help organization." Instead, it was "Davis's driving business ambition" that shaped AARP's politics, as he "wrapped Colonial Penn tentacles firmly around every aspect of the AARP operation," especially after Andrus passed away in 1967 at the age of 85.[129] Her personal fortune, according to her attorney Jack Fay, was valued at less than $100,000.[130]

AARP's political profile shrunk even more when Andrus sought to move the headquarters back to Long Beach in 1965, two years before her death.[131] That would soon change, however, when the office returned to Washington, D.C. and, in 1969, hired Bernard Nash as executive director and Peter Hughes as legislative counsel. Both had Washington experience—Nash as Deputy Commissioner of the U.S. Administration on Aging and Hughes as a Capitol Hill staffer—and they established connections that ultimately made AARP an established Washington insider, especially as the Colonial Penn era began winding down a decade later.[132]

The 1970s. Political mobilization and organization of older Americans took off in the 1970s, as the policy-participation cycle went into full swing. Nearly everyone aged 65 and over received Social Security benefits—82 percent in 1970, 90 percent by 1980[133]—and had health care coverage through Medicare. The Older Americans Act of 1965 had set up a government network of aging administrators and advocates, including the federal Administration on Aging, and both chambers of Congress had permanent special committees on aging by the mid-1970s. Older Americans now had a political identity and a clear stake in government. The 1971 White House Conference on Aging—the second such conference, held once a decade since 1961—was a major catalyst for the gray lobby and a forum for advocates to lay out their priorities and express their demands.[134] Aging-based political organizations, AARP and NCSC in particular, further expanded their network of contracts on the Hill and in the executive branch, as well as their policy expertise, enhancing their reputation for credible and informative advocacy. Their influence should not be exaggerated, Binstock suggested early in the decade. Their advocacy for the truly needy and disadvantaged was lacking; their "electoral bluff" was just that—a bluff—since older voters were far from behaving like a unified voting bloc; and their goals were largely incremental and defensive.[135] But defense is important too, wrote Demkovich in the *National Journal* a few years later: "without their efforts, many federal programs and policies for the elderly would have been allowed to lapse." "There's a New Kick in the Step of the Senior Citizen Lobbies," her headline declared.[136]

AARP was a rising star in the gray lobby, if not yet the premier organization. AARP's advocacy division aimed to shake its more conservative Republican orientation and present itself as strictly bipartisan, with an educational and nonconfrontational approach to lobbying. But it retained a business orientation because of the Colonial Penn connection, sometimes putting it at odds with the labor-affiliated NCSC. Leading up to the 1971 White House Conference, NCSC emphasized active government efforts to benefit the aging, while AARP focused more on working with the private and nonprofit sectors. While NCSC was the most active senior group lobbying for the 1972 Social Security legislation that increased benefits by 20 percent and indexed them to the cost of living starting in 1975, AARP "stayed more in the background," being "willing to accept arguments that major changes would prove inflationary."[137] The association did show its muscle on regulatory issues, generating thousands of letters from its expanding membership to the Federal Trade Commission about setting standards and fighting consumer fraud for products and services ranging from prescription eyeglasses to funerals.[138]

AARP's major policy accomplishment of the decade resulted from its push to end mandatory retirement, which Andrus in 1959 had called a "vast waste of manpower and/or production."[139] The 1967 Age Discrimination in Employment Act (ADEA), protecting workers between the ages of 40 and 65, became law the year that Andrus died, apparently without much interest-group influence. But in the 1970s AARP took the lead in lobbying to expand those protections and end mandatory retirement. Working with the strongest advocate in Congress on aging issues, Representative Claude Pepper of Florida, AARP helped move ADEA amendments through Congress in 1978 that extended the protections against discrimination and mandatory retirement to age 70. AARP was instrumental once again in pushing for further ADEA amendments in 1986 that abolished mandatory retirement at any age. It was an issue that bitterly divided AARP and NCSC at the 1971 White House Conference, and a position both organized and labor and the U.S. Chamber of Commerce—an unusual and powerful combination—continued to oppose into the 1980s. But in both efforts, AARP mobilized a flood of letters from constituents while applying pressure to congressional holdouts, ultimately gaining overwhelming bipartisan support.[140]

Despite the policy differences between AARP and other senior organizations including the NCSC, their alliance strengthened during the 1970s. AARP took a leading role in forming the Leadership Council of Aging Organizations in 1979, a coalition of 30 groups that has expanded to over 70 aging-based, social welfare, labor, and other allied organizations. "Senior power may yet become a reality" Demkovich wrote in 1976.[141] Indeed, AARP added another ten million members during the decade, now leading the pack in size and in wealth, and was on its way to becoming not only the leading gray lobby group, but one of the most prominent lobbies in Washington.

The 1980s. During the 1980s, AARP emerged from the shadow of Colonial Penn, nearly tripled in size to over 33 million to become the nation's largest secular membership organization, and lodged itself into the American consciousness. It also found itself fighting the "greedy geezer" stereotype, engaging in conflict with its own aging-based allies over major Social Security and Medicare reforms, and struggling to influence those policies even as its reputation as a Washington powerhouse grew. It was, in sum, a paradoxical decade for AARP.

The decade began with AARP still embroiled in controversy following the 1978 *60 Minutes* exposé of Colonial Penn's questionable practices and organizational control. In 1981, the association switched to Prudential for the group health insurance, and soon thereafter cut or replaced all remaining Colonial Penn products. Cyril Brickfield, twice executive director from 1967 to 1969 and again from 1977 to 1987, had been a close associate of Leonard Davis and served as legislative counsel in between stints as executive director. But now, popular with the staff and respected in Washington, he steered the organization through its revival. Financially strapped and chastened, AARP merged officially with NRTA in 1982 and expanded the association's membership base by lowering the age from 55 to 50 in 1984. Two years later AARP hired Rother and doubled the political division's budget and staff.[142] It also further energized the grassroots, developing its famous system for finding every 50-year-old, generating piles of mail to legislators, and activating networks of volunteers through its state and local chapters.[143]

AARP had bounced back, and not a moment too soon. President Ronald Reagan's administration, conservative in ideology and coming on the heels of late-1970s stagflation, was intent on slashing the federal budget. The movement for generational equity questioned whether older people were receiving more than their share in government benefits, at the expense of younger generations. But Social Security remained—and remains—overwhelmingly popular among Americans of all ages. When President Reagan proposed Social Security benefit cuts in order to shore up the trust fund in 1981, he was met with fierce resistance from both parties in both chambers of Congress after a flood of constituent phone calls. Save Our Security, a coalition of over one hundred labor and aging-based groups including AARP that had formed in 1979, kicked into high gear. When Reagan and Senate Republicans proposed $40 billion in cuts over three years in 1982, they withdrew the proposal after a flood of letters that Florida senator Lawton Chiles attributed to a bulletin from AARP.[144] Thus, AARP was instrumental, if not dominant, in stopping immediate benefits cuts.

But Social Security was no longer the third rail of politics: "touch it and you're dead." The third-rail metaphor—based on the danger of electrocution for anyone who steps on the high-voltage rail in electric railway tracks—came from Kirk O'Donnell, an aide to then-Speaker of the House Tip O'Neill, in the wake of those aborted attempts to cut Social Security benefits.[145] The next year, 1983, Congress passed legislation based on recommendations of the Reagan-created bipartisan National Commission on Social Security Reform chaired by Alan Greenspan. Political careers survived the third rail this time because benefit cuts were phased in more gradually and the pain was spread around: current beneficiaries saw a six-month delay in cost-of-living increases, future recipients would be subject to a gradual increase in the full-benefit retirement age to 67, and workers got a payroll tax increase. "No one was 'electrocuted' by the third rail, O'Donnell reportedly said, because 'if a Republican foot and a Democratic foot touch it simultaneously, nothing happens.'"[146] Although AARP and other groups opposed the benefit reductions, the organizations lacked unity on some of the provisions in the compromise legislation and on alternative proposals. In the end, the passage of the 1983 Social Security Act showed that "AARP is not an invincible political force."[147] AARP's star continued to rise throughout the decade as it grew in size and celebrity, extended its presence and member activism in states and localities throughout the country, and expanded its outreach to more vulnerable groups, including women and minority elderly, in addition to its traditional white middle-class professional base. It launched voter education programs, including forums and debates as well as ads and mass mailings, to energize the grassroots, and it intensified its efforts to build coalitions, ad hoc and permanent, not only horizontally with other senior groups but also vertically with children's advocates as a denial of greedy geezerdom.[148] But policy change, especially of the big-budget variety, is challenging, and in 1987, AARP embarked on a quixotic effort that to this day remains one of its leaders' greatest disappointments: the quest for long-term care coverage.[149] Teaming with the Villers Foundation—now Families USA—and bolstered by Representative Claude Pepper's steadfast leadership in attempting to win passage of major long-term care legislation in Congress, AARP launched the Long-Term Care Campaign to raise public and elite awareness and support. The campaign lost steam after the defeat of President Bill Clinton's health care reform effort in the mid-1990s, and while it remains high on AARP's wish list, universal coverage of long-term care in the current political environment remains a pipe dream.

"Politics is the art of the possible," Otto von Bismarck famously observed.[150] and AARP was growing more adept at pushing the boundaries of the possible. By the end of the 1980s, AARP had grown so prominent in aging policy circles that its endorsement had become vital, and its opposition fatal, to the passage of any aging-related policy. This was illustrated by its important role in the passage of the Medicare Catastrophic Coverage Act of 1988. The MCCA was a major victory for AARP. But in the end, it became a major defeat.

The Medicare Catastrophic Coverage Act was the first major expansion of Medicare since the program's creation in 1965, which would seem to be a unifying issue for the gray lobby. Indeed, the groups were unified in their general support for expansion and in their dislike of the financing mechanism, which laid the costs on seniors themselves through higher premiums and a surtax on higher-income beneficiaries. They also wanted the program to cover long-term care. But AARP was the most willing to compromise on those provisions in order to get the long-desired prescription drug coverage and other benefits, and its legislative staff worked closely, and effectively, with members of Congress to make sure drug coverage was not left out. This put it in conflict with the powerful Pharmaceutical Manufacturers Association, or PhRMA, and required more hard negotiations in order to overcome President Reagan's veto threat.[151] In the end, Richard Himelfarb's detailed study of the MCCA concludes that AARP's support was crucial to the bill's passage.[152]

Opponents of the MCCA, especially PhRMA and the National Committee to Preserve Social Security and Medicare, protested vigorously and led a campaign that triggered a barrage of letters and street demonstrations by older people convinced that the costs were too heavy and unfairly imposed on them alone. AARP's persistent efforts to counter the opposition and tout the benefits of the legislation failed, as Congress took the nearly unprecedented step of repealing major social legislation just a year after passing it overwhelmingly.[153] For AARP, it was an inauspicious end to a triumphant decade of expansion and political renown.

The 1990s. AARP began and ended the 1990s at the pinnacle of its perceived power in Washington. Conservative commentators in the late 1980s labeled it the "most dangerous" lobby in America, a label that stuck midway through the 2000s.[154] It was *America's Most Powerful Lobby,* proclaimed the title of Charles Morris's 1996 book, and it topped *Fortune* magazine's Power 25 in 1997, 1998, and 1999.[155] At the same time, the Medicare Catastrophic Coverage debacle shocked the leadership into adopting a more cautious approach to its political activities throughout the decade. "I've almost stopped thinking of them as a lobby," one congressional staffer told the *New York Times* in 2001. "They have all kinds of valuable member services and do really good research work. But in terms of being a tough lobby, they're not what they used to be."[156]

President Bill Clinton's aborted attempt at comprehensive health care reform in 1993 illustrates both AARP's influence and its post-MCCA cautious approach. AARP and the Clinton Administration shared a mutual interest in including prescription drug coverage and long-term care in the Health Security Act. With health care costs rising faster than inflation and consuming a growing proportion of the federal budget through Medicare and Medicaid, AARP figured the only way to gain drug and long-term care coverage would be through comprehensive health care reform, and it pushed for those provisions to be included. The Clintons wanted older people's support for their plan. Administration officials were particularly "eager to obtain the backing of AARP because of its potential ability to mobilize millions of older people."[157] The plan fell short of comprehensive long-term care coverage, instead focusing on home- and community-based services for the severely disabled. AARP still was willing to negotiate and compromise for a bipartisan bill that its Republican and Democratic members alike could support. Cautiously, AARP invested a great deal of time and energy gauging members' opinions and weighing the costs and benefits of the plan for both Medicare beneficiaries and those aged between 50 and 64, not yet Medicare-eligible. Its endorsement finally came, too late.[158]

Could AARP have engineered a victory for the Health Security Act with more vigorous and timely support? So many influential groups on both sides of the issue made it difficult to attribute victory or defeat to any one of them. Powerful conservative groups and health-related organizations opposed all or parts of the plan. The Health Insurance Association of America was especially effective in opposition, with its television ads featuring "Harry and Louise," a young couple expressing fear about the overbureaucratization of health care and the alleged lack of choice among doctors and health plans. Supporters of the status quo, at any rate, nearly always enjoy an advantage over groups pushing for change.[159] But AARP's long hesitation and ultimate place on the losing side was hardly consistent with being America's most powerful lobby.

Executive Director Horace Deets had risen to that position in 1988. Congenial and nonpartisan like Cyril Brickfield, he was nevertheless a contrast in style; while Brickfield was a "back- slapping hail fellow," Deets, his former chief of staff and a former Catholic priest, was more reserved and low-key. Touted by *Fortune* as "Washington's second most powerful man," he was still, "to many . . . Horace Who?"[160] Jack Carlson had served as executive director for 15 weeks in between them, hired for his brash and aggressive style, but that turned out to be a bad fit after all with AARP's "carefully cultivated image of moderation and bipartisanship."[161] AARP under Deets may have been seen as overly cautious after the Catastrophic Coverage catastrophe but was also thinking about the association's future. Only a decade before, Americans for Generational Equity was speaking on behalf of baby boomers, arguing that AARP's advocacy for old-age benefits was draining resources from younger groups. The nation, said one of AGE's pamphlets, was "raising a generation of young Americans who will live in financial slavery."[162] Now boomers themselves were becoming the AARP generation, with the first of them reaching age 50 in 1996, and AARP was taking steps to steer them toward AARP membership—steps that included revamping *Modern Maturity* magazine and dropping "retired" from its name, changing it to the now-familiar initials, AARP.

One distraction along the way was a series of congressional hearings held over two days in 1995, led by Senator Alan Simpson, on AARP's business practices and nonprofit status. The hearings and other investigations resulted in AARP paying to settle disputes with the IRS, and a provision in the 1996 Lobby Reform Bill, aimed at AARP, that prohibited 501(c)4 nonprofits that lobby government from receiving government grants. AARP never admitted any wrongdoing and did not oppose the lobbying reform; it separated its for-profit business arm and its charitable arm more formally from its advocacy division. However sincere the efforts to clean up corruption in the lobbying industry, the hearings were also at least partially politically motivated, as Senator Simpson and other Republicans "took vengeance" on AARP for its adamant defense of old-age entitlement programs.[163] But the hearings demonstrated that its critics in Congress viewed AARP as a force to be reckoned with in any future attempt to reduce or privatize Social Security or Medicare.[164]

Entitlement reform was already on the federal agenda. In 1994, President Clinton created the Bipartisan Commission on Entitlement and Tax Reform, chaired by Democratic senator Robert Kerrey and Republican senator John Danforth, which kicked off a decades-long series of efforts to address the federal deficit in the long term. Social Security, Medicare, and Medicaid together comprised the largest proportion of the budget, and would continue to expand with escalating medical costs and the aging of the population. AARP, then as now, staunchly opposed any changes made strictly for the purpose of balancing the budget. With Social Security and Medicare still widely popular among voters of all ages and in both parties, AARP could take strong positions against benefit cuts while remaining bipartisan. At the same time, entitlement reform was becoming an increasingly partisan issue, and proposals for partial privatization of Social Security and Medicare were becoming increasingly acceptable, among policy elites. Although not represented on the Kerrey-Danforth commission, AARP had observers and lobbyists at its meetings "ready to mount the barricades."[165]

Another strategy for increasing AARP's influence was to establish a permanent, professional presence in the states, beginning in the late 1990s. Previously, said Cheryl Matheis, a former senior executive who had been with AARP for 28 years, state-level lobbying and advocacy had been handled largely by volunteers, with professional staff "riding circuit." Opening offices in every state capital with paid staff allowed the association to become "truly national and nationwide."[166] So much of public policy affecting older Americans is "funded, regulated, or delivered at the state level," said Deets. "And you really have to be there to be a player. And so that enables us to have a staff that's there, that can support our volunteer cadre in every state, that can work more effectively with . . . government and with other organizations that serve our people."[167]

As the 1990s came to an end, so did AARP's cautious, laid back political period. William Novelli, a top executive under Deets who would soon succeed him, promised that AARP would once again live up to its reputation as a power player in Washington, expanding both its lobbying efforts and its grassroots mobilization. Even as aging policy moved increasingly front and center in polarized partisan politics, Novelli, like Deets and like Brickfield before him, was determined to remain politically bipartisan and relevant to members all across the partisan spectrum: "Try to work with both sides, bring them together, keep raising the bar in terms of what you want."[168]

Into the Twenty-First Century. Bill Novelli, a "marketing maestro," ascended to the CEO position in 2001 to help AARP "recapture some of the clout and luster it lost in the 1990s," said the *National Journal* early in 2002, reflecting much of Washington's perception that the association had become cautious and timid but now was roaring back.[169] Drawn to social causes early in his marketing and advertising career, Novelli had built a reputation as a social marketing innovator. He helped burnish the Peace Corps' image as its director of advertising and creative services, and then, with his boss Jack Porter, founded the highly successful marketing and public relations firm Porter Novelli. Retiring from the firm in 1990 to devote himself full time to social issues, he worked for the global antipoverty organization CARE, and then, as the first president of the Campaign for Tobacco-Free Kids, he designed a public awareness campaign that turned cigarette ad icons Joe Camel and the Marlboro Man into symbols of the ill effects of smoking.[170]

Novelli joined the AARP leadership in 2000 "as an opportunity to make social change"[171] by recharging and expanding the group's political advocacy and membership drives. In many ways he was picking up where Deets had left off: broadening the group's appeal to the politically diverse and individualistic boomer generation, expanding offices to all 50 U.S. states plus the District of Columbia and two territories, and crafting bipartisan responses to aging policy issues. But as Communications Director Lisa Davis put it, "we've seen that change get on steroids" once Novelli took over.[172] Stepping up the lobbying game while enhancing member services, Lynch suggests, causes some "tension between this consumer services brand and a more aggressive 'warrior brand.'"[173] But Novelli and Rother both energetically defend AARP's unique "hybrid" nature: the political advocacy, the grassroots mobilization, the charitable and philanthropic work, and the myriad member services and information giving Americans aged 50 and over more choice and more control are all "integrated," with each organizational aspect reinforcing the others.[174] Combining membership growth with active political advocacy requires true bipartisanship and pragmatism, and Novelli wanted to break away from AARP's now-liberal image and "pull AARP to the middle."[175]

Topping the political agenda was Medicare prescription drug coverage, especially with the increasing use and rapidly escalating costs of medications. In 2003 that turned out to be the ideal issue for AARP to both flex its muscles and pull to the center. Congressional Democrats, frustrated with the association's post-Catastrophic restraint, urged it to take a clear stand. "They're supportive-lukewarm about everything that comes out," one Democratic Senate aide said about prescription coverage proposals.[176] Democratic senator John D. Rockefeller IV "told Novelli that strong leadership from AARP, including some clear indications of what legislative provisions would be acceptable to its members, could bring the lawmakers back to productive discussions."[177] They got their wish, but not in the way they hoped.

President George W. Bush and the Republican congressional majority combined prescription drug coverage with provisions that would prohibit government price controls on pharmaceuticals and prohibit their reimportation from Canada—much to the delight of PhRMA—and would expand options for Medicare beneficiaries to choose private managed care plans over traditional Medicare, through Medicare Advantage. The Medicare Prescription Drug, Improvement, and Modernization Act (MMA) represented a compromise between conservative efforts to privatize Medicare and liberal efforts to expand Medicare benefits, but the lack of cost controls in particular alienated Democrats and made it mostly a

Republican bill. "We needed AARP's endorsement, because this was a difficult needle to thread," said one congressional leadership aide.[178] AARP used its influence to insist on drug coverage and to negotiate for provisions such as larger subsidies for low-income seniors and continued drug coverage for retirees in their employers' retirement plans. AARP spent millions of dollars on newspaper and television ads to convince Medicare beneficiaries and members of Congress to support MMA. It was a close vote, so close that the House leadership kept the vote open for an unprecedented three hours in order to drum up enough votes, and by all accounts AARP's endorsement made the win possible.[179] Congressional Democrats were furious, and tens of thousands of liberal members left the association.[180] But from AARP's perspective, it was an important display of nonpartisan pragmatism, for the sake of the big win: Medicare prescription drug benefits.

AARP's fight against Social Security privatization two years later swung it back to the Democratic side, and this time it was an easier win, though a costly one. President Bush proposed to allow workers to invest some of their Social Security payroll taxes in private investment accounts, making it the central domestic issue of his second term. In this battle, AARP was up against some of the most powerful business and corporate lobbies in Washington: the securities and investment industry, which stood to profit from the private accounts, and business groups like the U.S. Chamber of Commerce and the National Federation of Independent Business.[181] The president framed his proposal as both a way to keep Social Security solvent in the long term and a way to increase taxpayers' returns through the stock market. AARP and its labor and senior-organization allies countered that the stock market was too risky; traditional Social Security worked well and was popular; and the up-front costs of diverting payroll taxes into private accounts—up to two trillion dollars—were too high. AARP spent millions on an ad campaign to get the message out, and its audience was receptive. "This is our signature issue," said John Rother. "It's the No. 1 issue for our membership, by far. We'll devote whatever it takes, everything we can think of."[182] The membership was united this time, in opposition to private accounts. Public support for the Bush proposal, even among younger adults but especially among seniors, dropped precipitously,[183] and so did support among congressional Republicans. The proposal died.[184]

AARP emerged from the Social Security privatization battle with its Washington reputation stronger than ever. Political scientist James Thurber, an expert on interest group lobbying, called AARP "the largest, most effective lobbying group in D.C., and probably the world. It can stimulate people out there very quickly and get them to push back on issues. Just the threat of AARP against you gets people to change their minds."[185] In 2008, its membership peaked at over 40 million.

The battle over health care reform, a signature issue for newly elected President Barack Obama in 2009, tested AARP's vaunted influence. Health care reform was a much more complicated and controversial issue than Social Security privatization, involving multiple competing and overlapping interest group alliances and rivalries. Divided We Fail, the unusual coalition that AARP formed with business and labor groups in 2007 to promote health care reform, helped to place and keep it on the national agenda as Obama made it a campaign issue and then an early goal of his presidency. As Congress shaped the complicated Patient Protection and Affordable Care Act, or ACA, different interest groups, including those in Divided We Fail, split over various provisions. For AARP, a major goal was closing the gap in Medicare prescription drug coverage—the infamous "doughnut hole" that put limits on the coverage provided in the MMA. But making health insurance available and affordable to people aged over 50 but not yet 65 and eligible for Medicare—the age of one-third of its membership—was also a major goal. The various provisions for financing the ACA included measures to reduce growth in Medicare costs, which ACA opponents portrayed misleadingly as "Medicare cuts." Even more misleading were opponents' references to "death panels" and playing on older people's fears of health care rationing.[186] Setting priorities that differed across age groups—those aged 50–64 and those aged over 65—set AARP's leadership up for its "worst nightmare: that significant numbers of the 50+ population perceived [the ACA] as a zero-sum game, an 'us-versus-them' battle that jeopardized an already underfunded Medicare system by redistributing resources to young Americans."[187]

AARP's support for the ACA throughout most of the debate leading to its passage was publicly ambivalent, as it strove to maintain its bipartisan image. But its outspoken advocacy for closing the gap in prescription drug coverage was successful, as the doughnut hole was scheduled to be phased out by 2020. Ultimately AARP's support, along with that of the American Medical Association and other powerful health industry groups, was crucial to the ACA's passage, and its support was hailed by President Obama.[188] Where ACA supporters granted credit, its opponents leveled blame. "Thanks to just-released emails from the House Energy and Commerce Committee, we now know that AARP worked through 2009–2010 . . . toiling daily to pass [the] health bill," said the *Wall Street Journal*.[189]

AARP's efforts to explain and defend the ACA, and to fight numerous Republican efforts to repeal it since its passage, have been at least as critical as its initial support.[190] Both CEO Barry Rand, who succeeded Novelli in 2009, and CEO Jo Ann Jenkins since 2014, have presided over those efforts.[191] After the 2016 election, when Republicans controlled both chambers of Congress and the White House under President Donald Trump, Obamacare "repeal and replace" was declared a top priority of the newly unified government. When Republican Party leaders in the House introduced the American Health Care Act (AHCA) in March, 2017, AARP was ready to pounce. The new law would cause premiums to skyrocket for people aged over 50—an "age tax," AARP called it in membership communications and radio ads—and Medicaid's long-term services and supports for poor seniors would be slashed, while the wealthiest Americans would benefit from steep tax cuts. "AARP and its allies are bombarding congressional offices with objections," said the *New York Times*.[192] The AHCA "made a trio of powerful medical interest group enemies: the AARP, the American Medical Association (AMA), and the American Hospital Association (AHA)," said *Fortune* magazine.[193] AARP's letter to congressional leaders "—from one of the most influential groups in domestic policy—is the latest blow for a bill that has already seen opposition from many conservative leaders, media organizations and interest groups," said CNN.[194] "AARP does not lose many political battles," wrote Jennifer Rubin in the *Washington Post*.[195] It did not lose this one. The AHCA, hastily written, criticized from both the left and the right, and unpopular with the public at only 17 percent approval,[196] was withdrawn before it reached the House floor; subsequent repeal attempts also failed.

AARP did lose on one issue related to the ACA: coverage for long-term services and supports, or LTSS (now the term preferred to long-term care). The Community Living Assistance Services and Supports, or CLASS Act, a provision within the ACA when it passed, was a public LTSS insurance program funded by voluntary premiums. The CLASS Act was deemed financially unworkable and was never implemented; in 2012, it was repealed.[197] LTSS coverage remains a major goal for AARP, although early twenty-first century political realities make it more of a pipe dream. "It wouldn't be a brilliant strategy to storm the Hill for a major new entitlement" at this time, Executive Vice President Nancy LeaMond conceded, "but we are trying to create a constituency for that, and exploring the financing possibilities."[198] Caregiving has become a top priority, both politically and in terms of member services; it is a frequent topic in AARP publications. AARP leaders hope that by increasing awareness and mobilizing the millions of Americans who provide unpaid care to older or disabled adults, public support will grow for more government support. The need is growing, especially as baby boomers, with fewer children than previous generations, expand the ranks of retirees.[199]

Access to affordable home-based and community-based care is a top AARP priority at the state level as well, as is clearer coordination between hospitals and caregivers. Since AARP established offices in every state with professional staff in the late 1990s and early 2000s, other priority issues vary from state to state. Many of the state offices lobby at the state and local levels to hold down utility rates. After passage of the Affordable Care Act, state offices helped set up health insurance exchanges, and lobbied states to accept federal Medicaid expansion funds. Other issues tackled at the state level, with varying levels of success, include regulation of payday loans and consumer protection from scams often targeting older people.[200] Initially, said Cheryl Matheis, who helped open and direct the state offices, they followed the lead of the national office in lobbying state governments, but gradually they have become "more unique to individual states' needs."[201] Louisiana, for example, provides more funding for nursing home care than for home-based services by more than a two-to-one margin. AARP Louisiana has been trying to "rebalance toward home-based care," said State Director Denise Bottcher, for two reasons: because that is what most people want and because it is less expensive.[202] AARP struggles at the state level to match the lobbying power of business and industry groups, such as the nursing home industry and the payday loan industry. But nationwide, it is one of the most influential interest groups representing broad-based consumer interests and building comprehensive grassroots networks across the states.[203]

Politically, AARP's primary concern, its "paramount political mission,"[204] is protecting Social Security and Medicare. The association challenges opponents' assertion that either program is in "crisis," while promoting bipartisan, incremental changes to guarantee the programs' long-term sustainability without having to cut benefits. In an environment of partisan polarization, it is not always an easy position to promote, but at the same time it is the source of AARP's influence, backed by its massive size and ability to mobilize the grassroots.

AARP was a major, visible force in the budgetary negotiations that had the country careening from crisis to crisis in the wake of the Great Recession of 2007–2008. The resulting drop in revenue, along with President Obama's stimulus package to reverse the economic downturn, led to no fewer than five bipartisan attempts during his first term to address the ballooning deficit and expanding national debt. AARP's consistent message was: no cuts to Social Security or Medicare benefits for the sake of balancing the budget. Medicare savings can be achieved by slowing the growth of health care costs; Social Security adjustments for long-term solvency can be achieved without cutting benefits, AARP maintained.[205]

In 2010, President Obama appointed the National Commission on Fiscal Responsibility and Reform to "improve the fiscal situation in the medium term and to achieve fiscal sustainability over the long run."[206] The commission was informally known as Simpson-Bowles for its cochairs: Democrat Erskine Bowles, who had been President Clinton's chief of staff, and Republican Alan Simpson, the former Wyoming senator and one of AARP's most vocal critics for years. The commission's plan would eliminate the deficit by 2035 through tax adjustments and spending reductions including Social Security benefit cuts by gradually increasing the full retirement age and adopting the chained CPI that would reduce cost-of-living increases. The plan did not reach the 14-vote threshold required to send it to Congress, but it became a blueprint for future budget discussions.[207] While "an army" of interest groups and labor unions protested the commission's recommendations, "AARP may be the one player that can almost single-handedly block—or enable—changes to Social Security," said *The Fiscal Times*. Other groups in the "army" may be more stridently opposed, but AARP's "position is more nuanced and less partisan than many other advocacy groups on the right and the left. If there is any hope for a bipartisan agreement on Social Security, they say, it will need the AARP's support."[208]

Over the next three years, a series of ad hoc congressional committees and informal groups struggled to find bipartisan agreement on measures to raise the debt ceiling and to avoid the so-called "fiscal cliff" when previously enacted laws would take effect and cause another recession. Although these shorter-term problems were not affected by Social Security's longer-term outlook, congressional conservatives used the debates to promote entitlement reform, often invoking Simpson-Bowles. In 2012 Obama even offered to switch to the chained CPI in return for Republicans' agreement to cut taxes—a bargain Republicans refused. AARP ran million-dollar-plus ad campaigns, held meetings and candidate debates around the country, and mobilized the grassroots to oppose cutting benefits to reduce the deficit. None of the final budget agreements, in the end, touched Social Security.[209] Representative Paul Ryan's Medicare privatization proposal had also been rebuffed. By the end of Obama's second term, with the economy growing again and temporary stimulus spending winding down, the president even announced support for increasing Social Security benefits. AARP had played successful defense. At the same time, with public opinion still heavily on the side of saving old-age entitlements, most politicians would have had a hard time going on record against them: "Who wants to be blamed for any cuts that could be perceived as hurting grandma?"[210]

New challenges arrived with the election of Donald Trump to the presidency in 2016. During the campaign, Trump had pledged repeatedly not to cut Social Security or Medicare, reassuring voters that he would grow the economy enough to head off any potential threats to future solvency. His budget director, Mick Mulvaney, however, is a long-time advocate of overhauling the programs, with hopes of changing the president's mind.[211] AARP started with the mobilizing letters and e-mails, and launched another seven-figure television ad buy, just days after the inauguration, urging members and supporters to "protect Medicare" and to hold President Trump to his "promise" not to cut benefits.[212]

President Trump's first budget proposal contained several program reductions and eliminations that would particularly affect lower-income seniors and younger people with disabilities. Details in the initial proposal were still being fleshed out, but up for elimination were Community Development Block Grants that partially fund Meals on Wheels, and community service programs providing energy assistance for low-income households and help for older adults to get public service jobs. In addition, unspecified large cuts to the Department of Health and Human Services would surely reduce funding for programs under the Older Americans Act, which also provides funding for Meals on Wheels. Meals on Wheels, as a well-known program that provides food aid to needy older persons, immediately became a widely publicized symbol of the harm that could be done to society's most vulnerable.[213] Office of Management and Budget Director Mulvaney, hoping to focus on policy outcomes rather than symbols, suggested that the program is "just not showing any results."[214] But many studies do in fact find that home-delivered meal programs for seniors provide not only improved nutrition and food security but also opportunities for social interaction, psychological benefits, and the economic benefits of allowing people live at home who might otherwise have to move into costly nursing facilities, often funded by Medicaid.[215] One study conducted by researchers at Brown University, and funded by a grant from the AARP Foundation, found the same benefits for those receiving daily meals, as well as fewer falls and hospitalizations.[216] Said the *Washington Post* headline reporting all these findings: "Meals on Wheels is 'not showing any results' only if you ignore all these results."[217]

On large partisan issues like Social Security and Medicare, as well as smaller-budget issues like services provided through the Older Americans Act, AARP is recognized as a major player. With all of these issues heating up, and partisan polarization showing no sign of abating, AARP's influence will be increasingly important, and increasingly tested, through the remainder of the 2010s and beyond.

Lobbying the Private Sector

Interest-group lobbying and advocacy are generally associated with the government in people's minds: They involve contact with public sector officials, with the purpose of influencing public policy. But much of AARP's advocacy is with the private sector, lobbying companies to recognize the profit potential in marketing to Americans aged 50 and over, to develop and offer products meeting their needs and interests, and to advertise effectively to the 50+ demographic. This was, after all, how AARP got started in the first place. "Just as AARP's founder shook up the marketplace in the 1950s with pioneering group health insurance and a mail-order pharmacy, AARP Services is leveraging market forces to help people live healthier, more secure and happier lives," explains the annual report of AARP's for-profit division, ASI.[218] The 50+ market was a $7 trillion market in 2015, controlling 70 percent of the disposable income in the United States.[219]

AARP created the BankSafe initiative, for example, to help financial institutions guard against fraudulent practices that often target older persons, who are more likely to experience cognitive decline and to be vulnerable to exploitation. Banks themselves can lose money when their customers are scammed, and so they work with AARP to find and share solutions. AARP also offers online training to financial institution employees.[220] AARP has lobbied private-sector employers to offer high quality 401(k) accounts and to offer flexible work schedules to employees who are caring for family members at home; it has persuaded telephone companies to make sure that rural communities have service; it has demonstrated the value of developing easy-to-use mobile phones and worked with Intel to develop an easy-to-use tablet. "Movies for Grownups" spotlights movies for and about people aged over 50 in an effort to persuade Hollywood to target the older age group as much as teenage boys, as well as to hire more older actors and older writers.[221] Two teams within ASI, Media Sales and Influent50, work with companies to develop effective advertising that avoids ageist stereotypes and appeals to older consumers' interests and lifestyles.[222] Private-sector advocacy, Nancy LeaMond said, "is often more fruitful than lobbying government."[223]

As Leonard Davis learned when he teamed with Ethel Percy Andrus, there is serious money to be made in the 50+ market for those who appeal to the 50+ consumer. With the entire baby boom generation now past the age of 50, AARP's Media Sales notes, "boomers and older consumers will remain the dominant and most powerful consumer group for decades to come."[224]

Conclusion

AARP, by many measures, is one of the most influential advocacy groups in the United States. It has the largest membership among all advocacy groups, it has a large staff dedicated to politics and to policy research, and it has cultivated relationships with government decision makers through its reputation as a reliable provider of information about aging policy and the interests and opinions of Americans aged 50 and over. At least since the 1990s, it has consistently ranked high in measures of interest-group prominence including contacts with public officials, amount of money spent on lobbying, and reputation among Washington insiders.[225]

But metrics do not tell the whole story in Washington's complex of interests, issue networks, and coalitions. Lone-wolf lobbying is rare, which makes it even harder to evaluate the power of any single group.[226] AARP wins some and it loses some, by its leaders' own acknowledgment; for example, years of lobbying for government provision of long-term services and supports has borne little fruit beyond Medicaid coverage, which is for those in greatest financial need. The association had almost nothing to do with the creation of aging-based welfare state programs; it did not even exist when Social Security was created, and was not very politically active at the time that Medicare, Medicaid, and the Older Americans Act were passed. But AARP now is a widely recognized power in Washington. Other groups on both the political left and right seek it as a coalition partner, and policy makers hesitate to make any change in policy affecting Americans aged 50 and over without AARP's endorsement or approval. AARP's relatively moderate position among the aging-based membership organizations gives it the flexibility that, along with its huge membership and policy expertise, makes it a power broker in divisive policy debates. It has often been instrumental in getting issues on the agenda, helping to formulate and pass legislation, monitoring implementation, litigating in favor of older consumers and beneficiaries, and lobbying the private sector to produce and advertise products and services with older Americans in mind.

In the currency of U.S. politics, there is one resource that AARP neither possesses nor utilizes, namely the ability to endorse and financially support candidates for office. With a membership of 38 million people divided roughly evenly among Democrats, Republicans, and independents, specific candidate endorsements and contributions run the risk of alienating one-third to one-half of its membership. Its politically diverse membership does at times serve as a restraint on its advocacy, as taking bold stands on highly visible issues risks losing members. At the same time, since most members join for the discounts and other benefits rather than for the politics, AARP can and does take some of those risks, calculating when a policy victory outweighs the potential loss of thousands of members. At any rate, a group of tens of millions can lose even a few hundred thousands and still be "the biggest kid on the block."[227] That membership is AARP's most valuable political resource. The constant surveys of member opinions, and the mobilization of the grassroots across the country, are what make AARP's advocacy effective; they catch the attention of public officials and provide entrée for organization lobbyists.

Now with older Americans as Contenders—politically influential but often portrayed as receiving more than their share, especially as health care costs rise, the population ages, the national debt expands, and partisan polarization brings Social Security, Medicare, and Medicaid to the center of political debate—AARP's defensive power is both more important and increasingly tested. So is its ability to hold together a politically and socioeconomically diverse coalition of grassroots supporters.[228] "Looking back," said Christopher Howard, "one is led to conclude that AARP's power has been overrated. Looking ahead, however, is another matter."[229]

CHAPTER SIX

Business, Advocacy, and Service: Conflict or Convergence?

AARP is a multisector organization engaged in a wide variety of political, charitable, and commercial activities. Critics of AARP have long questioned whether its complex structure conceals conflicts of interest between its political advocacy and its profitable business relationships. They ask whether AARP's top priority in endorsing products is negotiating the best deals for its members or maximizing profits. Some critics have even asked whether the association manipulates its tax-exempt status in illegal or unscrupulous ways.

AARP and its supporters respond that the organization's various divisions and affiliates complement each other to fulfill its mission of advocacy, service, and "help[ing] people turn their goals and dreams into real possibilities."[1] Its revenues from business royalties and advertising provide funding for effective advocacy and member services while keeping membership dues low—at this writing, still only $16 per member or couple. There are times when AARP's political advocacy and its financial interests happen to coincide. But there are also times when its advocacy runs counter to what would be most profitable for its business. The political advocacy, AARP officials insist, is driven strictly by what they feel best meets the needs and interests of its members and of Americans aged 50 and over. The for-profit business affiliate, AARP Services, Inc., or ASI, pays income tax on its earnings. Neither its political advocacy nor its business practices violates AARP's tax-exempt status under subchapter 501(c)(4) of the Internal Revenue Code.

AARP values its role as a "trusted source for news and information."[2] When AARP is embroiled in controversy, it naturally opens itself to attack by those on the other side of whatever controversy that may be, and those attacks in turn may jeopardize trust among some segments of its constituency. That of course is a central tenet of democratic politics: building trust for one's own point of view while destroying the opposition's. In the combative political environment of the late twentieth and early twenty-first centuries, it is more difficult than ever to avoid controversy when engaging in political advocacy—especially for those whose advocacy is perceived as effective. This is the dilemma that Frederick Lynch describes as the tension between AARP's politically driven "warrior brand" and the broad appeal of its "consumer services brand."[3]

This chapter examines the evidence accumulated through years of investigations and reports examining the potential conflicts of interest inherent in AARP's complex and multifaceted organization, as well as the quality of its branded and endorsed products and services. AARP defends its practices, occasionally making changes in response to those queries but without admitting wrongdoing. Questions endure regarding the extent to which criticisms of AARP are politically motivated, or motivated by genuine concern for the 50+ constituency it represents.

AARP as a Nonprofit Organization

AARP is a 501(c)(4) nonprofit organization, defined in the Internal Revenue Code as a social welfare organization, operated exclusively for the promotion of social welfare and not organized for profit. AARP's charitable affiliate is the AARP Foundation, a 501(c)(3) affiliate of AARP that provides assistance to struggling seniors, particularly with housing, food, income, and personal connection, while also offering legal assistance and raising public awareness of the challenges facing the most vulnerable older Americans.[4] Both are exempt from federal income taxes as long as they do not violate Internal Revenue Service rules. Nonprofit organizations, in contrast to business organizations, must serve a public rather than private benefit, with no private dividend payments. The funds that they raise must be used to support the purpose of the nonprofit organizations and not paid out to directors, members, or staff beyond reasonable compensation. Charitable donations to a 501(c)(3) organization are tax deductible, while donations to a 501(c)(4) organization generally are not deductible.[5] In addition, 501(c)(3) charitable organizations may receive government grants, but 501(c)(4) organizations that lobby government may not.

Organizations classified as 501(c)(4)s like AARP may engage in unlimited political or lobbying activities related to the purpose of the organization, while 501(c)(3) charities are permitted only very limited political activities. Thus, there is nothing illegal or questionable about the extent of AARP's lobbying activity as a 501(c)(4). The most controversial political activity that 501(c)(4)s engage in is campaign finance. This is controversial, first of all, because they can raise and spend unlimited funds in support of candidates, as long as they run their ads independently of the candidates' campaigns and spend less than half of their money on such ads. Second, 501(c)(4)s do not need to disclose who their donors are; thus they serve as a conduit for anonymous individuals and organizations to support candidates without public disclosure.[6] These controversies related to campaign finance do not affect AARP, however, because AARP neither endorses candidates for office nor spends money to help elect them.

AARP Services, Inc., or ASI, is AARP's for-profit, taxable business subsidiary. ASI is in charge of the business relationships through which it offers its branded and endorsed products, from the flagship health insurance products—Medicare Supplement, Medicare Advantage, and Medicare Part D prescription drug coverage—to a variety of other products and services available for sale. ASI explores, selects, and expands member benefits and services, contracts with companies to provide member discounts, and offers marketing development and consultation to companies interested in appealing to 50+ consumers.

AARP's total budget is over a billion and a half dollars; total revenue in 2015 was $1,542,639,000.[7] More than half of AARP's operating revenue (54%) comes from the royalties paid by third-party providers for the use of AARP's name, logo, and mailing list. In 2015, two-thirds of those royalties came from UnitedHealthcare, the provider of the Medicare Supplement and Medicare Advantage insurance products as well as Medicare Part D prescription drug coverage. Nineteen percent of AARP's operating revenues came from membership dues; another 10 percent came from advertisements in AARP's publications. Six percent was grant revenue, awarded to the Foundation—not to the parent 501(c)(4) organization—from the federal government and private organizations. The largest grant programs were the Senior Community Service Employment Program, providing job training for low-income seniors, and AARP's long-lived tax assistance program, Tax-Aide. The remaining 11 percent of revenue came from contributions and program income (see Figures 6.1 and 6.2.).

ASI's business income from royalties and advertising revenue supports AARP's member services and political advocacy, while keeping membership dues low so that more people can afford to join and take advantage of

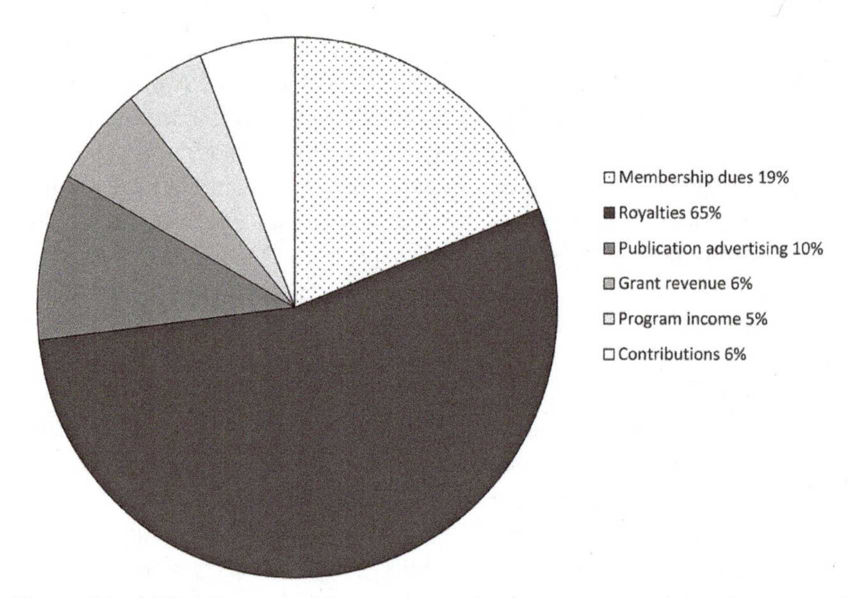

Figure 6.1 AARP Operating Revenues, 2015 (AARP, Consolidated Financial Statements Together with Report of Independent Certified Public Accountants, December 31, 2015 and 2014. Available at http://www.aarp.org/content/dam/aarp/about_aarp/annual_reports/2016/2015-financial-statements-AARP.pdf.)

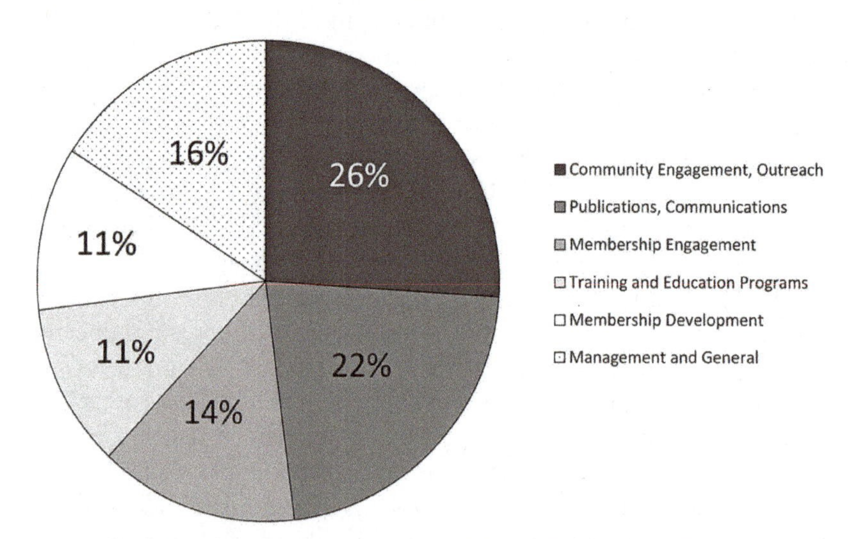

Figure 6.2 AARP Operating Expenses, 2015 (AARP, Consolidated Financial Statements Together with Report of Independent Certified Public Accountants, December 31, 2015 and 2014. Available at http://www.aarp.org/content/dam/aarp/about_aarp/annual_reports/2016/2015-financial-statements-AARP.pdf.)

the membership benefits. Thus AARP can be said to follow the social enterprise model, a profit/nonprofit hybrid that uses its proceeds to address social problems. Social entrepreneurship often targets disadvantaged or vulnerable populations, or it may benefit the broader population by addressing problems often caused by, or ignored by, pure business activities, as, for example, with environmental entrepreneurship.[8] Ethel Percy Andrus acted as a social entrepreneur when she sought to offer reasonably priced insurance products and travel discounts to older Americans and use the earnings to further expand services and advocacy on behalf of retirees.[9]

A successful social enterprise, write Roger Martin and Sally Osberg in the *Harvard Business Review*, must meet two objectives: it must adhere to its social goals and it must be financially sustainable without depending, in the long term, on subsidies from government or private philanthropy.[10] Many nonprofits adopt the social enterprise model for that reason: so they can support their social goals without relying on outside grants and contributions. AARP is certainly not alone. But it is singularly successful. "No organization has perfected the art of monetization better than AARP," wrote Peter Murray in the *Stanford Social Innovation Review*, describing its success at aggregating consumers in order to negotiate deals with insurance and other businesses. Those deals in turn allow them to market the products to consumers at lower group rates, while providing royalties for AARP to pursue its social mission.[11]

Horace Deets, AARP's executive director throughout the 1990s, responded in the same way when asked, in an interview, about the increasing proportion of AARP's revenues that came from its business ventures. "I think one of the things that's always been different about AARP has been . . . the reluctance to rely on soft money. This is an organization that was built on a financial model as a membership organization—not to stand on foundations and grants for revenues." Responding to criticisms that AARP is more of a business than a nonprofit, Deets noted that "if you look at the definition of nonprofit, it's not where the money comes from. It's what you do with the money."[12] As ASI's President and CEO Lawrence Flanagan put it: "In a virtuous cycle, the royalties AARP receives from providers for the use of AARP's name make a significant contribution to 'fueling' the social mission of AARP."[13]

AARP's critics put quite a different spin on the three-to-one ratio of money coming in from the royalties and advertising revenues, relative to revenue from membership dues. AARP, they contend, puts its business profit before its members. It is an insurance company, not a social welfare organization or an organization concerned primarily with the welfare of its members, they say. The overwhelming emphasis on business income as a source of revenue creates conflicts of interest with its purported social mission.[14] These alleged conflicts of interest have been examined, famously and perhaps in greatest detail, in two Republican-led congressional investigations, one in 1995 and another in 2011. Many others have made the same claims along the way, usually conservatives, although liberals also have questioned AARP's motives and charged it with conflicts of interest, for example, when AARP endorsed the Republican-backed Medicare Modernization Act in 2003. AARP and its supporters counter that the conflict-of-interest claims are motivated by ideology and partisanship. They also suggest that AARP's detractors lack understanding of the complex multisector nature of AARP, and how it all works to promote the interests of older Americans—and ultimately, all Americans, given that, barring tragedy, we all eventually reach the age at which we receive the invitation to join AARP.[15]

Conflicts of Interest? The 1980s and 1990s

Ethel Andrus's motto for AARP—"what we do, we do for all"—is consistent with social entrepreneurship, and so was her vision of an organization that would uplift older Americans' independence, well-being, self-esteem, and sense of purpose. Finding a company that would sell reasonably priced health insurance policies to retirees was one of her top priorities in those pre-Medicare days. She recognized the need, and when she met Leonard Davis in 1955, that need was finally fulfilled. The policies were so popular with the teachers in Andrus's National Retired Teachers Association that other older people began requesting them too, and Andrus and Davis founded the American Association of Retired Persons in 1958. But, as Andy Rooney put it, "Andrus's interest was old people. Davis's interest was money."[16] Andrus died in 1967 and Davis's interest in money became the overriding force, corrupting the organization's mission and resulting in a "hailstorm of bad press, lawsuits and investigations,"[17] including Rooney's *60 Minutes* exposé in 1978. AARP by then was offering poor-quality products through Davis's company Colonial Penn. The life and health insurance products were among the worst on the market, with high premiums and low payouts.[18] In 1981, AARP severed ties with Colonial Penn, inviting competitive bids and awarding its group health insurance to Prudential.

The association sought to revamp its image, emphasizing Ethel Andrus's legacy while distancing itself from that of Leonard Davis. By the end of the 1980s, it had a widespread reputation for skillful and pragmatic advocacy and coalition building, extensive policy expertise, a broader and much improved array of membership benefits, and 33 million members. But it had not left controversy behind. The Internal Revenue Service investigated the association's tax-exempt status, and the United States Post Office investigated its use of nonprofit rates for mass mailings advertising its insurance products. By the mid-1990s, AARP had settled with both, for a total of well over $100 million, and was under investigation by a U.S. Senate panel headed by the most colorful of AARP critics, Senator Alan Simpson of Wyoming.[19]

A dispute between AARP and the Internal Revenue Service erupted in the late 1980s over its tax exemptions. Both AARP and the IRS agreed that legally, a nonprofit's unrelated business income, or UBIT, is taxable, but they disagreed over which income was "unrelated." AARP conceded that the advertising revenues from its publications, as well as income from products other than health insurance, constituted unrelated income. But it argued that the royalty fees collected for the use of its name by other companies fell under the royalty exclusion in the federal tax code, making them tax-exempt. In addition, AARP contended that income from health insurance was not unrelated to its mission. After all, provision of health insurance had been a central purpose of the organization ever since Andrus and Davis had teamed up to found it, when such insurance was otherwise not commercially available to its older constituency.[20] Executive Director Deets testified during the 1995 Senate hearings that the IRS had determined that income to be nontaxable in 1978, and AARP had continued to follow that ruling,[21] but the IRS rules had tightened since then. In 1994, AARP settled with the IRS by paying $135 million in lieu of taxes for the years 1985–1993. The payment was not an admission of guilt, but rather a settlement to avoid further negative publicity. In 1999, AARP finally settled with the IRS once again with a payment of $52 million in lieu of taxes after 1993, and agreed to form AARP Services, Inc. as its taxable for-profit subsidiary. The creation of ASI as a separate unit not only ended the dispute with the IRS; it also opened the door to further revenue-raising ventures. As tax attorney Albert R. Rodriguez noted, "when you are willing to pay taxes, you can pretty much do whatever you want."[22]

The U.S. Postal Service (USPS) had its own beef with AARP around the same time, over AARP's use of nonprofit rates for mailings that advertised its insurance products. It was not the first time. In the late 1970s, when AARP was still affiliated with Colonial Penn, postal inspectors began a long investigation, recommending in 1981 that AARP and Colonial Penn be indicted for criminal fraud. Fearing criminal intent would be too difficult to prove, the U.S. district attorney declined to prosecute. After the Postal Service Appropriations Act for 1991 further restricted the use of nonprofit postal rates, AARP lobbied USPS to cooperate in trying to get the legislation amended. But the USPS refused, and it issued preliminary rules clarifying that AARP's product advertisements had to be mailed at regular rates. AARP continued to use the nonprofit rates until the new rules were made final. In 1994, AARP paid $2.8 million to settle with the Postal Service.[23]

AARP's expanding size and lobbying prowess during this time had made it a big target for its policy opponents and, in particular, for those who favored reducing or privatizing Social Security and Medicare. In the early 1990s, even with its cautious approach following the Medicare Catastrophic Coverage Act debacle in 1988–1989, AARP had flexed its muscles in President Clinton's health care reform effort and in opposing Republican efforts to slow growth in Medicare spending.[24] When Republicans won a majority in both chambers of Congress in 1994, it was their turn to flex. A Senate Finance subcommittee chaired by Senator Simpson spent two days in June, 1995 holding hearings on AARP's tax-exempt status while it was receiving government grants and earning business income. Simpson's goals in holding the hearings, he said, were "to cut off all 501(c)(4)'s from administering Federal grants" and "to ensure that 501(c)(4) status only follows upon direct financial dependence on membership or contribution direct support, and not upon businesses."[25]

Democratic senators David Pryor and John Breaux took issue with the partisan nature of the hearings. Many groups across the ideological spectrum are more dependent than AARP on grants and business income, with less of their revenue coming from member dues, they pointed out, including conservative groups like the National Rifle Association. "I think we have to raise it to a much higher level. Having political parties go after groups or organizations that differ with our political philosophy, we have to be very careful when we move into this area of free speech," said Breaux.[26] There are hundreds of thousands of nonprofits, including 140,000 501(c)(4) organizations, Pryor noted, and "I think our work is just beginning."[27] Simpson agreed. "Please do not feel that I am picking on the AARP," he said in his opening statement.[28]

But Simpson made no bones about his feelings toward the group—"I have been a long-time critic of AARP"[29]—or about his view that Social Security and Medicare were careening toward crisis. "Medicare will go broke in the year 2002. . . . Social Security will go broke in the year 2031, and will begin its swan dive of disaster in the year 2013. . . . And this particular senior group, the AARP, not only continually asks for more from the Treasury, that is their theme, their motif. . . . Break the bank."[30] Although his proposed changes to nonprofit tax exemptions would affect "several organizations . . . to me, [AARP] is the most grievous example of a group because they get less than 45 percent of their money from dues, and the rest of it comes from commercial operations."[31] In response, AARP's Deets testified that his organization still received a much larger proportion of its income from member dues than the average 501(c)(4); the average, Senator Breaux had said, was about 10 percent. More importantly, Deets noted, many nonprofits keep their membership dues very low. "Many of them represent very low-income constituents and people who do not have a lot of money." Income from other sources enables organizations like AARP "to carry out a purpose which we would all think is very important" while holding down the price of membership and enabling more people to join.[32]

"If this empire is not what our nonprofit laws were intended to facilitate," Simpson said of AARP outside the hearings, "then we may need to change the law."[33] And he did get a provision inserted into the 1995 Lobbying Disclosure Act that prohibits 501(c)(4) organizations that lobby government from receiving government grants. No problem, said AARP. It simply moved all grant activity—primarily programs for job training and for aiding seniors with their tax returns—into the AARP Foundation, its 501(c)(3) charitable affiliate.[34] The National Rifle Association, which used federal grants to run hunting and fishing training programs, had no problem with Simpson's provision either. "That's fine with us," said the NRA's top lobbyist.[35] And so, by the end of the 1990s, AARP had separate affiliates within the organization for its philanthropic work—the AARP Foundation—and its business operations—AARP Services, Inc.—in response to challenges to its mix of political, commercial, and charitable activities.[36]

AARP leaders contend that its detractors challenge its complex, hybrid structure and its tax-exempt status not only because of its political positions but also because it is a big and powerful force in Washington,[37] and Senator Simpson conceded as much during the 1995 hearings. "There are some organizations which are extraordinary, one called the National Council of Senior Citizens. . . . It is a left-wing operation, 96-percent funded by the Federal Government. . . . But they are small potatoes. They have very few members. And this group [AARP] allegedly has 33 million members. That is why I am directing my attention here."[38] The hearings reinforced the central position of AARP in aging-related policy debates in Washington.[39] It was not the last time that AARP would be challenged on its alleged conflicts of interest.

Conflicts of Interest? The 2000s and 2010s

The twenty-first century brought a flurry of new challenges centered on the notion that AARP's lobbying activities are driven more by its bottom line than by the needs and interests of Americans aged 50 and over. It is not always conservatives who question AARP's motives—usually, but not always. "America's two main parties take turns being angry at AARP," said Peter Overby on National Public Radio.[40] In 2003, it was the Democrats' turn.

When AARP lobbied in support of the Republicans' 2003 Medicare Modernization Act (MMA), liberals objected that the new law was more business-friendly than helpful to Medicare beneficiaries. The MMA created a new prescription drug benefit under Medicare, called Medicare Part D, something that had long been on AARP's wish list. But liberal senior organizations that had also pushed for Medicare prescription drug coverage wanted to hold out for fuller coverage and government price controls, as did Democrats in Congress who opposed the bill. Part D drug coverage is offered only by private-sector plans, another provision drawing liberal opposition; it was the first part of Medicare requiring beneficiaries to sign up with private insurers. The MMA also expanded Medicare Part C, offering private-insurance competition to traditional Medicare, and renamed it Medicare Advantage. Republican supporters argued that the private market competition would bring Medicare costs down, but in fact Medicare Advantage turned out to cost more, per enrollee, than traditional Medicare.[41]

There was potential profit in both Part C and Part D, and in supporting the business-friendly bill, AARP's liberal critics claimed that the association was supporting new business opportunities for itself, in Part C Medicare Advantage plans, and in Part D prescription drug insurance plans.[42] That support was a reflection of the corporate culture that then-CEO William Novelli and his executive team had brought to AARP, said Barbara Dreyfuss in The *American Prospect*—"people much more comfortable with Republicans, open to private plans and market-oriented policies and more willing to make deals than many of the veteran staff."[43] "AARP would stand to gain many millions of dollars in new income under the Republican Medicare bill," stated consumer advocacy group Public Citizen. "Maximizing corporate-related income and profits poses a significant conflict of interest for an organization trying to represent the best interest of its members."[44]

AARP did in fact introduce a Part D prescription drug plan, the AARP MedicareRx Plan, which quickly became one of the top choices among enrollees. It offers a Medicare Advantage plan as well, AARP MedicareComplete. Both are administered by UnitedHealthcare, the same third-party provider that insures the AARP Medicare Supplement Plans, AARP's lucrative Medigap policies for which AARP retains 4.95 percent of premiums.[45] Together, the UnitedHealthcare insurance products provide about two-thirds of the royalty income AARP receives for licensing with third-party providers.[46] So AARP's critics were right about the profit potential, but were they right about the group's motives?

AARP's policy positions and priorities are driven by the needs and interests of its older constituents, not by the profit potential, AARP insists. While Congress was still debating over the MMA, AARP spokesman Steve Hahn noted that it could actually be a money-loser for AARP, which was earning over $100 million on Medicare supplement policies and mail-order pharmaceuticals. The drug benefit in the MMA would reduce the need for both.[47] The fact that AARP later offered successful Medicare drug-coverage policies and Medicare Advantage policies was not only a happy coincidence, it also supports AARP's service and advocacy for the benefit of its constituency. "Our public policy is not dictated by products. The only reason why we produce them is because our members want them," said Cheryl Matheis, a senior vice president who was with AARP for 28 years.[48] "Policy always takes precedence over marketing," Novelli emphasized.[49] The MMA bill was imperfect, he and AARP Policy Director John Rother conceded, but in 2003, with a Republican president and Republican majorities in both chambers of Congress, it was the best shot at getting Medicare drug coverage. Prescription drugs, Rother noted, had become increasingly important to overall health care since Medicare's creation in 1965, and something had to be done.[50] Members wanted Medicare drug coverage, and opposing legislation with that benefit would have been hard to explain to the membership.[51] Even Ron Pollack, executive director of Families USA, which opposed MMA, defended AARP's motives, rejecting the charge that AARP's support "was predicated on conflicts of interest or other improper factors. . . . I believe those improvements are real, even if I believe they were wholly inadequate."[52]

Still, Democratic leaders felt betrayed. "AARP's credibility is severely wounded," and now "they're trying to look like they want to improve it," said House Minority Leader Nancy Pelosi after the MMA passed.[53] But AARP did want to improve the prescription drug benefit, in particular by eliminating the "doughnut hole" that left a gap in Part D drug coverage. Lobbying successfully for that provision in the Affordable Care Act (ACA), or Obamacare, six years later, AARP once again took fire from Republicans, who once again charged AARP with conflicts of interest.

Republican members of the Ways and Means Committee of the House of Representatives issued a report in 2011 called *Behind the Veil: The AARP America Doesn't Know*, raising many of the same issues as the Senate Finance hearings of 1995.[54] AARP, the report says, is essentially an insurance company, "operat[ing] as a massive for-profit enterprise" that earns the bulk of its revenue from business ventures, not membership dues.[55] The report also questions AARP's tax-exempt status, and asks the IRS to investigate whether it should be stripped of its tax exemption, although there seems to have been no response or follow-up by the IRS, by any other agency, or even by Congress itself.[56] In its executive summary, the report even takes a swipe at AARP's sponsorship of NASCAR driver Jeff Gordon, without revealing that the AARP Foundation had teamed with NASCAR for its Drive to End Hunger campaign to raise awareness and donations for its antihunger programs.[57] Former Republican Congressman Billy Tauzin, who had been instrumental in passing the Medicare Modernization Act in 2003, wrote an op-ed opposing the effort to have AARP's tax-exempt status nullified. The short-term political gain for Republicans, he said, would be outweighed by the threat to nonprofits in general, conservative as well as liberal.[58]

Finally, *Behind the Veil* asserts that AARP's advocacy pursues profit for AARP more than policies benefiting Americans aged 50+. The report's conflict-of-interest argument centers on AARP's support for the ACA, President Barack Obama's health insurance reform legislation, which AARP supported and helped to shape, and which passed Congress without a single Republican vote. The ACA contains various provisions for raising revenue and holding down costs, in an attempt to extend coverage to nearly all Americans without adding to the federal deficit. Funding for the Medicare Advantage program was reduced, on the grounds that it is more expensive, per enrollee, than traditional Medicare. As demand declines for Medicare Advantage plans and more beneficiaries return to traditional Medicare, demand for Medigap insurance policies is likely to increase. AARP would stand to make a "windfall" of up to $166 million in 2014, the report says, from the increased Medigap business, even with the loss of its Medicare Advantage customers, because the association receives royalties for every Medigap enrollee, while UnitedHealthcare pays AARP an annual fee for use of the AARP name in selling Medicare Advantage plans.[59] Marilyn Moon, a widely respected health policy expert who directed the AARP Policy Institute from 1986 to 1989, and who is cited in *Behind the Veil*, acknowledges that "there's an inherent conflict of interest. A lot of people there are trying to do good, but they're ending up becoming very dependent on sources of income."[60]

Nevertheless, in the complex world of U.S. health care, with its tangled mix of public, nonprofit, and for-profit insurers and providers, it is impossible to know just how much any company or organization would stand to win or lose with any given change in policy.[61] "We wouldn't know it, and we wouldn't really care," said AARP's Director of Legislative Policy David Certner during the Obamacare debate. "The advocacy is what drives what we do here, and not the other way around."[62] AARP officials point out that it even lost a piece of the insurance market, for people between the ages of 50 and 64 who are not eligible for Medicare, with the passage of the ACA. The authors of *Behind the Veil* suggested that AARP stood to gain new business with that age group by participating in the ACA health insurance exchanges.[63] But it did not participate in the exchanges because officials did not perceive a need. The ACA enables Americans in that age group to buy insurance through the exchanges, and prohibits the previous practice of private insurance companies charging older customers much higher rates because of their age. That was a major factor in AARP's decision to support the ACA.[64]

Conservatives' conflict-of-interest accusations persisted beyond the passage of the ACA. During the 2011 budget negotiations over the federal debt ceiling, Republican leaders and President Obama discussed at least two proposals to cut Medicare costs. One proposal was to limit Medigap coverage by not allowing it to cover some copays and deductibles, thereby reducing demand for unnecessary doctor visits and tests; another was to increase the eligibility age from 65 to 67 years. AARP opposed both changes. The Medigap limits were especially controversial, because the change would have lowered Medigap premiums and saved many customers a significant amount of money. AARP opposed both measures, its detractors argued, because both would lead to reduced revenue from its Medigap policies. Novelli, now the former CEO, conceded that AARP stood to lose revenue; although he "never saw financial incentives come into play" in AARP's advocacy, he conceded that "it's fair to say that AARP does have a financial interest in Medigap insurance because it's a significant revenue-raiser for them."[65] But many people would be hurt by having to wait two more years for Medicare, AARP responded. Further, limiting Medigap policies might reduce the premiums, but it would also reduce coverage, and increase the financial burden on those who needed health care. "These proposals fail to take into account that people choose these policies because they provide certainty and health security—the peace of mind that even if they have a health crisis or frequent, ongoing health care needs that they will be able to manage financially," then-CEO Barry Rand wrote to the congressional "supercommittee" charged with forging a deficit reduction plan in 2011.[66]

Conservatives were not the only ones challenging AARP on alleged conflicts of interest. Liberal supporters of a more universal, government-funded single-payer health insurance system raised that challenge as well. AARP would not support a single-payer system, wrote Sidney Wolfe of the consumer group Public Citizen in 2014, because it makes too much money on private insurance. "AARP is clearly more like a business than an advocacy group for Americans 50 and older," he wrote. "The time has come for AARP, the most powerful citizen lobbying group in Washington, to speak out loud and clear in favor of single payer health care reform in the United States."[67] Public officials and political organizations across the ideological spectrum could benefit from the support of "the most powerful citizen lobbying group in Washington." It is when they confront AARP's opposition that they are most likely to call the group out for conflict of interest.

A Social Change Organization, Not an Insurance Company

AARP strenuously objects to any suggestion that profit trumps good policy in its decision making. Sometimes the group's advocacy and its financial interests may coincide. But often, CEO Jo Ann Jenkins and Executive Vice President Kevin Donnellan said that AARP's social mission and advocacy conflict with the potential for profit, and when that happens, the social mission and advocacy always win.[68] There is no conflict of interest, but rather an integrative approach to improving the lives of Americans aged 50 and over—an integrative approach that dates back to the partnership between Ethel Andrus and Leonard Davis that led to AARP's founding. "We don't just advocate for government or public policy solutions; we also seek to promote marketplace solutions—just as Dr. Andrus did," then-CEO Rand testified in response to the House Ways and Means Committee's 2011 report. "We seek to move the market by lending our name to products and services . . . [and we] provide people 50-plus with valuable information and educational resources to help them live their best lives."[69] Cheryl Matheis, who worked "just about everywhere at AARP" during her years there, including as a liaison to ASI, also emphasized the goal of making the market more responsible to AARP's consumer policies: "People go to work at AARP not for profit, but for the mission."[70]

Revenue from the taxable subsidiary ASI supports the social mission and the political advocacy, AARP officials emphasize consistently—not the other way around. Further, revenue from ASI helps to keep the dues low, so that more people can join and take advantage of the membership benefits, and those tens of millions of members in turn make AARP a powerful advocate for its 50+ constituency.[71]

Critics on both the right and the left often characterize AARP as an insurance company. But AARP is not an insurance company. It does not take on risk. The fact that it licenses its name to private companies and earns money from those licenses does not make it an insurance company; in fact, writes Bruce Collins, corporate vice president and general counsel of C-SPAN, nonprofit licensing in exchange for royalty payments "has always been deemed a lawful noncommercial activity for [tax-]exempt organizations"[72] The boards of directors of AARP, the AARP Foundation, and ASI include a few overlapping members, but officials emphasize the "strict firewall" between ASI and the other aspects of AARP.[73] *Behind the Veil* and other critiques of AARP's hybrid structure often highlight the high salaries of AARP CEOs, noting in particular the $1.6 million paid to Novelli in 2009, including a large severance payment.[74] But the salaries at AARP are not out of line with other nonprofits, especially considering AARP's size and wealth. Over a dozen charitable nonprofits paid their CEOs seven-figure salaries in 2015,[75] and the median salary for nonprofits with budgets of $200 million and above was $526,679, maxing out at nearly $4 million.[76] The year in which *Behind the Veil* was released, CEO Barry Rand's salary did not make it to the list of the top 25 association executive salaries in Washington, D.C.[77] No one at AARP, including CEO Jo Ann Jenkins whose 2015 salary was $870,501,[78] comes remotely close to CEO compensation at the top five health insurance companies, which in 2014 ranged from $10.1 million at Humana to $15 million at Aetna.[79] "We're a consumer advocacy organization; we're not an insurance firm," Certner emphasized. "That drives everything we do. It's got to be good for our members, or we don't endorse it."[80]

Hybrid profit/nonprofit organizations, and nonprofits with for-profit subsidiaries, are not uncommon. There are many nonprofits with taxable business subsidiaries and with strong corporate ties that help fund their service and advocacy functions: the National Geographic Society, the American Cancer Society, the American Red Cross, the Nature Conservancy, and the National Rifle Association, to name just a few. But AARP is unusual in its size and influence, which makes it a frequent political target, as well as a valued political coalition partner. There is a growing trend toward both business organizations and nonprofit organizations becoming—or trying to become—more like AARP, said Matheis, because businesses feel increasingly compelled to appear socially responsible and philanthropic, while nonprofits, in an environment of increasing competition for grants and donations, must be cognizant of their bottom line. "But AARP was the pioneer in public-private partnerships."[81]

A Trusted Brand?

AARP's product endorsements often are portrayed as similar to the Good Housekeeping Seal of Approval for older Americans, built on the trust in AARP that it does the research on product quality and value.[82] People do trust AARP. A series of Harris Polls conducted between 2007 and 2012 found AARP to be consistently among the most trusted large organizations that influence U.S. politics and business.[83] That trust derives in part from its large, diverse membership; people do not perceive AARP to be "serving an ideology or a narrow economic agenda."[84] Trust in the AARP brand is important, said Barbara Shipley, AARP's senior vice president of brand integration. It is important not simply for selling products, but for the service and advocacy missions as well.[85] Because of the cross-sector connections—the multiple ways in which AARP's service, advocacy, charitable, and financial aspects influence and support each other—a lack of trust in one aspect of the organization could be detrimental to the others. Conversely, a high degree of trust in one aspect of the brand—in this case, the insurance and other product offerings—can have a positive effect on the others.

AARP applies very stringent quality control on the products for which it licenses its name and receives royalties, said CEO Jenkins and Executive Vice President and Chief of Staff Donnellan. The products that AARP endorses and markets are not necessarily the cheapest on the market, but AARP feels they are the best. The focus, naturally, is on finding products and services especially suited for the aging, and in the process, AARP "is very active in driving the marketplace to provide better products for fifty-plus," said Donnellan.[86] Sometimes AARP even develops and introduces its own products, such as the easy-to-use tablet developed in conjunction with Intel. Both Jenkins and former CEO Novelli singled out AARP's relationship with United Healthcare—by far its most lucrative partnership—for praise. "United Healthcare executives said AARP had made them a better company by pushing them" as part of ASI's oversight role, Jenkins said.[87] United Healthcare "has been a good partner to AARP and the partnership has endured" for a long time, Novelli agreed.[88] But the association also invites people to shop around. The group's website and publications offer information and helpful hints for choosing the best Medigap policy and other products to fit individual needs, even if the choice does not lead them to buy products for which AARP receives royalties. "We always encourage people to study, research and choose on their own," Jenkins said.[89] Although AARP's licensing agreements are not necessarily for the cheapest products on the market, AARP is in a good position to push for good deals, Rother noted, for the obvious reason of size and scale.[90]

There have been some missteps along the way, but by far the biggest was the Colonial Penn affair. Although the relationship with Leonard Davis started out well as AARP through its partnership offered health insurance that was otherwise largely unavailable to retirees, Colonial Penn took advantage of people's trust in AARP as competition grew from other insurers. By the mid-1970s, several years after Andrus passed away, both a U.S. Senate subcommittee hearing and an analysis by *Money* magazine found AARP's insurance offerings through Colonial Penn to be among the worst on the market. *Consumer Reports* magazine came to the same conclusion after a more detailed analysis in 1976, and the same year, *Forbes* magazine revealed that Colonial Penn was the most profitable company in the country.[91] Colonial Penn virtually controlled the organization, but there was growing dissension within the ranks as well as increased media scrutiny, and finally AARP severed ties with Colonial Penn and Davis, put the health insurance up for bid, and signed on with Prudential Insurance in 1981.[92] One thing that AARP insisted on in the deal was community rating on its Medigap policies, or offering the same rates for everyone in a given area regardless of age, so that older members are not so easily priced out of the market.[93]

Charles Morris reviewed AARP's major products in the mid-1990s, and compared them with other products on the market, for his book, *The AARP: America's Most Powerful Lobby and the Clash of Generations*.[94] Morris is a former attorney and banker who has written numerous books, newspaper articles, and magazine articles, mostly about U.S. business and finance from the industrial revolution to the 2008 economic crisis and postcrisis recovery. "Overall," he said of AARP, "the product offerings are quite creditable."[95] He was impressed with AARP's biggest money-maker, the Medigap policies offered through Prudential; their premiums were competitive and not adversely affected by age, the policies did not require medical examinations, their service was excellent, and their payouts were high. The major medical and long-term care policies, also offered through Prudential, also fared well. The hospital supplement insurance, though, like many hospital supplement plans at the time, did not seem worth the money. The mutual funds, he found, were somewhat lackluster in performance overall. The rest of the products he reviewed—home, automobile, and life insurance, bank cards and annuities, mail-order pharmaceuticals, and travel discounts—all had good value, he found, and in particular, they offered prices and services that were helpful to older, less advantaged, and less sophisticated members. Morris notes that few such products are one-size-fits-all in any market. As any comparison shopper knows, it is impossible to find a product that offers the best value for every potential customer. But in general, Morris found AARP products to offer excellent value, especially for older consumers.[96]

In 1995, Prudential announced rate increases in its Medigap policies averaging 30 percent, and up to 40 percent in several states. It was not the only insurance company to do so. After an independent review of Prudential's pricing calculations, AARP concluded that the rate increases were justified.[97] A year and a half later, however, United Healthcare outbid Prudential for renewal of the agreement, and won AARP's health insurance business beginning in 1998. The agreement added more than $4 billion in premiums to United Healthcare's business, and was "a big blow" to Prudential. United Healthcare, AARP's membership director said, not only offered favorable premium prices but also 24-hour medical advice and other new services and products.[98]

AARP's products came under scrutiny again a decade later when, in 1998, U.S. senator Chuck Grassley, an Iowa Republican, contacted CEO Novelli and state commissioners with questions about AARP/United-Healthcare's policies for members aged 50–64. The policies were basically supplemental health insurance policies for those not yet old enough for Medicare. Grassley had received complaints from constituents who discovered the policies did not provide catastrophic coverage, although marketing materials did not make that very clear. Novelli agreed to suspend marketing and sales of the policies immediately, and hire an outside expert to investigate. That incident, however, led Bloomberg News to review a wider array of AARP products. The good news for AARP was that Bloomberg found AARP/UnitedHealthcare's prized Medigap policies to be excellent bargains, with the lowest or nearly the lowest premiums in many states. The AARP-branded life-insurance premiums tended to be high, however, and the financial services were not particularly good deals. Mutual funds were expensive, and annuities generated relatively lower payment streams than could be found elsewhere. Yet when viewed from the perspective of many AARP members, even those products were not bad deals, because they were priced to serve people who might otherwise have a hard time buying such products at all. The life insurance policies required less health information up front, for example, and the investment services generally required lower initial investments than most. In general, AARP sought products and services more easily accessible for older and lower-income consumers than those widely available in the broader market. Thus, while not all products were the cheapest or best deals generally, they were good deals for many AARP constituents.[99]

The controversy over Grassley's investigation and the Bloomberg review faded quickly, said Lynch. Even better, a four-part series on CBS Moneywatch in 2008 and 2009 delivered positive reviews of AARP's mutual funds, life insurance and annuities, auto and homeowners' insurance, and health and long-term care insurance.[100] The Moneywatch series found the products to be generally competitive and, again, especially helpful and attractive to 50+ consumers.[101]

AARP's branded and licensed products, in sum, receive generally good, even excellent, ratings and reviews from analysts and experts over the years—at least since it parted ways with Leonard Davis's company Colonial Penn after what Morris calls "the disgraceful profit-mongering of AARP's first two decades."[102] But as Morris also points out, "it is to Davis's lasting credit that he blazed the trail for marketing to the elderly."[103] It is a trail that AARP continues to follow, with an eye toward providing products and member services that Americans aged 50+ can trust.

Conclusion

AARP is a nonpartisan nonprofit tax-exempt social welfare organization with a taxable for-profit business subsidiary and a charitable foundation all wrapped into one. Hybrid nonprofit/for-profit organizations are not uncommon in the complex American system of advocacy groups, membership associations, businesses, and social enterprises that use their business proceeds to address social problems. What makes AARP unique is its huge size, which gives it outsized influence, enhanced by the integration of its business, politics, service, and philanthropy. Its big size makes it a big target, leading to allegations of conflicts of interest: between AARP's nonprofit status and its profit orientation; between its nonprofit status and its political activities; between its lobbying activities and its receipt of government grants; and above all, between its pursuit of profit and its interest in the well-being of its 50+ constituency.

There is no conflict, AARP and its supporters respond. All aspects of the organization interact, they say, to fulfill AARP's mission of improving the quality of life for Americans aged 50 and over, helping them "turn their goals and dreams into real possibilities."[104] That mission is itself complex, given the diversity of older Americans, and their wide variety of interests and needs.

AARP works with the private sector to find, develop, and advertise products geared toward the needs of Americans who are 50+. Its for-profit subsidiary, AARP Services, Inc., or ASI, manages the business side of the organization. It licenses with other companies to provide AARP-branded products, primarily insurance and financial products, and receives royalties for the use of its name and logo. AARP also arranges with a wide variety of companies to offer discounts on products and services to its 38 million members, and accepts advertisements in its print and online publications, including *AARP The Magazine*—the largest-circulation magazine in the country. AARP's business proceeds support the organization's member services, political advocacy, and charitable activities, while keeping the annual dues low so that more people can take advantage of the membership benefits. Its political advocacy includes extensive policy research and member surveys, which the board of directors uses to set issue positions and priorities, and it engages in direct and grassroots lobbying and litigation in pursuit of policies the organization feels will best benefit the 50+ population today and in the future. A small portion of its income is from government grants, which help fund activities of its charitable wing, the AARP Foundation, especially its job-training program for low-income seniors and its Tax-Aide program for helping low- and moderate-income seniors with their tax returns.

AARP's combination of service, business, and political pursuits dates back to its origins. Ethel Percy Andrus, an accomplished and progressive retired school principal, founded AARP's precursor, the National Retired Teachers Association, in 1947, to organize retired teachers, many of whom were trying to survive on meager pensions. She quickly discovered that health insurance was a primary need in those pre-Medicare years. She worked long and hard to persuade private insurance companies to sell insurance to retirees at a reasonable price, until she met Leonard Davis, who already was selling group insurance to retired teachers in New York. Ethel Andrus was "a visionary," said former CEO Bill Novelli. Today many people are envious of AARP's successful model of business and member services, which "grew up like Tinkertoys," piece by piece over time, in a way that is impossible to duplicate.[105] Leonard Davis was something of a visionary too. He may have run the group off the rails for a time, putting profit before service, but he understood the business advantages of marketing to older consumers at a time when most others did not. Since severing ties with Davis and then switching to another insurance company in 1981, AARP officials insist, its business relationships are driven entirely by its interest in improving the lives of its 50+ constituency, not by what will make the most money.

As a 501(c)(4) social welfare organization under the Internal Revenue Code, AARP is not limited by law in its political advocacy. Its charitable affiliate, the AARP Foundation, a 501(c)(3) organization, is permitted only very limited political activities. That is why donations to the Foundation are tax-deductible, while those to the parent organization are not, and that is also why the Foundation can accept government grants. What makes the parent organization legally a nonprofit organization is that its proceeds go into service and advocacy. It is not a for-profit insurance company that sells policies and assumes risks. The boards of directors of AARP, ASI, and the Foundation have some overlap but are separated by a "strict firewall," AARP officials insist, that prevents political and constituency service decisions from being driven by business concerns. AARP's executive compensation is not out of line with other nonprofits, especially considering the association's size and wealth, and its leaders are paid a tiny fraction of the compensation typical of major insurance companies. "We reinvest all our resources in our social programs," then-CEO Novelli asserted. "We're not paying dividends here. We're investing in social change."[106]

Intrigued by the scandals of the 1970s, and especially by Andy Rooney's exposé of AARP's business practices on the popular television show *60 Minutes* in 1978, Charles Morris decided to dig deeper and expose more, for his 1996 book *The AARP: America's Most Powerful Lobby and the Clash of Generations*.[107] But he concluded that "after an awful start [under the control of Leonard Davis and Colonial Penn] they had become squeaky clean."[108] His review of AARP-branded and endorsed products, like other reviews, found them generally to be good deals. It is impossible for any one product to be the best deal available, and the best fit, for every possible consumer. But AARP works hard at research and quality control, its leaders maintain, to negotiate the best deals and offer the most useful products and services for older Americans.

Conservative and liberal critics alike have accused AARP of supporting political policies that, above all, improve AARP's bottom line. But AARP strenuously objects to any suggestion that its policy positions are profit-driven. It may happen that AARP lobbies for policy change that creates or expands a business opportunity, but its policy priorities and positions do not always coincide with its business interests. AARP's social mission always comes before business, they insist; policy always trumps profit.

Conflict-of-interest accusations tend to come from those opposed to AARP's politics. In the current polarized political environment, conservatives are generally more likely than liberals to oppose AARP's political positions, as AARP defends the current structure of Social Security and Medicare programs from conservative proposals to pare back or privatize benefits. Two major congressional investigations of AARP's business practices—Senate Finance subcommittee hearings in 1995 led by Republican senator Alan Simpson and a report by Republican subcommittee chairs in the House Ways and Means Committee in 2011—followed AARP's efforts to support Democrat-sponsored health care reform and oppose Medicare benefit reductions. But Democrats also accused AARP of pursuing profitable policies when it supported the Republican-sponsored Medicare Modernization Act in 2003, which added prescription drug coverage to Medicare. In the wake of AARP's support for President Barack Obama's health insurance reform package, the Affordable Care Act, conservatives claimed that AARP stood to make money from resulting policy changes that would enhance its Medigap insurance business, while some liberals claimed that AARP supported the ACA, and failed to support a single-payer health insurance system, for the same reason.

Taking heat from all sides, AARP stands by its affirmation that, in the tradition of Ethel Percy Andrus, all of its parts work together, as an integrated whole, for the purpose of enhancing the lives and well-being of older Americans.

CHAPTER SEVEN

Conclusion

How can one organization represent a membership of tens of millions—not to mention a broader constituency of well over a hundred million—that is so diverse and fragmented by income, education, race, ethnicity, gender, religion, employment status, and family and household composition, and so politically divided along partisan and ideological lines? For AARP this question presents numerous dilemmas, especially in the polarized and divisive American political system of the early twenty-first century. It presents opportunities as well, with the 50+ population united by a common desire for income and health security as the realities of retirement and advancing age hit home.

It is no secret how AARP achieved and maintains a membership in the tens of millions. AARP's membership benefits are legendary; the product and service discounts and the publications and information attract members, and the advocacy and social mission help to keep them. It is no secret, yet even among the many hybrid organizations that combine service, advocacy, and business, AARP's formula for growth and influence is difficult to duplicate. It began when Ethel Percy Andrus recognized needs—for access to health insurance, affordable prescription drugs, travel discounts, and more fundamentally, basic security and life fulfillment—and worked to meet them. Today, said AARP's brand manager, Emilio Pardo, the organization does nothing that "does not pass the Ethel test."[1]

Proceeds from AARP's business activities, managed by its taxable subsidiary, AARP Services, Inc., support the member services and the political advocacy, while keeping membership dues low and obviating the need to seek outside support from grants and donations. AARP's critics sometimes level conflict-of-interest allegations, asserting that AARP lobbies for policies most likely to increase its business profits. AARP officials maintain that its advocacy is always for the purpose of improving the lives of

Americans who are 50+. Policy, they insist, trumps profit. The conflict-of-interest allegations, they note, generally come from political adversaries, including public officials and political commentators on the right and on the left. Liberals and Democrats tend to make those allegations when AARP is supporting Republican policies, while conservatives and Republicans are more likely to criticize when AARP is supporting Democratic policies. The association took hits from both sides by supporting the 2010 Affordable Care Act, known as Obamacare, as many on the right preferred the less-regulated status quo, while many on the left preferred a single-payer or more universal health care system similar to those in other industrialized Western countries. As the major entitlement programs directly benefiting older and retired Americans, Social Security and Medicare, continue to move toward the front and center of domestic policy debates, AARP tends to support Democratic efforts to maintain and even increase benefits against Republican efforts to reduce or radically reform the programs. But it remains officially nonpartisan and open to policies generated by either party that improve the well-being of the 50+ population.

AARP's political influence derives primarily from its enormous membership base. The numbers give it clout, and when even a small percentage of its members are mobilized to contact Congress, to attend rallies and candidate forums and town hall meetings, and to lobby public officials in state capitals across the country, the numbers are impressive. The association's policy expertise and Washington insider status are important as well. The most successful advocacy organizations combine grassroots mobilization with well-informed direct lobbying. Grassroots mobilization without well-informed direct lobbying is often dismissed as "Astroturf," while lobbying with little evidence of widespread public support tends to have limited effect, especially on major redistributive policies. Money does talk in Washington and in the state capitals, and in a political advocacy system dominated by well-heeled business-related organizations, AARP is one of the few consumer groups with the wealth and clout to compete at that level.

AARP has long been in the happy position of defending programs that are extremely popular among Americans of all ages, but now they are growing more contentious and partisan as the population ages and health care costs escalate. AARP will continue to play an important but increasingly delicate advocacy role, more liberal and Democratic than conservative and Republican, but pragmatic and realistic. Maintaining a stance of nonpartisan pragmatism is not easy in the early twenty-first century. The group has drawn criticism—including from its own members—for being too liberal or too conservative, and for taking bold stands that are not universally popular, as well as for being too cautious about taking bold stands.

Government spending on older and retired Americans is already approaching half the federal budget and is six times as high as government spending on children.[2] AARP's conservative adversaries point to these facts to justify reducing or privatizing old-age benefits, or means-testing them so that benefits can be focused on those with the greatest need. But social insurance programs like Social Security and Medicare have done much more to lift people out of poverty and provide security than the generally more meager and stigmatized means-tested public assistance programs. Already a few policy compromises have been made in that direction, such as higher Medicare premiums and partial taxation of Social Security benefits for higher-income retirees. A disproportionate number of older Americans live near the poverty line and struggle to make ends meet. Economic inequality is at least as great among older adults as among the young, and the needs among the most vulnerable older groups, such as low-income women living alone, still go largely unmet. "There is no shortage of needs, and no end to the need for advocacy," said AARP's long-time former policy director John Rother.[3]

The best approach to defending old-age benefits, AARP officials stress, is to think and act intergenerationally. Older and younger Americans are connected through intergenerational family and community relationships. Older people's health and income security takes a good deal of financial pressure off younger family members. Programs that help older and disabled persons live independently at home are much less costly for taxpayers than institutional long-term care. "Older people are not primarily interested in discounts," said former CEO William Novelli; "they are interested in their kids and grandkids. And younger people have a lot of reverence toward parents and grandparents."[4] In addition, those younger people are aging too. That is one thing that sets older people apart as an interest group: everybody, barring untimely demise, will one day be part of that group if they are not already there. AARP has an interest in maintaining good will among younger generations—its future constituency—as well as among those who are currently 50+. In the 1980s, AARP helped create the intergenerational coalition, Generations United. In 2017, AARP awarded a grant to the Association of Young Americans, founded the previous year to get young adults politically engaged and in touch with public officials.[5] Nevertheless, all the intergenerational good will in the world will not provide easy answers to the budgetary pressures on Social Security, Medicare, and Medicaid.

Maintaining AARP's greatest political resource—its membership—is also a challenge in the early twenty-first century, as younger generations, including the baby boomers, who are now all old enough to join AARP, are more individualistic and less prone than older generations to join organizations. Jo Ann Jenkins, AARP's CEO, and Kevin Donnellan, AARP's executive vice president and chief of staff, emphasize the need for personal "relevance": providing information to facilitate individual choices, and a wide array of options for individuals to get what they want from AARP by phone and by mail, through the Internet and social media, and through state and local offices and chapters. "We're constantly working on personalizing the AARP experience, at the personal and community levels," said Jenkins.[6]

The Livable Communities project, promoting everything to make life at the local level easier, from transportation and safe streets to quality housing, infrastructure, and disaster recovery, is "overwhelmingly generational," noted Nancy LeaMond, AARP's chief advocacy and engagement officer.[7] Caregiving is another issue with intergenerational appeal, as an aging population with fewer children puts increasing pressure on younger adults, millions of whom provide unpaid care to older and disabled relatives and loved ones. More comprehensive coverage of long-term services and supports has long been on AARP's political agenda, but the chances of the federal government creating major new entitlement programs are slim in the foreseeable future. AARP offers information and tools for helping those who need the care, and those who provide the care, to navigate the daily challenges.

"We must involve all sectors of society," says Jenkins, not only about caregiving but about AARP's engagement with its 50+ constituency more generally. "I refer to this as the three Ps . . . the public sector, government at all levels; the private sector, business, organizations and non-profit institutions; and the personal sector, each of us individually."[8]

AARP's evolution and growth have been phenomenal, in ways Ethel Andrus could hardly have foreseen. "Since its inception," says AARP's website, "AARP has grown and changed dramatically in response to societal changes, while remaining true to its founding principles:

- To promote independence, dignity and purpose for older persons
- To enhance the quality of life for older persons
- To encourage older people "To serve, not to be served"[9]

Remaining true to those principles is complicated in today's polarized political environment, when there is so much conflict over which policies best "enhance the quality of life for older persons." Diverse and divided though they may be, Americans aged 50 and older have interests that unite them, and AARP is their primary collective voice. Its influence in the twenty-first century will be both increasingly challenging and increasingly consequential.

Notes

Chapter 1 Introduction

1. Barbara Shipley, Senior Vice President of Brand Integration, AARP, personal interview, July 23, 2015.

2. Dave Barry, *Dave Barry Turns 50* (New York: Ballantine Books, 1998), 161.

3. Bill Geist, *The Big Five-Oh! Facing, Fearing, and Fighting Fifty* (New York: William Morrow, 1997), 7.

4. Paul Schwartzman, "At 50, AARP Enters Its Golden Years; with Boomers on Board, Seniors Lobby Flexes Its Muscle," *Washington Post*, September 4, 2008, http://www.washingtonpost.com/wp-dyn/content/article/2008/09/03/AR2008090303785.html.

5. Alison Mitchell, "Clinton Has $10 Million Wish for Birthday Bash," *New York Times*, August 19, 1996, http://www.nytimes.com/1996/08/19/us/clinton-has-10-million-wish-for-birthday-bash.html.

6. Julie Pace, "Obama Celebrates 50th Birthday at White House," *Seattle Times*, August 4, 2011, http://www.seattletimes.com/seattle-news/politics/obama-celebrates-50th-birthday-at-white-house/.

7. "Jo Ann Jenkins, Age Disruptor," *Insight News*, November 7, 2016, http://www.insightnews.com/2016/11/07/jo-ann-jenkins-age-disruptor/.

8. Craig Walker and Bret Bradigan, "The Age of Reformation: Dr. Ethel Percy Andrus and the Founding of the AARP," *Ojai History*, Winter, 2011–2012, 120–125.

9. Ibid., 123.

10. Ibid.; AARP, "AARP History," May 10, 2010, http://www.aarp.org/about-aarp/company/info-2016/history.html; Frederick R. Lynch, *One Nation under AARP: The Fight over Medicare, Social Security, and America's Future* (Berkeley: University of California Press, 2011), 129–130.

11. Charles R. Morris, *The AARP: America's Most Powerful Lobby and the Clash of Generations* (New York: Times Books, 1996).

12. Ibid.; Julie Kosterlitz, "Test of Strength," *National Journal*, October 24, 1987, 2652–2657.

13. Barry, *Dave Barry Turns 50*, 161–162.

14. John Rother, Chief Executive Officer, National Coalition on Health Care, telephone interview, September 18, 2014.

15. Jain World, "Elephant and the Blind Men," Jainism Global Resource Center, http://www.jainworld.com/education/stories25.asp (accessed June 25, 2016).

16. Rother, interview.

Chapter 2 AARP's History: Growing Up and Branching Out

1. Charles R. Morris, *The AARP: America's Most Powerful Lobby and the Clash of Generations* (New York: Times Books, 1996).

2. Carroll L. Estes, *The Aging Enterprise* (San Francisco: Jossey-Bass, 1979), 2.

3. Julie Kosterlitz, "The World According to AARP," *National Journal*, March 10, 2007, 28–35; Morris, *The AARP*; Craig Walker and Bret Bradigan, "The Age of Reformation: Dr. Ethel Percy Andrus and the Founding of the AARP," *Ojai History*, Winter, 2011–2012, 120–125.

4. See the ad at www.youtube.com/watch?v=4PM6pAnHKLs (accessed June 22, 2014).

5. The NRTA became a de facto subunit of AARP, until they merged officially in 1982. During that time, the organization was variously referred to as NRTA/AARP, AARP/NRTA, or simply AARP; I have chosen the latter convention to keep it simple.

6. Henry J. Pratt, *The Gray Lobby* (Chicago: University of Chicago Press, 1976); Alexander Guerin, Media Relations Associate, AARP, e-mail message to author, June 8, 2016.

7. Ethel Percy Andrus, "The Aged and Retired," in *Who Is My Neighbor?*, ed. Esther Pike (Greenwich, CT: Seabury Press, 1960), 119–136.

8. Frederick R. Lynch, *One Nation under AARP: The Fight over Medicare, Social Security, and America's Future* (Berkeley: University of California Press, 2011); Morris, *The AARP*.

9. Morris, *The AARP*, 26.

10. Morris, *The AARP*; Pratt, *The Gray Lobby*.

11. Information about AARP's relationship with Colonial Penn during this time is drawn largely from Morris, *The AARP*, chapter 2. Morris had "use of an extensive file of primary sources compiled by Andy Rooney and his staff at CBS" (269).

12. Morris, *The AARP*, 33.

13. Ibid., 37.

14. *Miller v. Davis*, 464 F. Supp. 458 (1978), United States District Court, District of Columbia, November 18, 1978.

15. Andy Rooney, *Sincerely, Andy Rooney* (New York: Public Affairs, 2001).

16. Morton Mintz, "Two Groups for Elderly May Lose Nonprofit Postal Status," *Washington Post*, January 3, 1979, 2A.

17. Dale Van Atta, *Trust Betrayed: Inside the AARP* (Washington, DC: Regnery, 1998), 55.

18. Ibid.

19. Robert J. Samuelson, "Benefit Programs for the Elderly—Off Limits to Federal Budget Cutters?" *National Journal*, October 3, 1981, 1757–1762.

20. Julie Kosterlitz, "Test of Strength," *National Journal*, October 24, 1987, 2652–2657; Henry J. Pratt, *Gray Agendas: Interest Groups and Public Pensions in Canada, Britain, and the United States* (Ann Arbor: University of Michigan Press, 1993); Jack L. Walker, *Mobilizing Interest Groups in America: Patrons, Professions, and Social Movements* (Ann Arbor: University of Michigan Press, 1991).

21. Robert B. Hudson, "The 'Graying' of the Federal Budget and Its Consequences for Old Age Policy," *Gerontologist* 18, no. 4 (1978): 428–440.

22. Andrea Louise Campbell, *How Policies Make Citizens: Senior Political Activism and the American Welfare State* (Princeton, NJ: Princeton University Press, 2003); Christine L. Day, *What Older Americans Think: Interest Groups and Aging Policy* (Princeton, NJ: Princeton University Press, 1990); Pratt, *The Gray Lobby*; Walker, *Mobilizing Interest Groups*.

23. W. Andrew Achenbaum, *Old Age in the New Land: The American Experience Since 1790* (Baltimore: Johns Hopkins University Press, 1978); Edwin Amenta, *When Social Movements Matter: The Townsend Plan and the Rise of Social Security* (Princeton, NJ: Princeton University Press, 2005); David Hackett Fischer, "The Politics of Aging in America: A Short History," *Journal of the Institute for Socioeconomic Studies* 4 (1979): 51–66; Abraham Holtzman, *The Townsend Movement: A Political Study* (New York: Bookman, 1963); Pratt, *The Gray Lobby*; John B. Williamson, Linda Evans, and Lawrence A. Powell, *The Politics of Aging: Power and Policy* (Springfield, IL: Charles C. Thomas, 1982).

24. Pratt, *The Gray Lobby*.

25. Michael Kaye Carlie, "The Politics of Age: Interest Group or Social Movement?" *Gerontologist* 9, no. 4, Part 1 (1969): 259–264; Abraham Holtzman, "Analysis of Old Age Politics in the United States," *Journal of Gerontology* 9, no. 1 (1954): 56–66; see Pratt, *The Gray Lobby*, 39–40.

26. Linda Evans and John B. Williamson, "Social Control of the Elderly," in *Readings in the Political Economy of Aging*, ed. Merry Minkler and Carroll L. Estes (Farmingdale, NY: Baywood, 1984), 47–72.

27. Robert B. Hudson and Judith G. Gonyea, "The Shifting Political Construction of Older Americans as a Target Population," in *The New Politics of Old Age Policy*, 3rd ed., ed. Robert B. Hudson (Baltimore: Johns Hopkins University Press, 2014), 99–116.

28. Robert H. Binstock, "From Compassionate Ageism to Intergenerational Conflict?" *Gerontologist* 50, no 5 (2010): 574–585.

29. Hudson and Gonyea, "Shifting Political Construction."

30. Pratt, *The Gray Lobby*, 87; see also Robert H. Binstock, "Interest-Group Liberalism and the Politics of Aging," *Gerontologist* 12, no. 3, Part 1 (1972): 265–280.

31. Christine L. Day, "Old-Age Interest Groups in the 1990s: Coalition, Competition, and Strategy," in *New Directions in Old-Age Policies*, ed. Janie S. Steckenrider and Tonya M. Parrott (Albany: State University of New York Press, 1998), 131–150; Christine L. Day, "Aging Policy: A Partisan Paradox," in *Polarized Politics: The Impact of Divisiveness in the U.S. Political System*, ed. William Crotty (Boulder, CO: Lynne Rienner, 2014), 285–307; David Dirck Van Tassel and Jimmy Elaine Wilkinson Meyer, *U.S. Aging Policy Interest Groups: Institutional Profiles* (Westport, CT: Greenwood, 1982).

32. Jeffrey M. Berry and Clyde Wilcox, *The Interest Group Society*, 5th ed. (New York: Routledge, 2008); Allan J. Cigler and Burdett C. Loomis, eds., *Interest Group Politics*, 4th ed. (Washington, DC: CQ Press, 1995); R. Kenneth Godwin, *The Direct Marketing of Politics: $1 Billion of Influence* (Chatham, NJ: Chatham House, 1988); Walker, *Mobilizing Interest Groups.*

33. Pratt, *Gray Agendas*; Walker, *Mobilizing Interest Groups.*

34. Campbell, *How Policies Make Citizens.*

35. Linda E. Demkovich, "There's a New Kick in the Step of the Senior Citizen Lobbies," *National Journal*, October 2, 1976, 1382–1389.

36. Cheryl Matheis, former Senior Vice President of Policy, Strategy, and International Affairs, AARP, telephone interview, January 25, 2016; Lynn Mento, former Senior Vice President of Membership and Member Engagement, telephone interview, February 26, 2016; Morris, *The AARP*, 33.

37. Jo Ann Jenkins, Chief Executive Officer, AARP, and Kevin Donnellan, Executive Vice President and Chief of Staff, AARP, personal interview, Washington, DC, July 22, 2015; Barbara Shipley, Senior Vice President of Brand Integration, AARP, personal interview, July 23, 2015; Paul Light, *Artful Work: The Politics of Social Security Reform* (New York: Random House, 1985).

38. Robert H. Binstock, "The Aged as Scapegoat," *Gerontologist* 23, no. 2 (1983): 136–143; Binstock, "From Compassionate Ageism to Intergenerational Conflict?"

39. Andrus, "The Aged and Retired," 122.

40. Birnbaum, Jeffrey H., "Washington's Power 25: Which Pressure Groups Are Best at Manipulating the Laws We Live By?" *Fortune*, December 8, 1997. http://archive.fortune.com/magazines/fortune/fortune_archive/1997/12/08/234927/index.htm.; Matt Grossmann, *The Not-So-Special Interests: Interest Groups, Public Representation, and American Governance* (Stanford: Stanford University Press, 2012); Morris, *The AARP.*

41. Campbell, *How Policies Make Citizens*, 78–79; Pratt, *The Gray Lobby*, 51–52.

42. Walker and Bradigan, "The Age of Reformation."

43. Andrus, "The Aged and Retired," 133.

44. Walker and Bradigan, "The Age of Reformation."

45. Pratt, *The Gray Lobby*; Binstock, "Interest-Group Liberalism."

46. Pratt, *The Gray Lobby*, 97.

47. Martha Derthick, *Policymaking for Social Security* (Washington, DC: Brookings, 1979); Theodore R. Marmor, *The Politics of Medicare*, 2nd ed. (New York: Aldine DeGruyter, 2000); Paul Starr, *Remedy and Reaction: The Peculiar American Struggle over Health Care Reform*, 2nd ed. (New Haven, CT: Yale University Press, 2013); James L. Sundquist, "For the Old, Health Care," in *Politics and Policy: The Eisenhower, Kennedy, and Johnson Years*, ed. James L. Sundquist (Washington, DC: Brookings, 1968); Williamson, Evans, and Powell, *The Politics of Aging.*

48. Binstock, "Interest-Group Liberalism"; Day, *What Older Americans Think*, 94–96; Pratt, *The Gray Lobby*; Pratt, *Gray Agendas*, 85–86.

49. Demkovich, "There's a New Kick," 1382.

50. Binstock, "Interest-Group Liberalism"; Pratt, *The Gray Lobby.*

51. Binstock, "Interest-Group Liberalism"; Day, *What Older Americans Think*; Demkovich, "There's a New Kick"; Pratt, *The Gray Lobby*; Pratt, *Gray Agendas.*

52. Demkovich, "There's a New Kick," 1386.

53. Neal E. Cutler, "Political Characteristics of Elderly Cohorts in the Twenty-First Century," in *Aging: Social Change*, ed. Sarah B. Kiesler, James N. Morgan, and Valerie Kincaid Oppenheimer (New York: Academic Press, 1981); Arthur H. Miller, Patricia Gurin, and Gerald Gurin, "Age Consciousness and Political Mobilization of Older Americans," *Gerontologist* 20 (1980): 691–700.

54. Day, *What Older Americans Think*; Neal R. Peirce and Peter C. Choharis, "The Elderly as a Political Force—26 Million Strong and Well Organized," *National Journal*, September 11, 1982, 1559–1562; Pratt, *Gray Agendas.*

55. Hudson, "The 'Graying' of the Federal Budget."

56. Barbara Boyle Torrey, "Guns vs. Canes: The Fiscal Implications of an Aging Population," *American Economic Review* 72, no. 2 (1982): 309–313.

57. Samuelson, "Benefit Programs for the Elderly."

58. Light, *Artful Work.*

59. Day, *What Older Americans Think*, 26.

60. Samuelson, "Benefit Programs for the Elderly," 1759.

61. Campbell, *How Policies Make Citizens*, 78.

62. Day, *What Older Americans Think.*

63. Kosterlitz, "Test of Strength."

64. Day, *What Older Americans Think.*

65. Jeffrey H. Birnbaum and Natasha Graves, "Follow the Money," *Fortune*, December 6, 1999, 206–208.

66. Morris, *The AARP.*

67. Day, *What Older Americans Think*; Day, "Old-Age Interest Groups"; Pratt, *Gray Agendas.*

68. Van Atta, *Trust Betrayed.*

69. Morris, *The AARP*, 3.

70. James Dau, Media Relations Director, AARP, personal interview, July 22, 2015.

71. Grossmann, *The Not-So-Special Interests*, 118–123.

72. Binstock, "From Compassionate Ageism to Intergenerational Conflict?"; Larry Polivka and Carroll L. Estes, "The Economic Meltdown and Old Age Politics," *Generations* 33, no. 3 (2009): 56–62; Jill Quadagno, "Generational Equity and the Politics of the Welfare State," *Politics and Society* 17, no. 3 (1989): 353–376; James H. Schulz and Robert H. Binstock, *Aging Nation: The Economics and Politics of Growing Older in America* (Baltimore: Johns Hopkins University Press, 2006).

73. Quadagno, "Generational Equity"; Schulz and Binstock, *Aging Nation.*

74. David DeVoss, "Who Will Pay? Two Views on How—or Whether—America Can Afford a Rapidly Aging Population," *Los Angeles Times Magazine*, May 25, 1986. http://www.articles.latimes.com/1986-05-25/magazine/tm-7032_1_social-security-benefits.

75. Day, "Aging Policy: A Partisan Paradox"; Marilyn Werber Serafini, "Senior Schism," *National Journal*, May 6, 1995, 1089–1093.

76. Lynch, *One Nation under AARP*, 131; Morris, *The AARP*, 13, 237–242; Bara Vaida, "AARP's Big Bet," *National Journal*, March 13, 2004, 796–802.

77. Morris, *The AARP*; Bennett Roth, "GOP Probe of AARP Could Ensnare Other Nonprofits," *Roll Call*, April 1, 2011, http://www.rollcall.com/news/gop_probe_of_aarp_could_ensnare_other_nonprofits-204534-1.html; Vaida, "AAARP's Big Bet."

78. Richard Himelfarb, *Catastrophic Politics: The Rise and Fall of the Medicare Catastrophic Coverage Act of 1988* (University Park, PA: Penn State University Press, 1995); Christine L. Day, "Older Americans' Attitudes Toward the Medicare Catastrophic Coverage Act of 1988," *Journal of Politics* 55, no. 1 (1993): 167–177.

79. Steven A. Holmes, "The World According to AARP," *New York Times*, March 21, 2001. http://www.nytimes.com/2001/03/21/jobs/the-world-according-to-aarp.html.

80. Lynch, *One Nation under AARP*; Kosterlitz, "The World According to AARP"; Vaida, "AARP's Big Bet."

81. Vaida, "AARP's Big Bet," 797.

82. Lynch, *One Nation under* AARP, especially chapters 4–5; Vaida, "AARP's Big Bet."

83. Barbara T. Dreyfuss, "The Seduction: The Shocking Story of How AARP Backed the Medicare Bill," *American Prospect* 15, no. 6 (2004): 18–23;. Lynch, *One Nation under AARP.*

84. Lynch, *One Nation under AARP.*

85. Ibid., 136.

86. Lynch, *One Nation under AARP*, 138; Bara Vaida, "AARP's Chief: Giving Back," *National Journal*, July 31, 2010, 43–44.

87. Vaida, "AARP's Chief," 43; see also Binstock, "From Compassionate Ageism to Intergenerational Conflict"; Day, "Aging Policy: A Partisan Paradox"; Lynch, *One Nation under AARP.*

88. Vaida, "AARP's Chief," 44.

89. Jo Ann Jenkins, *Disrupt Aging: A Bold New Path to Living Your Best Life at Every Age* (New York: Public Affairs, 2016).

90. Barbara Shipley, Senior Vice President of Brand Integration, personal interview, July 23, 2015. Shipley said they realized "Real Possibilities" happened to coincide with the last two letters of the organization's name after they had already adopted it as a tag line.

91. Vaida, "AARP's Chief."

92. Michael A. Fletcher and Zachary A. Goldfarb, "AARP Uses Its Power to Oppose Social Security, Medicare Benefit Cuts for Retirees," *Washington Post*, November 17, 2012, https://www.washingtonpost.com/business/economy/aarp-uses-its-power-to-oppose-social-security-medicare-benefit-cuts-for-retirees/2012/11/17/affb5874–2aa6–11e2-bab2-eda299503684_story.html?utm_term=.d3340ebabcf6.

93. Daniel Marans, "Why AARP's New Social Security Campaign Is Upsetting Progressives," *Huffington Post*, February 16, 2016, http://www.huffingtonpost.com/entry/aarp-social-security-campaign_us_56c3854fe4b0c3c55052e81e.

94. Grossmann, *The Not-So-Special Interests*, 118.

95. Lynch, *One Nation under AARP*.

Chapter 3 AARP and Its Members: Maintaining America's Largest Interest Group

1. Steve Kroll-Smith, Vern Baxter, and Pam Jenkins, *Left to Chance: Hurricane Katrina and the Story of Two New Orleans Neighborhoods* (Austin: University of Texas Press, 2015); Tom Wooton, *We Shall Not Be Moved: Rebuilding Home in the Wake of Katrina* (Boston: Beacon Press, 2012).

2. Nancy LeaMond, Executive Vice President and Chief Advocacy and Engagement Officer, AARP, personal interview, Washington, DC, July 23, 2015; Denise Bottcher, State Director, Louisiana State AARP, telephone interview, March 20, 2015; Jason Tudor, Director of Outreach, Louisiana State AARP, personal interview, New Orleans, LA, March 31, 2015.

3. LeaMond, interview.

4. Kroll-Smith, Baxter, and Jenkins, *Left to Chance*; Wooton, *We Shall Not Be Moved*.

5. Paul Baricos, Founder, Carrollton Hollygrove Community Development Corporation and Hollygrove Market and Farm, New Orleans, LA, personal interview, New Orleans, September 25, 2015

6. Kevin Brown, former Executive Director, Trinity Christian Community, New Orleans, LA, personal interview, New Orleans, September 18, 2015.

7. Brad Edmondson, "A Comeback Story in New Orleans," *AARP Bulletin*, August 23, 2010, http://www.aarp.org/home-garden/livable-communities/info-08-2010/a_comeback_in_new_orleans.html.

8. Brown, interview.

9. Baricos, interview.

10. Brown, interview.

11. Edmondson, "A Comeback Story in New Orleans."

12. Brown, interview.

13. Richard A. Webster, "$3.4M Hollygrove Senior Center Opens," *New Orleans Times-Picayune*, October 16, 2015, http://www.nola.com/politics/index.ssf/2015/10/34m_hollygrove_senior_center_o.html.

14. Kroll-Smith, Baxter, and Jenkins, *Left to Chance*, 126.

15. Baricos, interview; Brown, interview.

16. Brown, interview.

17. Jo Ann Jenkins, "Walking the Walk: Renewal in New Orleans Ten Years After Katrina," AARP blog, posted August 25, 2015, http://blog.aarp.org/2015/08/25/walking-the-walk-renewal-in-new-orleans-10-years-after-katrina/.

18. Jo Ann Jenkins, CEO, AARP, and Kevin Donnellan, Executive Vice President and Chief of Staff, AARP, personal interview, Washington, DC, July 22, 2015; Barbara Shipley, Senior Vice President of Brand Integration, AARP, personal interview, July 23, 2015.

19. Mancur Olson, Jr., *The Logic of Collective Action* (Cambridge, MA: Harvard University Press, 1965); Peter B. Clark and James Q. Wilson, "Incentive Systems: A Theory of Organizations," *Administrative Science Quarterly* 6 (1961), 129–166; Robert H. Salisbury, "An Exchange Theory of Interest Groups," *Midwest Journal of Political Science* 13 (1969): 1–32.

20. Jeffrey M. Berry and Clyde Wilcox, *The Interest Group Society*, 5th ed. (New York: Routledge, 2008); Matt Grossmann, *The Not-So-Special Interests: Interest Groups, Public Representation, and American Governance* (Stanford: Stanford University Press, 2012); Robert H. Salisbury, "Interest Group Representation: The Dominance of Institutions," *American Political Science Review* 78 (1984): 64–76; Jack L. Walker, *Mobilizing Interest Groups in America: Patrons, Professions, and Social Movements* (Ann Arbor: University of Michigan Press, 1991); James Q. Wilson, *Political Organizations* (New York: Basic Books, 1973).

21. http://www.aarp.org/benefits-discounts/?intcmp=DSO-HDR-BENEFITS-EWHERE.

22. Frederick R. Lynch, *One Nation under AARP: The Fight over Medicare, Social Security, and America's Future* (Berkeley: University of California Press, 2011), 137.

23. Lynch, *One Nation under AARP*; Charles R. Morris, *The AARP: America's Most Powerful Lobby and the Clash of Generations* (New York: Times Books, 1996).

24. Jenkins and Donnellan, interview; Shipley, interview.

25. Morris, *The AARP*, 242.

26. Anne Tergesen, "Sure, It's from AARP. But Is It a Good Deal?" *Bloomberg Businessweek*, February 13, 2008, http://www.bloomberg.com/news/articles/2008-02-13/sure-its-from-aarp-dot-but-is-it-a-good-deal.

27. Lynch, *One Nation under AARP*, 142.

28. Jenkins and Donnellan, interview.

29. Ibid.

30. The Harris Poll, "American Red Cross, Nature Conservancy, Consumers Union and AARP Are Organizations inside the Beltway Most Trusted by Public," January 17, 2012, http://www.theharrispoll.com/search?keywords=most+trusted+beltway.

31. "Largest U.S. Magazines by Circulation," http://www.statisticbrain.com/largest-u-s-magazines-by-circulation/ (accessed April 2, 2017).

32. Peter Murray, "The Secret of Scale," *Stanford Social Innovation Review* (Fall, 2013), http://ssir.org/articles/entry/the_secret_of_scale.

33. Morris, *The AARP.*

34. Lynch, *One Nation under AARP*; Paul Gough, "AARP to Combine *Modern Maturity*, *My Generation*," *Online Media Daily*, August 28, 2002, http://www.mediapost.com/publications/article/3337/aarp-to-combine-modern-maturity-my-generation.html.

35. Shafaq Hasan, "AARP Bars Right-to-Die Group from Annual Exposition in San Diego," *Nonprofit Quarterly*, September 4, 2014, https://nonprofitquarterly.org/2014/09/04/aarp-bars-right-to-die-group-from-annual-exposition-in-san-diego/; see also Charles Trainor, Jr., "AARP Conference Attendees Do a Little Learning, a Little Shopping," *Miami Herald*, May 15, 2015, www.miamiherald.com/news/local/community/miami-dade/article21118479.html.

36. Hasan, "AARP Bars Right-to-Die Group."

37. Wesley L. Smith, "AARP Excludes Suicide Pushers From Expo," *National Review*, September 6, 2014, http://www.nationalreview.com/human-exceptionalism/387294/aarp-exclude-suicide-pushers-expo-wesley-j-smith.

38. Jenkins and Donnellan, interview; Shipley, interview; Paul Light, *Artful Work: The Politics of Social Security Reform* (New York: Random House, 1985).

39. LeaMond, interview.

40. Christine L. Day, *What Older Americans Think: Interest Groups and Aging Policy* (Princeton: Princeton University Press, 1990).

41. Lynch, *One Nation under AARP,* 6; see also 152–158, 166–196 for more on Life@50+.

42. Trainor, "AARP Conference Attendees."

43. Jason Weinstein, Vice President of Event Strategy and Services, AARP, and Jessica Winn, Media Relations Manager, AARP, telephone interview, June 3, 2016.

44. Ibid.

45. Ibid.

46. Dues are the same for individuals and for couples, and members who live with spouses or partners do not necessarily report the presence of additional age-eligible household members. Therefore, AARP calculates its membership numbers using a formula based on the proportion of respondents to their membership surveys who report having a spouse or partner. That is why *AARP The Magazine*'s circulation (23.5 million) is less than the number of members

(37,689,000 in 2015). Kristin Palmer, vice president of Media Relations, AARP, e-mail message to author, December 27, 2015.

47. Scholars and journalists have long described AARP as the largest membership organization aside from the Catholic Church; Church-affiliated groups do lobby government, of course. More recently, the American Automobile Association, which does lobby government on transportation-related issues such as speed limits and fuel taxes, has surpassed AARP with a membership of over fifty million, although it is more of a commercial enterprise, a dot-com rather than a dot-org. Regardless of how one defines a political or membership organization, AARP has been at or near the top for decades in terms of numbers, far exceeding almost every other group.

48. Joel N. Axelrod, "Attitude Measures That Predict Purchase," *Journal of Advertising Research* 8 (1968): 3–17; John J. Coleman and Paul F. Manna, "Congressional Campaign Spending and the Quality of Democracy," *Journal of Politics* 62, no. 3 (2000): 757–789; Thomas E. Mann and Raymond E. Wolfinger, "Candidates and Parties in Congressional Elections," *American Political Science Review* 74, no. 3 (1980): 617–632.

49. Shipley, interview.

50. See Jo Ann Jenkins, *Disrupt Aging: A Bold New Path to Living Your Best Life at Every Age* (New York: Public Affairs, 2016).

51. Lynn Mento, former Senior Vice President of Membership and Member Engagement, telephone interview, February 26, 2016.

52. Cheryl Matheis, former Senior Vice President of Policy, Strategy, and International Affairs, AARP, telephone interview, January 25, 2016.

53. Mento, interview.

54. Morris, *The AARP*, 11. See also Lynch, *One Nation under AARP*, 136; Bara Vaida, "AARP's Big Bet," *National Journal*, March 13, 2004, 796–802.

55. Morris, *The AARP*, 23–43.

56. Dale Van Atta, *Trust Betrayed: Inside the AARP* (Washington, DC: Regnery, 1998), 68.

57. Julie Kosterlitz, "Test of Strength," *National Journal*, October 24, 1987, 2652–2657.

58. Robert H. Binstock, "From Compassionate Ageism to Intergenerational Conflict?" *Gerontologist* 50, no 5 (2010): 574–585; Andrea Louise Campbell, *How Policies Make Citizens: Senior Political Activism and the American Welfare State* (Princeton, NJ: Princeton University Press, 2003); James H. Schulz and Robert H. Binstock, *Aging Nation: The Economics and Politics of Growing Older in America* (Baltimore: Johns Hopkins University Press, 2006).

59. Morris, *The AARP.*

60. Neal E. Cutler, "Demographic, Social-Psychological, and Political Factors in the Politics of Aging: A Foundation for Research in Political Gerontology," *American Political Science Review* 71, no. 3 (1977): 1011–1025; Day, *What Older Americans Think*, Henry J. Pratt, *The Gray Lobby* (Chicago: University of Chicago Press, 1976).

61. Robert B. Hudson, "The 'Graying' of the Federal Budget and Its Consequences for Old Age Policy," *Gerontologist* 18, no. 4 (1978): 428–440.

62. Robert J. Samuelson, "Benefit Programs for the Elderly—Off Limits to Federal Budget Cutters?" *National Journal*, October 3, 1981, 1757–1762.

63. Nancy Gibbs, "Living: Grays on the Go," *Time*, February 22, 1988, 66–75.

64. Henry Fairlie, "Talkin' 'Bout My Generation," *New Republic*, March 28, 1988, 19–22.

65. Lee Smith, "The Tyranny of America's Old," *Fortune*, January 13, 1992, 68–72.

66. Larry Polivka and Carroll L. Estes, "The Economic Meltdown and Old Age Politics," *Generations* 33, no. 3 (2009): 56–62; Jill Quadagno, "Generational Equity and the Politics of the Welfare State," *Politics and Society* 17, no. 3 (1989): 353–376; Schulz and Binstock, *Aging Nation*.

67. Kosterlitz, "Test of Strength"; Morris, *The AARP.*

68. Berry and Wilcox, *The Interest Group Society.*

69. Alexis de Tocqueville, *Democracy in America* (New York: Vintage Books, 1972 [1840]).

70. James Madison, Alexander Hamilton, and John Jay, *The Federalist Papers* (Auckland, New Zealand: The Floating Press, 2011 [1787]).

71. R. Kenneth Godwin and Robert Cameron Mitchell, "The Implications of Direct Mail for Political Organizations," *Social Science Quarterly* 65, no. 3 (1984): 829–845; Walker, *Mobilizing Interest Groups.*

72. Robert D. Putnam, *Bowling Alone: The Collapse and Revival of American Community* (New York: Simon and Schuster, 2000); Robert D. Putnam, "Bowling Alone: America's Declining Social Capital," *Journal of Democracy* 6, no. 1 (1995): 65–78.

73. Putnam, "Bowling Alone," 71.

74. Roger A. Lohmann, "An Interview: Horace Deets of AARP," *Nonprofit Management and Leadership* 12, no. 1 (2001): 87–94.

75. Ibid., 91.

76. Day, *What Older Americans Think*; Kosterlitz, "Test of Strength"; Lynch, *One Nation under AARP.*

77. Thomas L. Gais, Mark A. Peterson, and Jack L. Walker, "Interest Groups, Iron Triangles, and Representative Institutions in American National Government," *British Journal of Political Science* 14 (1984): 161–185.

78. Day, *What Older Americans Think*; Kosterlitz, "Test of Strength"; Lynch, *One Nation under AARP*, 1985; Neal R. Peirce and Peter C. Choharis, "The Elderly as a Political Force—26 Million Strong and Well Organized," *National Journal*, September 11, 1982, 1559–1562.

79. Steven A. Holmes, "The World According to AARP," *New York Times*, March 21, 2001. http://www.nytimes.com/2001/03/21/jobs/the-world-according-to-aarp.html.

80. Richard Himelfarb, *Catastrophic Politics: The Rise and Fall of the Medicare Catastrophic Coverage Act of 1988* (University Park, PA: Penn State University Press, 1995); Holmes, "The World According to AARP."

81. Lynch, *One Nation under AARP.*

82. Ibid., 213.

83. Paul C. Light, *Baby Boomers* (New York: W. W. Norton, 1990); Lynch, *One Nation under AARP*, 28–32; Putnam, *Bowling Alone.*

84. Michael X. Delli Carpini, "Baby Boomers," *The Forum* 12, no. 3 (2014): 417–445.

85. Robert Prisuta, "Enhancing Volunteerism among Aging Boomers," prepared for the Conference on Baby Boomers and Retirement: Impact on Civic Engagement, October 8–10, 2003, Cambridge, MA, www.agingsociety.org/agingsociety/links/AARPboomers.pdf., 50.

86. Ibid., 51.

87. The meaning of "entitlement programs" is often misunderstood, or confused, with the pejorative notion of feeling "entitled" to government largesse. Technically, an entitlement program is one that provides individual benefits according to a formula, with eligibility requirements set by law, so that the government is obligated to provide those benefits and must estimate how much they will cost when crafting the annual budget. Entitlements are distinct from discretionary spending categories for which Congress annually appropriates specific amounts. Examples of entitlement programs include Social Security and Medicare—the two largest—as well as Medicaid, unemployment insurance, veterans' benefits, and the Supplemental Nutrition Assistance Program.

88. Jacob S. Hacker, *The Great Risk Shift: The New Economic Insecurity and the Decline of the American Dream* (New York: Oxford University Press, 2006); Lynch, *One Nation under AARP*; Schulz and Binstock *Aging Nation.*

89. Anne L. Alstott, *A New Deal for Old Age* (Cambridge: Harvard University Press, 2016).

90. Stephen Crystal and Dennis Shea, "Cumulative Advantage, Cumulative Disadvantage, and Inequality Among Elderly People," *Gerontologist* 30, no. 4 (1990): 437–443.

91. Lynch, *One Nation under AARP*, 147.

92. Marilyn Werber Serafini, "AARP's New Direction," *National Journal*, January 5, 2002, 28–31.

93. Lynch, *One Nation under AARP*; Julie Kosterlitz, "The World According to AARP," *National Journal*, March 10, 2007, 28–35; Paul Schwartzman, "At 50, AARP Enters Its Golden Years," *Washington Post*, September 4, 2008, http://www.washingtonpost.com/wp-dyn/content/article/2008/09/03/AR2008090303785.html; Vaida, "AARP's Big Bet."

94. Shipley, interview.

95. Lynch, *One Nation under AARP*; Kosterlitz," The World According to AARP"; Vaida, "AARP's Big Bet."

96. John Rother, Chief Executive Officer, National Coalition on Health Care, telephone interview, September 18, 2014.

97. Jenkins and Donnellan, interview.

98. Robert Pear, "AARP, Eye on Drug Costs, Urges Change in New Law," *New York Times*, January 17, 2004, A12; Tierney Plumb, "AARP Loses 300,000 Members over Health Care Reform Debate," *Washington Business Journal*, April 8, 2011, http://www.bizjournals.com/washington/print-edition/2011/04/08/aarp-loses-300000-members-over-health.html.

99. Plumb, "AARP Loses 3000,000 Members."

100. David Certner, Legislative Counsel and Legislative Policy Director for Government Affairs, AARP; Cindy Lewin, Executive Vice President and General Counsel, AARP; and Sarah Mika, Senior Vice President, AARP Services, Inc., personal interview, Washington, DC, July 22, 2015.

101. Lynch, *One Nation under AARP*, 143.

102. Holmes, "The World According to AARP"; Jeffry H. Birnbaum, "Washington's Second Most Powerful Man Horace Deets Heads the Most Fearsome Force in Politics, the American Association of Retired Persons," *Fortune*, May 12, 1997, http://archive.fortune.com/magazines/fortune/fortune_archive/1997/05/12/226236/htm.

103. Michael T. Heaney, "Identity Crisis: How Interest Groups Struggle to Define Themselves in Washington," in *Interest Group Politics*, 7th ed., ed. Allan J. Cigler and Burdett A. Loomis (Washington, DC: CQ Press, 2006), 279–300; Lynch, *One Nation under AARP*.

104. Putnam, *Bowling Alone*; Laura Stoker, "Reflections on the Study of Generations in Politics," *The Forum* 12, no. 3 (2014): 377–396.

105. David Karpf, *The MoveOn Effect: The Unexpected Transformation of American Political Advocacy* (New York: Oxford University Press, 2012), 3; see also David Karpf, "How Will the Internet Change American Interest Groups?" in *New Directions in Interest Group Politics*, ed. Matt Grossmann (New York: Routledge, 2014), 122–143.

106. Bruce Bimber, Andrew Flanagin, and Cynthia Stohl, *Collective Action in Organizations: Interaction and Engagement in an Era of Technological Change* (Cambridge: Cambridge University Press, 2012).

107. Jenkins and Donnellan, interview; Jenkins, *Disrupt Aging*.

108. A. Barry Rand, "Our Age of Possibilities," *AARP Bulletin*, July-August 2014, 38.

109. Jenkins and Donnellan, interview.

110. Jo Ann Jenkins, "Own Your Age—and Resist Ageism," AARP blog, May 14, 2015, http://blog.aarp.org/2015/05/14/own-your-age-and-fight-back-against-ageism/.

111. William Novelli, *Voices of Social Change: Selected Speeches of Bill Novelli* (Washington, DC: AARP, 2009), 33–34.

112. Fredrick Kunkle, "Mid-Life Crisis Becomes 'Life Reimagined' with AARP Program," *Washington Post*, March 16, 2015, https://www.washingtonpost.com/news/local/wp/2015/03/16/mid-life-crisis-becomes-life-reimagined-with-aarp-program/?utm_term=.60740c2a6e1e.

113. Shipley, interview.

114. Kunkle, "Mid-Life Crisis."

115. Lynch, *One Nation under AARP*, 190.

116. Schulz and Binstock, *Aging Nation*, chapter 7.

117. Alstott, *A New Deal for Old Age*; Lynch, *One Nation under AARP.*

118. Susan C. Reinhard, Lynn Friss Feinberg, Rita Choula, and Ari Houser, "Valuing the Invaluable: 2015 Update," *Insight on the Issues*, no. 104 (Washington, DC: AARP Institute, 2015), http://www.aarp.org/content/dam/aarp/ppi/2015/valuing-the-invaluable-2015-update-new.pdf; see also Denys Dukhovnov and Emilio Zagheni, "Who Takes Care of Whom in the United States? Time Transfers by Age and Sex," *Population and Development Review* 41, no. 2 (2015): 183–206.

119. Al-Jen Poo with Ariane Conrad, *The Age of Dignity: Preparing for the Elder Boom in a Changing America* (New York: New Press, 2015).

120. Jenkins and Donnellan, interview; see also "Special Report: Caregiving in America," *AARP Bulletin*, November 2015.

121. LeaMond, interview.

122. Nancy R. Hooyman and Judith G. Gonyea, "A Feminist Model of Family Care: Practice and Policy Directions," *Journal of Women and Aging* 11, no. 2–3 (1999): 149–169.

123. Laura Katz Olson, *The Not-So-Golden* Years (New York: Rowman & Littlefield, 2003), 242–243.

124. Sandra J. Tanenbaum, "Work and Family, Round Two: The Political Construction of Elders' Working Daughters," presented at the annual meeting of the American Political Science Association, September 3, 2015, San Francisco; Amy Goyer, *Juggling Work and Caregiving* (Washington, DC: AARP and the American Bar Association, 2013).

125. Tanenbaum, "Work and Family," 9.

126. Jenkins and Donnellan, interview.

127. Dale Van Atta, "This Isn't the Old AARP," *Los Angeles Times*, November 4, 2003, http://articles.latimes.com/print/2003/nov/24/opinion/oe-vanatta24.

128. Ibid.

129. Hannah F. Pitkin, *The Concept of Representation* (Berkeley: University of California Press, 1967), 16.

130. Heinz Eulau, "The Legislator as Representative: Representational Roles," in *The Legislative System: Explorations in Legislative Behavior*, ed. John C. Wahlke, Heinz Eulau, William Buchanan, and LeRoy C. Ferguson (New York: John Wiley); Howard Schweber, "The Limits of Representation," *American Political Science Review* 110, no. 2 (2016): 382–396.

131. Kay Lehman Schlozman and Philip Edward Jones, "How Membership Associations Change the Balance of Representation in Washington (and How They Don't)," in *New Directions in Interest Group Politics*, ed. Matt Grossmann (New York: Routledge, 2014), 39.

132. Alexander Guerin, Media Relations Associate, AARP, e-mail message to author, July 11, 2016.

133. Martin Gilens, *Affluence and Influence: Economic Inequality and Political Power in America* (Princeton, NJ: Princeton University Press, 2012), 123.

134. Dara Z. Strolovich, *Affirmative Advocacy: Race, Class, and Gender in Interest Group Politics* (Chicago: University of Chicago Press, 2007).

135. Gilens, *Affluence and Influence*, 155.

136. Lynch, *One Nation under AARP*, 133–135; Kosterlitz, "The World According to AARP"; Vaida, "AARP's Big Bet," 798–800.

137. Theda Skocpol, *Diminished Democracy: From Membership to Management in American Civic Life* (Norman, OK: University of Oklahoma Press, 2013).

138. Vaida, "AARP's Big Bet," 800.

139. Maryann Barakso and Brian F. Schaffner, "Exit, Voice, and Interest Group Governance," *American Politics Research* 36, no. 2 (2008): 186–209.

140. Lynch, *One Nation under AARP*, chapter 5.

141. Lynch, *One Nation under AARP*; Heaney, "Identity Crisis," 297.

142. Craig Walker and Bret Bradigan, "The Age of Reformation: Dr. Ethel Percy Andrus and the Founding of the AARP," *Ojai History*, Winter, 2011–2012, 120–125.

143. Kosterlitz, "Test of Strength"; Vaida, "AARP's Big Bet."

144. Rother, interview; Certner, Lewin, and Mika, interview.

145. Kosterlitz, "Test of Strength"; Certner, Lewin, and Mika, interview.

146. Lynch, *One Nation under AARP*.

Chapter 4 A Pragmatic and a Powerful Ally

1. Henry Fairlie, "Talkin' 'Bout My Generation," *New Republic*, March 28, 1988, 19–22. Fairlie, in this article, coined the term "greedy geezers."

2. James H. Schulz and Robert H. Binstock, *Aging Nation: The Economics and Politics of Growing Older in America* (Baltimore: Johns Hopkins University Press, 2006), 216; Paul Schwartzman, "At 50, AARP Enters Its Golden Years; with Boomers on Board, Seniors Lobby Flexes Its Muscle," *Washington Post*, September 4, 2008, http://www.washingtonpost.com/wp-dyn/content/article/2008/09/03/AR2008090303785.html; Bara Vaida, "AARP's Big Bet," *National Journal*, March 13, 2004, 796–802.

3. Frederick R. Lynch, *One Nation under AARP: The Fight over Medicare, Social Security, and America's Future* (Berkeley: University of California Press, 2011), 171.

4. Ibid., 163–171.

5. Katherine Weber, "American Family Association Warns Christian Seniors against Joining AARP," *Christian Post*, May 17, 2013, http://www.christianpost.com/news/american-family-association-warns-christian-seniors-against-joining-aarp-96139/.

6. Bob Robb, "Does AARP Still Want Your Guns?" *NRA American Rifleman*, April 10, 2013, https://www.americanrifleman.org/articles/2013/4/10/does-the-aarp-still-want-your-guns/.

7. John H. Aldrich and David W. Rohde, "The Consequences of Party Organization in the House: The Role of the Majority and Minority Parties in Conditional Party Government," in *Polarized Politics: Congress and the President in*

a Partisan Era, ed. Jon R. Bond and Richard Fleisher (Washington, DC: CQ Press, 2000), 31–72; Sarah Binder, *Stalemate: Causes and Consequences of Legislative Gridlock* (Washington, DC: Brookings, 2003).

8. American Political Science Association, "Toward a More Responsible Party System: A Report of the Committee on Political Parties," *American Political Science Review* 44 (Supplement) (1950).

9. Thomas E. Mann and Norman J. Ornstein, *It's Even Worse Than It Looks: How the American Constitutional System Collided with the New Politics of Extremism*, expanded ed. (New York: Basic Books, 2016).

10. Binder, *Stalemate*; William Crotty, ed., *Polarized Politics: The Impact of Divisiveness in the U.S. Political System* (Boulder, CO: Lynne Rienner, 2014); Jeffrey M. Stonecash, ed., *New Directions in American Political Parties* (New York: Routledge, 2010).

11. Nolan McCarty, Keith T. Poole, and Howard Rosenthal, *Polarized America: The Dance of Ideology and Unequal Riches*, 2nd ed. (Cambridge, MA: MIT Press, 2016).

12. Pew Research Center, "Partisanship and Political Animosity in 2016," June22,2016,http://www.people-press.org/2016/06/22/partisanship-and-political-animosity-in-2016/.

13. Mann and Ornstein, *It's Even Worse Than It Looks.*

14. Matt Grossmann and David Hopkins, *Asymmetric Politics: Ideological Republicans and Group Interest Democrats* (New York: Oxford University Press, 2016).

15. Christine L. Day, "Aging Policy: A Partisan Paradox," in *Polarized Politics: The Impact of Divisiveness in the U.S. Political System*, ed. William Crotty (Boulder, CO: Lynne Rienner, 2014), 285–307; Schulz and Binstock, *Aging Nation*.

16. Debra Whitman, Executive Vice President and Chief Public Policy Officer, AARP, and James Dau, Media Relations Director, AARP, personal interview, Washington, DC, July 23, 2015.

17. "Ryan at the AARP," *Wall Street Journal*, September 26, 2012, http://www.wsj.com/articles/SB10000872396390444813104578014243421799324.

18. Meghan McCarthy, "The GOP's Senior Moment," *National Journal*, September 29, 2012, 41.

19. Robert H. Binstock, "From Compassionate Ageism to Intergenerational Conflict?" *Gerontologist* 50, no. 5 (2010): 574–585.

20. Daniel Béland, *Social Security: History and Politics from the New Deal to the Privatization Debate* (Lawrence, KS: University of Kansas Press, 2005); Schulz and Binstock, *Aging Nation*, chapter 3.

21. Theodore R. Marmor, *The Politics of Medicare*, 2nd ed. (Hawthorne, NY: Aldine de Gruyter, 2000); Colleen M. Grogan and Christina M. Andrews, "The Politics of Aging within Medicaid," in *The New Politics of Old Age Policy*, 2nd ed., ed. Robert B. Hudson (Baltimore: Johns Hopkins University Press, 2010), 275–306.

22. For discussion and critique of disengagement theory, see Arlie Russell Hochschild, "Disengagement Theory: A Critique and Proposal," *American Sociological Review* 40, no. 5 (1975): 553–569; W. Andrew Achenbaum and Vern L. Bengtson, "Re-engaging the Disengagement Theory of Aging: On the History and Assessment of Theory Development in Gerontology," *Gerontologist* 34, no. 6 (1994): 756–763.

23. Craig Walker and Bret Bradigan, "The Age of Reformation: Dr. Ethel Percy Andrus and the Founding of the AARP," *Ojai History*, Winter, 2011–2012, 120–125.

24. Ibid.; Craig Walker, "Ethel Andrus: How One Woman Changed America," a talk given to the Ojai Valley Museum, May 1, 2011, www.ojaihistory.com/ethel-percy-andrus-how-one-woman-changed-america/.

25. Walker and Bradigan, "The Age of Reformation"; Charles R. Morris, *The AARP: America's Most Powerful Lobby and the Clash of Generations* (New York: Times Books, 1996).

26. Henry J. Pratt, *The Gray Lobby* (Chicago: University of Chicago Press, 1976), 90–91.

27. Robert H. Binstock, "Interest-Group Liberalism and the Politics of Aging," *Gerontologist* 12, no. 3, Part 1 (1972): 265–280; quote on p. 270.

28. Binstock, "Interest-Group Liberalism"; Pratt, *The Gray Lobby.*

29. Ibid.; Linda E. Demkovich, "There's a New Kick in the Step of the Senior Citizen Lobbies," *National Journal*, October 2, 1976, 1382–1389.

30. Demkovich, "There's a New Kick"; Pratt, *The Gray Lobby.*

31. Pratt, *The Gray Lobby.*

32. Binstock, "Interest-Group Liberalism"; David Hackett Fischer, "The Politics of Aging in America: A Short History," *Journal of the Institute for Socioeconomic Studies* 4 (1979): 51–66; John B. Williamson, Linda Evans, and Lawrence A. Powell, *The Politics of Aging: Power and Policy* (Springfield, IL: Charles C. Thomas, 1982).

33. Carroll L. Estes, *The Aging Enterprise* (San Francisco: Jossey-Bass, 1979); Meredith Minkler and Carroll L. Estes, *Critical Gerontology: Perspectives from Political and Moral Economy* (New York: Baywood, 1999).

34. Roger Sanjek, *Gray Panthers* (Philadelphia: University of Pennsylvania Press, 2009).

35. Christine L. Day, *What Older Americans Think: Interest Groups and Aging Policy* (Princeton: Princeton University Press, 1990); Neal R. Peirce and Peter C. Choharis, "The Elderly as a Political Force—26 Million Strong and Well Organized," *National Journal*, September 11, 1982, 1559–1562; Henry J. Pratt, *Gray Agendas: Interest Groups and Public Pensions in Canada, Britain, and the United States* (Ann Arbor: University of Michigan Press, 1993).

36. Paul Light, *Artful Work: The Politics of Social Security Reform* (New York: Random House, 1985).

37. Ibid., 202; see also Béland, *Social Security*, 157–163.

38. Julie Kosterlitz, "Test of Strength," *National Journal*, October 24, 1987, 2652–2657; Morris, *The AARP.*

39. Carmen DeNavas-Watt and Bernadette D. Proctor, "Income and Poverty in the United States: 2014," U.S. Census Bureau, Current Population Reports, P60–252 (Washington, DC: U.S. Government Printing Office, 2015), https://www.census.gov/content/dam/Census/library/publications/2015/demo/p60–252.pdf.

40. Andrea Louise Campbell, *Trapped in America's Safety Net: One Family's Struggle* (Chicago: University of Chicago Press, 2014); Christopher Howard, *The Welfare State Nobody Knows: Debunking Myths about U.S. Social Policy* (Princeton, NJ: Princeton University Press, 2008); Jill Quadagno, "Generational Equity and the Politics of the Welfare State," *Politics and Society* 17, no. 3 (1989): 353–376.

41. Robert B. Hudson, "The 'Graying' of the Federal Budget and Its Consequences for Old Age Policy," *Gerontologist* 18, no. 5, Part 1 (1978): 428–440; see also David Broder, "Budget Funds for Elderly Grow Rapidly," *Washington Post*, January 30, 1973, A-16; Barbara Boyle Torrey, "Guns vs. Canes: The Fiscal Implications of an Aging Population," *American Economic Review* 72, no. 2 (1982): 309–313; Robert B. Samuelson, "Benefit Programs for the Elderly—Off Limits to Federal Budget Cutters?" *National Journal*, October 3, 1981, 1757–1762.

42. Julia Isaacs, Sara Edelstein, Heather Hahn, Ellen Steele, and C. Eugene Steuerle, *Kids' Share 2015: Report on Federal Expenditures on Children in 2014 and Future Projections* (Washington, DC: Urban Institute, 2015), http://www.urban.org/sites/default/files/alfresco/publication-pdfs/2000422-Kids-Share-2015-Report-on-Federal-Expenditures-on-Children-Through-2014.pdf; Schulz and Binstock, *Aging Nation.*

43. Robert J. Samuelson, "Benefit Programs for the Elderly," 1759, 1757.

44. Robert H. Binstock, "The Aged as Scapegoat," *Gerontologist* 23, no. 2 (1983): 136–143.

45. Lee Smith, "The Tyranny of America's Old," *Fortune*, January 13, 1992, 68.

46. Fairlie, "Talkin' 'Bout My Generation."

47. Phillip Longman, "Justice between Generations," *Atlantic Monthly*, June, 1985, 73–91; see also Phillip Longman, *Born to Pay: The New Politics of Aging in America* (Boston: Houghton Mifflin, 1987).

48. Lawrence Kotlikoff, *Generational Accounting: Knowing Who Pays, and When, for What We Spend* (New York: Free Press, 1992); Peter G. Peterson, *Gray Dawn: How the Coming Age Wave Will Transform America—and the World* (New York: Times Books, 1999); Samuel H. Preston, "Children and the Elderly in the United States," *Scientific American* 251, no. 6 (1984): 44–49; Robert J. Samuelson, "Off Golden Pond," *National Review*, April 12, 1999, 44.

49. David DeVoss, "Who Will Pay? Two Views on How—or Whether—America Can Afford a Rapidly Aging Population," *Los Angeles Times Magazine*, May 25, 1986, www.articles.latimes.com/1986–05–25/magazine/tm-703_1_social-security-benefits/2.

50. Ibid.

51. Binstock, "The Aged as Scapegoat"; Eric Laursen, *The People's Pension: The Struggle to Defend Social Security Since Reagan* (Oakland, CA: AK Press, 2012), 141; Quadagno, "Generational Equity."

52. Eric R. Kingson, Barbara A. Hirshorn, and John M. Cornman, *The Ties That Bind: The Interdependence of Generations* (Washington, DC: Seven Locks Press, 1986); John B. Williamson and Diane M. Watts-Roy, "Framing the Generational Equity Debate," in *The Generational Equity Debate*, ed. John B. Williamson, Diane M. Watts-Roy, and Eric Kingson (New York: Columbia University Press, 1999), 3–38; John B. Williamson and Diane M. Watts-Roy, "Aging Boomers, Generational Equity, and the Framing of the Debate over Social Security," in *Boomer Bust? Economic and Political Issues of the Graying Society*, ed. Robert B. Hudson (Westport, CT: Praeger, 2008), 153–172.

53. Howard Fineman, "Can Social Security Be Cut?" *Newsweek*, May 13, 1985. Quoted in Laursen, *The People's Pension*, 157.

54. Steven Greenhouse, "Passing the Buck from One Generation to the Next," *New York Times*, August 17, 1986, http://www.nytimes.com/1986/08/17/weekinreview/passing-the-buck-from-one-generation-to-the-next.html.

55. Day, *What Older Americans Think*; Williamson and Watts-Roy, "Aging Boomers."

56. Laursen, *The People's Pension*; Quadagno, "Generational Equity"; Joseph White, *False Alarm: Why the Greatest Threat to Social Security and Medicare Is the Campaign to "Save" Them* (Baltimore: Johns Hopkins University Press, 2001).

57. Peter G. Peterson, "The Morning After," *Atlantic Monthly*, October, 1987, 44.

58. Preston, "Children and the Elderly."

59. Quadagno, "Generational Equity," 360.

60. Max Rose and Frank R. Baumgartner, "Framing the Poor: Media Coverage and U.S. Poverty Policy, 1960–2008," *Policy Studies Journal* 41, no. 1 (2013): 22–53.

61. Fred C. Pampel, "Population Aging, Class Context, and Age Inequality in Public Spending," *American Journal of Sociology* 100, no. 1 (1994): 153–195; see also Campbell, *Trapped in America's Safety Net*.

62. Quadagno, "Generational Equity"; Williamson and Watts-Roy, "Framing the Generational Equity Debate"; Campbell, *Trapped in America's Safety Net*.

63. Greenhouse, "Passing the Buck."

64. John Rother, "Closing Remarks," in *Justice Across Generations: What Does It Mean?* ed. Lee M. Cohen (Washington, DC: Public Policy Institute, American Association of Retired Persons, 1993), 291.

65. Richard Himelfarb, *Catastrophic Politics: The Rise and Fall of the Medicare Catastrophic Coverage Act* (University Park, PA: Penn State University Press, 1995); Joshua M. Wiener, Carroll L. Estes, Susan M. Goldenson, and Sheryl C. Goldbert, "What Happened to Long-Term Care in the Health Reform Debate of 1993–1994? Lessons for the Future," *Milbank Quarterly* 79, no. 2 (2001): 207–252; Day, *What*

Older Americans Think, 102–104; Julie Rovner, "Catastrophic-Costs Conferees Irked by Lobbying Assault," *Congressional Quarterly Weekly Report*, March 26, 1988, 777.

66. Himelfarb, *Catastrophic Politics*; see also Christine L. Day, "Older Americans' Attitudes toward the Medicare Catastrophic Coverage Act of 1988," *Journal of Politics* 55, no. 1 (1993): 167–177; Lawrence Haas, "Fiscal Catastrophe," *National Journal*, October 7, 1989, 2453–2456; Julie Rovner, "Catastrophic-Insurance Law: Costs vs. Benefits," *Congressional Quarterly Weekly Report*, December 3, 1988, 3450–3452.

67. Himelfarb, *Catastrophic Politics*; Rovner, "Catastrophic-Insurance Law"; Julie Rovner, "The Catastrophic-Costs Law: A Massive Miscalculation," *Congressional Quarterly Weekly Report*, October 14, 1989, 2712–2715.

68. Himelfarb, *Catastrophic Politics*, 81.

69. Pratt, *Gray Agendas*, 193–198; Rovner, "Catastrophic-Costs Conferees."

70. Himelfarb, *Catastrophic Politics*, 98; Morris, *The AARP*, 105–113.

71. George A. Quattrone and Amos Tversky, "Contrasting Rational and Psychological Analyses of Political Choice," *American Political Science Review* 82 (1988): 719–736.

72. Steven A. Holmes, "The World According to AARP," *New York Times*, March 21, 2001. http://www.nytimes.com/2001/03/21/jobs/the-world-according-to-aarp.html; see also Morris, *The AARP*, 111.

73. Himelfarb, *Catastrophic Politics*, 96–100; Morris, *The AARP*, 111.

74. Lynch, *One Nation under AARP*; Morris, *The AARP*; Pratt, *Gray Agendas*; Wiener et al., "What Happened to Long-Term Care . . .?"

75. Holmes, "The World According to AARP."

76. Himelfarb, *Catastrophic Politics*, 99–101; Haas, "Fiscal Catastrophe"; Wiener, et al., "What Happened to Long-Term Care . . .?" 211–212.

77. Himelfarb, *Catastrophic Politics*; Paul Starr, "What Happened to Health Care Reform?" *American Prospect*, Winter, 1995, 20–31; Clifford Krauss, "Clinton's Health Plan: Interest Groups, Lobbyists of Every Stripe Turning to the Grass Roots," *New York Times*, September 24, 1993, http://www.nytimes.com/1993/09/24/us/clinton-s-health-plan-interest-groups-lobbyists-every-stripe-turning-grass-roots.html?pagewanted=all; Wiener, et al., "What Happened to Long-Term Care . . .?"

78. Day, "Aging Policy: A Partisan Paradox."

79. Williamson and Watts-Roy, "Introduction," in *The Generational Equity Debate*, ed. John B. Williamson and Diane M. Watts-Roy (New York: Columbia University Press, 1999), 1–37; Jill Quadagno, "Social Security and the Myth of the Entitlement 'Crisis,'" in *The Generational Equity Debate*, ed. John B. Williamson and Diane M. Watts-Roy (New York: Columbia University Press, 1999), 140–156.

80. Fay Lomax Cook and Edith J. Barrett, *Support for the American Welfare State: The Views of Congress and the Public* (New York: Columbia University Press, 1992).

81. Campbell, *Trapped in the American Safety Net*; Joe Soss, Richard C. Fording, and Sanford S. Schram, *Disciplining the Poor: Neoliberal Paternalism and the*

Persistent Power of Race (Chicago: University of Chicago Press, 2011); R. Kent Weaver, *Ending Welfare as We Know It* (Washington, DC: Brookings, 2000); U.S. Department of Health and Human Services, Administration for Children and Families, Office of Family Assistance, "TANF Caseload Data 2014," May 22, 2015, www.acf.hhs.gov/ofa/resource/caseload-data-2014.

82. Day, "Aging Policy: A Partisan Paradox."

83. See, for example, Robert J. Samuelson, "Why Are We in This Debt Fix? It's the Elderly, Stupid," *Washington Post*, July 28, 2011, http://www.washington post.com/opinions/why-are-we-in-this-debt-fix-its-the-elderly-stupid. But see also Robert J. Samuelson, "It's the Welfare State, Stupid," *Washington Post*, November 11, 2012, https://www.washingtonpost.com/opinions/robert-samuel son-its-the-welfare-state-stupid/2012/11/11/e392868a-2ab0-11e2-bab2-eda 299503684_story.html?utm_term=.797cdb90cd98.

84. Theodore R. Marmor, Fay Lomax Cook, and Stephen Scher, "Social Security and the Politics of Generational Conflict," in *The Generational Equity Debate*, ed. John B. Williamson and Diane M. Watts-Roy (New York: Columbia University Press, 1999), 185–203; Quadagno, "Generational Equity."

85. Jacob S. Hacker, *The Great Risk Shift: The New Economic Insecurity and the Decline of the American Dream*, revised ed. (New York: Oxford University Press, 2008).

86. Peter G. Peterson, "How Will America Pay for the Retirement of the Baby Boom Generation?" in *The Generational Equity Debate*, ed. John B. Williamson and Diane M. Watts-Roy (New York: Columbia University Press, 1999), 41–57; Peter G. Peterson, *Will America Grow Up before It Grows Old? How the Coming Social Security Crisis Threatens You, Your Family, and Your Country* (New York: Random House, 1996).

87. Social Security and Medicare Boards of Trustees, "Status of the Social Security and Medicare Programs: A Summary of the 2016 Annual Reports," Social Security Administration, Washington, DC (2016), https://www.ssa.gov/oact/TRSUM/index.html.

88. Raymond E. Wolfinger and Steven J. Rosenstone, *Who Votes?* (New Haven: Yale University Press, 1980).

89. Robert H. Binstock, "Older Voters and the 2008 Election," *Gerontologist* 49, no. 5 (2009): 697–701; Andrea Louise Campbell and Robert H. Binstock, "Politics and Aging in the United States," in *Handbook of Aging and the Social Sciences*, 7th ed., ed. Robert H. Binstock and Linda K. George (New York: Elsevier, 2011), 265–280.

90. Laurie A. Rhodebeck, "The Politics of Greed? Political Preferences among the Elderly," *Journal of Politics* 55, no. 2 (1993): 342–364.

91. Robert H. Binstock, "Older Voters and the 2010 U.S. Election: Implications for 2012 and Beyond?" *Gerontologist* 52, no. 3 (2012): 408–417; Pew Research Center for People and the Press, "The Generation Gap and the 2012 Election," November 3, 2011, www.people-press.org/2011/11/03/section-2-gene rations-and-the-2012-election/.

92. Paul Taylor and Pew Research Center, *The Next America: Boomers, Millennials, and the Looming Generational Showdown* (New York: Public Affairs, 2016).

93. Schulz and Binstock, *Aging Nation*; White, *False Alarm*.

94. Béland, *Social Security*.

95. Lawrence J. Kotlikoff and Scott Burns, *The Clash of Generations: Saving Ourselves, Our Kids, and Our Economy* (Cambridge, MA: MIT Press, 2014); Peter G. Peterson, *Running on Empty: How the Democratic and Republican Parties Are Bankrupting Our Future and What Americans Can Do About It* (New York: Farrar, Straus and Giroux, 2004).

96. In 2001, NCSC was reconfigured into the nonpartisan Alliance for Retired Americans, still affiliated with the AFL-CIO.

97. Lynch, *One Nation under AARP*; Christine L. Day, "Old-Age Interest Groups in the 1990s: Coalition, Competition, and Strategy," in *New Directions in Old-Age Policies*, ed. Janie S. Steckenrider and Tonya M. Parrott (Albany: State University of New York Press, 1998), 131–150; Laursen, *The People's Pension*, 304–305; Schulz and Binstock, *Aging Nation*.

98. Thomas B. Edsall, "High Drug Prices Return as Issue That Stirs Voters," *Washington Post*, October 15, 2002, https://www.washingtonpost.com/archive/politics/2002/10/15/high-drug-prices-return-as-issue-that-stirs-voters/d528c46b-1a89–4da7–8d08-aeb6d94ef002/; Jonathan Tilove, "Seniors Group Says No to Demo Health Bills," *New Orleans Times Picayune*, November 17, 2009, A1, A6; see also Schulz and Binstock, *Aging Nation*.

99. Matea Gold, "Koch-Backed Political Network, Built to Shield Donors, Raised $400 Million in 2012 Elections," *Washington Post*, January 5, 2014, https://www.washingtonpost.com/politics/koch-backed-political-network-built-to-shield-donors-raised-400-million-in-2012-elections/2014/01/05/9e7cfd9a-719b-11e3–9389–09ef9944065e_story.html.

100. 60 Plus, https://60plus.org/about/ (accessed July 27, 2016).

101. Laursen, *The People's Pension*, 304.

102. Association of Mature American Citizens, http://amac.us/about-us/ (accessed July 27, 2016).

103. For the classic work on issue networks, see Hugh Heclo, "Issue Networks and the Executive Establishment," in *The New American Political System*, ed. Anthony King (Washington, DC: American Enterprise Institute, 1978), 87–124.

104. Alan A. Abramowitz, *The Disappearing Center: Polarization and American Democracy* (New Haven: Yale University Press, 2010); Jeffrey M. Stonecash, "Changing American Political Parties," in *New Directions in American Political Parties*, ed. Jeffrey M. Stonecash (New York: Routledge, 2010), 3–10

105. Day, "Aging Policy: A Partisan Paradox."

106. Nancy LeaMond, Executive Vice President and Chief Advocacy and Engagement Officer, AARP, personal interview, Washington, DC, July 23, 2015.

107. Edmund Andrews, "AARP Looms as Key Player in Deficit Panel Debate," *Fiscal Times*, August 31, 2010, www.thefiscaltimes.com/Articles/

2010/08/31/AARP-Looms-as-Key-Player-in-Deficit-Panel-Debate; Laursen, *The People's Pension*, 348.

108. Andrea Louise Campbell and Julia Lynch. "Whose 'Gray Power'? Elderly Voters, Elderly Lobbies, and Welfare Reform in Italy and the United States," *Italian Politics and Society* 53 (2000): 11–39.

109. Barbara T. Dreyfuss, "The Seduction: The Shocking Story of How AARP Backed the Medicare Bill," *American Prospect* 15, no. 6 (2004): 18–23; Kimberly J. Morgan and Andrea Louise Campbell, *The Delegated Welfare State: Medicare, Markets, and the Governance of Social Policy* (New York: Oxford University Press, 2011).

110. Holmes, "The World According to AARP"; Lynch, *One Nation under AARP.*

111. Marilyn Werber Serafini, "AARP's New Direction," *National Journal*, January 5, 2002, 29.

112. Ibid.

113. Reneé L. Beard and John B. Williamson, "Symbolic Politics, Social Policy, and the Senior Rights Movement," *Journal of Aging Studies* 25, no. 1 (2011): 22–33; Dreyfuss, "The Seduction"; Lynch, *One Nation under AARP*; Thomas R. Oliver, Philip R. Lee, and Helene L. Lipton, "A Political History of Medicare and Prescription Drug Coverage," *Milbank Quarterly* 82, no. 2 (2004): 283–354; Vaida, "AARP's Big Bet."

114. Centers for Medicare and Medicaid Services, "President Signs Medicare Legislation: Remarks by the President at Signing of the Medicare Prescription Drug, Improvement and Modernization Act of 2003," https://www.cms.gov/about-cms/agency-information/history/downloads/bushsignmma2003.pdf.

115. Sheryl Gay Stolberg and Milt Freudenheim, "A Final Push in Congress: AARP Support Came as Group Grew 'Younger,'" *New York Times*, November 26, 2003, www.nytimes.com/2003/11/26/us/a-final-push-in-congress-the-endorsement-aarp-support-came-as-group-grew-younger.html.

116. Vaida, "AARP's Big Bet," 802.

117. William Novelli, Professor, McDonough School of Business, Georgetown University, and former CEO, AARP, telephone interview, January 22, 2016.

118. John Rother, Chief Executive Officer, National Coalition on Health Care, telephone interview, September 18, 2014.

119. Schulz and Binstock, *Aging Nation*, 217.

120. Lynch, *One Nation under AARP*, 141–142; Robert Pear, "In Ads, AARP Criticizes Plan on Privatizing," *New York Times*, December 30, 2004, www.nytimes.com/2004/12/30/politics/in-ads-aarp-criticizes-plan-on-privatizing.html.

121. Beard and Williamson, "Symbolic Politics."

122. Lynch, *One Nation under AARP*, 158–163.

123. Rother, interview.

124. Lawrence R. Jacobs and Theda Skocpol, *Health Care Reform and American Politics: What Everyone Needs to Know*, 3rd ed. (New York: Oxford University Press, 2016), 74.

125. Julie Hirschfeld Davis, "The Influence Game: Labor and Business, Joined in Health Care Cause, Now at Odds on Specifics," *Chicago Tribune*, February 16, 2009, http://www.chicagotribune.com/news/nationworld/sms-ap-health-care-strange-bedfellows,0,6877237.story.

126. *National Federation of Independent Business v. Sebelius*, 567 U.S. ___ (2012), 183 L. Ed. 2d 450, 132 S.Ct. 2566.

127. Jacobs and Skocpol, *Health Care Reform*, 153–159.

128. Binstock, "From Compassionate Ageism to Intergenerational Conflict?"; Angie Drobnic Holan, "The PolitiFact Guide to Medicare Attack Lines," *PolitiFact*, May 6, 2012, http://www.politifact.com/truth-o-meter/article/2012/may/06/politifact-guide-medicare-attack-lines/.

129. Binstock, "From Compassionate Ageism to Intergenerational Conflict?"

130. Angie Drobnic Holan, "PolitiFact's Lie of the Year: 'Death Panels,'" *PolitiFact*, December 18, 2009, http://www.politifact.com/truth-o-meter/article/2009/dec/18/politifact-lie-year-death-panels/.

131. Paul Starr, *Remedy and Reaction: The Peculiar American Struggle over Health Care Reform*, revised ed. (New Haven: Yale University Press, 2013), 274–275.

132. Andrew Gelman, Daniel Lee, and Yair Ghitza, "Public Opinion on Health Care Reform," *The Forum* 8, no. 1, article 8 (2010), http://www.bepress.com/forum/vol8/iss1/art8.

133. Lynch, *One Nation under AARP.*

134. Vaida, "AARP's Chief: Giving Back," *National Journal*, July 31, 2010, 43–44.

135. LeaMond, interview.

136. Glenn Kessler, "Paul Ryan's False Claim That 'Because of Obamacare, Medicare Is Going Broke,'" *Washington Post*, November 14, 2016, https://www.washingtonpost.com/news/fact-checker/wp/2016/11/14/paul-ryans-false-claim-that-because-of-obamacare-medicare-is-going-broke/.

137. Lynch, *One Nation under* AARP, 189; see also Jacobs and Skocpol, *Health Care Reform*, 187.

138. Laura Johannes, "AARP Faces Competition from Conservative Leaning Groups," *Wall Street Journal*, March 30, 2014, http://www.wsj.com/articles/SB10001424052702304704504579433343591891948; Vaida, "AARP's Chief."

139. Vaida, "AARP's Big Bet," 802.

140. Johannes, "AARP Faces Competition."

141. Laursen, *People's Pension*, 304; Lynch, *One Nation under AARP*, 185; Schulz and Binstock, *Aging Nation*, 216–217.

142. David Certner, Legislative Counsel and Legislative Policy Director for Government Affairs, AARP; Cindy Lewin, Executive Vice President and General Counsel, AARP; and Sarah Mika, Senior Vice President, AARP Services, Inc., personal interview, Washington, DC, July 22, 2015.

143. "The Moment of Truth: Report of the National Commission on Fiscal Responsibility and Reform" (Washington, DC: White House, December 2010),

http://www.washingtonpost.com/wp-srv/politics/documents/TheMomentofTruth.pdf.

144. "AARP Ramps Up Grassroots Advertising in Opposition to Fast Track Debt Commission," AARP Media Relations/Press Center, January 26, 2010, http://www.aarp.org/about-aarp/press-center/info-03–2010/aarp_activities_conrad_gregg.html.

145. Michael A. Fletcher and Zachary A. Goldfarb, "AARP Uses Its Power to Oppose Social Security, Medicare Benefit Cuts for Retirees," *Washington Post*, November 17, 2012, https://www.washingtonpost.com/business/economy/aarp-uses-its-power-to-oppose-social-security-medicare-benefit-cuts-for-retirees/2012/11/17/affb5874–2aa6–11e2-bab2-eda299503684_story.html; Laursen, *The People's Pension*.

146. Stephanie Condon, "Alan Simpson: Social Security Is Like a 'Milk Cow with 310 Million Tits,'" CBS News, August 25, 2010, http://www.cbsnews.com/news/alan-simpson-social-security-is-like-a-milk-cow-with-310-million-tits/.

147. David Harrison, "Advocates for Seniors Fight Potential CPI Shift," *CQ Today Online News*, October 21, 2011, http://public.cq.com/docs/news/news-000003967448.html; see also Daniel Marans, Ryan Grim, and Arthus Delaney, "Barack Obama Once Proposed Cutting Social Security. Here's What Changed His Mind," *Huffington Post*, June 3, 2016, http://www.huffingtonpost.com/entry/barack-obama-grand-bargain-social-security-expansion_us_5751f92de4b0eb20fa0e0142.

148. "Op-Ed: Reforming Social Security Is Easy—But It Won't Be for Long," Committee for a Responsible Federal Budget, June 4, 2013, http://www.crfb.org/papers/op-ed-reforming-social-security-easy-%E2%80%94-it-wont-be-long.

149. AARP, "Updating Social Security for the 21st Century: 12 Proposals You Should Know About," October, 2015, http://www.aarp.org/work/social-security/info-05–2012/future-of-social-security-proposals.html.

150. George J. Church and Richard Lacayo, "Social Insecurity," *Time*, March 20, 1995, http://content.time.com/time/magazine/article/0,9171,982700,00.html.

151. Laursen, *The People's Pension*, 227.

152. Laura Meckler, "Key Seniors Association Pivots on Benefit Cut," *Wall Street Journal*, June 17, 2011, http://www.wsj.com/articles/SB10001424052702304186404576389760955403414.

153. Zeiler, Shawn, "AARP Members: A Say Earned, but Forgone?" *Congressional Quarterly Weekly Report*, April 30, 2012, 846.

154. Lyneka Little, "AARP Wobbles on Social Security Benefits," ABC News, June 17, 2011, http://abcnews.go.com/Business/aarp-denies-social-security-cuts/story?id=13859214.

155. Jim Meyers, "Wall Street Journal: AARP Flips Position, Agrees to Social Security Cuts," *Newsmax*, June 17, 2011, http://www.newsmax.com/Newsfront/AARP-socialsecurity-cuts-benefits/2011/06/17/id/400411/.

156. Stephen Ohlemacher, "AARP Slammed for Not Fighting Social Security Cuts," NBC News, June 17, 2011, http://www.nbcnews.com/id/43445777/ns/

politics/t/aarp-slammed-not-fighting-social-security-cuts/%20-%20.WD-mXtIr Lcs#.WPuG6zdgncs.

157. Carla Fried, "Did AARP Really Sell Out Seniors on Social Security?" CBS News, June 21, 2011, http://www.cbsnews.com/news/did-aarp-really-sell-out-seniors-on-social-security/.

158. Stephen Ohlemacher, "AARP in the Midst of Social Security Controversy," *Fort Wayne News-Sentinel*, June 18, 2011, www.news-sentinel.com/apps/pbcs.dll/article?AID=/SE/20110618/NEWS/106180343.

159. Ibid.

160. Meckler, "Key Seniors Association Pivots."

161. Ohlemacher, "AARP in the Midst of Social Security Controversy."

162. Ibid.

163. Ibid.

164. Erik Wasson, "AARP Says Some Social Security Cuts Could Be Acceptable," *The Hill*, June 17, 2011, http://thehill.com/policy/healthcare/167125-aarp-says-some-social-security-cuts-acceptable.

165. Ohlemacher, "AARP in the Midst of Social Security Controversy."

166. Ibid; see also Wasson, "AARP Says Some Social Security Cuts Could be Acceptable."

167. Meckler, "Key Seniors Association Pivots."

168. Ibid.

169. Certner, Lewin, and Mika, interview.

170. Laura Meckler, "Why John Rother, AARP's Policy Chief, Is Leaving," *Wall Street Journal*, September 8, 2011, http://blogs.wsj.com/washwire/2011/09/08/why-john-rother-aarps-policy-chief-is-leaving/; Rother, interview.

171. Nancy Cook and Chris Frates, "Thanks to AARP, Grandma's Got Influence," *National Journal*, October 1, 2011, 5.

172. Ibid.

173. Fletcher and Goldfarb, "AARP Uses Its Power."

174. See the ad at https://www.ispot.tv/ad/AodA/aarp-services-inc-social-security-answer-the-call (accessed March 17, 2017).

175. "Take a Stand," AARP advertisement, *AARP Bulletin*, October 2016, 54–55.

176. Daniel Marans, "Nation's Largest Seniors Group Is Using Conservative Scare Tactics on Social Security," *Huffington Post*, October 16, 2016, http://www.huffingtonpost.com/entry/aarp-conservative-social-security_us_57fbe10be4b068ecb5e0d0f3.

177. Ibid.

178. "Seniors Group Responds to Ominous Social Security and Medicare Trust Fund Report," 60 Plus Association, June 22, 2016, https://60plus.org/seniors-group-responds-to-ominous-social-security-and-medicare-trust-fund-report/.

179. "AARP's Rival Has Good Social Security Plan," Association of Mature American Citizens, January 15, 2014, www.amac.us/aarps-rival-good-social-security-plan/.

180. Scott Wong and Mike Lillis, "Ten Public Policy Issues That Divide Trump and Ryan," *The Hill*, May 7, 2016, http://thehill.com/homenews/campaign/279067–10-issues-dividing-donald-trump-and-paul-ryan.

181. "Take a Stand," AARP advertisement, *AARP Bulletin*, October 2016, 54–55; "Trump and Clinton: Find Out Where They Stand on Social Security," *AARP Bulletin*, June 27, 2016, http://www.aarp.org/politics-society/government-elections/info-2016/election-2016-and-social-security.html.

182. Nancy J. Altman and Eric R. Kingson, *Social Security: How Expanding It Will Help Us All* (New York: The New Press, 2015); Robert Kuttner, "Why Social Security Beats All Rivals—And the Case for Expanding It," *Huffington Post*, July 26, 2015, http://huffingtonpost.com/robert-kuttner/why-social-security-beats-all-rivals_b_7876090.html.

183. Marans, Grim, and Delaney, "Barack Obama Once Proposed Cutting Social Security."

184. Daniel Marans, "Why AARP's New Social Security Campaign Is Upsetting Progressives," *Huffington Post*, February 16, 2016, http://www.huffingtonpost.com/entry/aarp-social-security-campaign_us_56c3854fe4b0c3c55052e81e; Marans, "Nation's Largest Seniors Group"; Marans, Grim, and Delaney, "Barack Obama Once Proposed Cutting Social Security."

185. Alexander Hertel-Fernandez, "Who Passes Business's 'Model Bills'? Policy Capacity and Corporate Influence in U.S. State Politics," *Perspectives on Politics* 12, no. 3, (2014): 582–602.

186. Michael Hitzik, "A Shamed AARP Withdraws from Right-Wing Lobbying Organization," *Los Angeles Times*, August 5, 2016, 2016, http://www.latimes.com/business/hiltzik/la-fi-hiltzik-aarp-alec-20160805-snap-story.html; Kim LaCapria, "Is the AARP Funding ALEC?" *Snopes.com*, August 4, 2016, http://www.snopes.com/2016/08/04/is-the-aarp-funding-alec/; Daniel Marans, "AARP to Withdraw From Controversial Conservative Group Amid Rising Pressure," *Huffington Post*, August 5, 2016, http://www.huffingtonpost.com/entry/aarp-to-withdraw-from-alec_us_57a4c72de4b03ba6801233e5.

187. "ALEC and AARP," AARP Online Community, http://community.aarp.org/t5/Introduce-Yourself/ALEC-and-AARP/td-p/1747998 (accessed August 2, 2016).

188. Jean Card, "'Shut Up' Politics: AARP's Decision to Leave ALEC Due to Left-Wing Bullying Means Leaving the Political Conversation," *U.S. News*, August 11, 2016, http://www.usnews.com/opinion/articles/2016-08- 11/aarp-yielded-to-shut-up-politics-by-ending-its-alec-membership.

189. Thomas T. Holyoke, *Competitive Interests: Competition and Compromise in American Interest Group Politics* (Washington, DC: Georgetown University Press, 2011).

190. Beard and Williamson, "Symbolic Politics."

191. Frederick R. Lynch, "How AARP Can Get Its Groove Back," *New York Times*, June 23, 2011, http://www.nytimes.com/2011/06/24/opinion/24lynch.html?_r=2; see also Lynch, *One Nation under AARP.*

192. Mary Clare Jalonick, "Sam Johnson, Key Republican on House Ways and Means Subcommittee, Looks to Overhaul Social Security," *Washington Times*, December 13, 2016, http://www.washingtontimes.com/news/2016/dec/13/republican-lawmaker-floats-social-security-overhaul/; Michael Hitzik, "The GOP Unveils a 'Permanent Save' for Social Security—With Massive Benefit Cuts," *Los Angeles Times*, December 9, 2016, http://www.latimes.com/business/hiltzik/la-fi-hiltzik-social-security-gop-20161209-story.html.

193. Jo Ann Jenkins, "After the Storm, We All Need to Get to Work," *AARP Bulletin*, December, 2016, 38.

Chapter 5 AARP's Influence: 38 Million Members, Washington Insider Status, and No Campaign Dollars

1. Julie Kosterlitz, "Test of Strength," *National Journal*, October 24, 1987, 2652–2657. The phrase "gray lobby" was coined by Henry Pratt in his book *The Gray Lobby* (Chicago: University of Chicago Press, 1976).

2. Charles R. Morris, *The AARP: America's Most Powerful Lobby and the Clash of Generations* (New York: Times Books, 1996); see also Jeffrey H. Birnbaum and Natasha Graves, "Follow the Money," *Fortune*, December 6, 1999, 206–208.

3. Robert J. Samuelson, "AARP's America Is a Mirage," *Washington Post*, November 16, 2005, http://www.washingtonpost.com/wp-dyn/content/article/2005/11/15/AR2005111501308.html; John Tierney, "Old Money, New Power," *New York Times Magazine*, October 23, 1988, www.nytimes.com/1988/10/23/magazine/old-money-new-power.html?pagewanted=all.

4. Charles P. Blahous, *Reforming Social Security: For Ourselves and Our Posterity* (New York: Praeger, 2000), 82; Margot Hornblower, "AARP's Gray Power!" *Time*, January 4, 1988, 36–37; Naureen Khan, "Is the AARP the '900-pound Invisible Gorilla' in the Room?" Aljazeera America, March 22, 2014, http://alj.am/1hSz1xt; Sheryl Gay Stolberg, "Ideas and Trends: An 800-Pound Gorilla Changes Partners over Medicare," *New York Times*, November 23, 2003, www.nytimes.com/2003/11/23/weekinreview/ideas-trends-an-800-pound-gorilla-changes-partners-over-medicare.html; "AARP Looms as a Key Player in Deficit Panel Debate," *Fiscal Times*, August 31, 2010, http://www.thefiscaltimes.com/articles/2010/08/31/AARP-Looms-as-Key-Player-in-Deficit-Panel-Debate.

5. Kosterlitz, "Test of Strength."

6. Frederick R. Lynch, *One Nation under AARP: The Fight over Medicare, Social Security, and America's Future* (Berkeley: University of California Press, 2011), 145.

7. Eric Laursen, *The People's Pension: The Struggle to Defend Social Security since Reagan* (Oakland, CA: AK Press, 2012), 303.

8. Robert H. Binstock, "Interest-Group Liberalism and the Politics of Aging," *Gerontologist* 12, no. 3, Part 1 (1972): 265–280; Pratt, *The Gray Lobby*.

9. Christopher Howard, *The Welfare State Nobody Knows: Debunking Myths about Social Policy* (Princeton, NJ: Princeton University Press, 2007), 147–148.

10. Alexander Hamilton, James Madison, and John Jay, *The Federalist Papers*, ed. Lawrence Goldman (New York: Oxford University Press, 2008 [1787–1788]).

11. Alexis de Tocqueville, *Democracy in America*, Vol. I (New York: Vintage Books, 1945 [1835]), 204.

12. Robert A. Dahl, *Who Governs?* (New Haven: Yale University Press, 1961); David B. Truman, *The Governmental Process*, 2nd ed. (New York: Alfred A. Knopf, 1971).

13. G. William Domhoff, *Who Rules America: The Triumph of the Corporate Rich*, 7th ed. (New York: McGraw-Hill, 2013); Kay Lehman Schlozman and John T. Tierney, *Organized Interests and American Democracy* (New York: Harper and Row, 1986); Kay Lehman Schlozman, Sidney Verba, and Henry E. Brady, *The Unheavenly Chorus: Unequal Political Voice and the Broken Promise of American Democracy* (Princeton, NJ: Princeton University Press, 2012).

14. E. E. Schattschneider, *The Semi-Sovereign People: A Realist's View of Democracy in America* (New York: Holt, Rinehart, and Winston, 1960), 35.

15. Ken Godwin, Scott H. Ainsworth, and Erik Godwin, *Lobbying and Policymaking: The Public Pursuit of Private Interests* (Washington, DC: CQ Press, 2012), 39.

16. Andrew S. McFarland, *Neopluralism: The Evolution of Political Process Theory* (Lawrence, KS: University of Kansas Press, 2004); Frank R. Baumgartner, Jeffrey M. Berry, Marie Hojnacki, David C. Kimball, and Beth L. Leech, *Lobbying and Policy Change: Who Wins, Who Loses, and Why* (Chicago: University of Chicago Press, 2009).

17. Godwin, Ainsworth, and Godwin. *Lobbying and Policymaking*, especially chapter 8; Richard L. Hall and Alan V. Deardorff, "Lobbying as Legislative Subsidy," *American Political Science Review* 100, no. 1 (2006) 69–84.

18. Baumgartner, et al., *Lobbying and Policy Change*, 212.

19. Ibid., 66.

20. Tierney, "Old Money, New Power."

21. *National Federation of Independent Business v. Sebelius*, 567 U.S. ___ (2012), 183 L. Ed. 2d 450, 132 S.Ct. 2566.

22. Lawrence R. Jacobs and Theda Skocpol, *Health Care Reform and American Politics: What Everyone Needs to Know*, 3rd ed. (New York: Oxford University Press).

23. Jeffrey H. Birnbaum, "Washington's Power 25: Which Pressure Groups Are Best at Manipulating the Laws We Live By?" *Fortune*, December 8, 1997, http://archive.fortune.com/magazines/fortune/fortune_archive/1997/12/08/234927/index.htm; Jeffrey H. Birnbaum and Russell Newell, "Fat and Happy in D.C.," *Fortune*, May 28, 2001, 94–100; Jeffrey H. Birnbaum and Natasha Graves, "Follow the Money," *Fortune*, December 6, 1999, 206–208.

24. Martin Gilens, *Affluence and Influence: Economic Inequality and Political Power in America* (Princeton, NJ: Princeton University Press, 2012), 263.

25. Michelle Leach, "10 Most Powerful Special Interest Groups in America," *Listosaur.com*, July 2, 2014, http://listosaur.com/politics/10-powerful-special-interest-groups-america/.

26. Ibid.

27. Baumgartner, et al., *Lobbying and Policy Change*, 224.

28. Matt Grossmann, *The Not-So-Special Interests: Interest Groups, Public Representation, and American Governance* (Stanford: Stanford University Press, 2012).

29. Ibid., 118.

30. Ibid., 187–188.

31. Ibid., 80.

32. Linda E. Demkovich, "There's a New Kick in the Step of the Senior Citizen Lobbies," *National Journal*, October 2, 1976, 1382–1389; Pratt, *The Gray Lobby*; Binstock, "Interest-Group Liberalism."

33. AARP, *Consolidated Financial Statements Together with Report of Independent Certified Public Accountants, AARP, December 31, 2015 and 2014*, 2016. www.aarp.org/content/dam/aarp/about_aarp/annual_reports/2016/2015-financial-statements-AARP.pdf.

34. Lynch, *One Nation under AARP*, 130; see also Bara Vaida, "AARP's Big Bet," *National Journal*, March 13, 2004, 796–802.

35. Jo Ann Jenkins, Chief Executive Officer, AARP, and Kevin Donnellan, Executive Vice President and Chief of Staff, AARP, personal interview, Washington, DC, July 22, 2015; Lynn Mento, former Senior Vice President of Membership and Member Engagement, telephone interview, February 26, 2016.

36. David Certner, Legislative Counsel and Legislative Policy Director for Government Affairs, AARP; Cindy Lewin, Executive Vice President and General Counsel, AARP; and Sarah Mika, Senior Vice President, AARP Services, Inc., personal interview, Washington, DC, July 22, 2015.

37. Nancy LeaMond, Executive Vice President and Chief Advocacy and Engagement Officer, AARP, personal interview, Washington, DC, July 23, 2015.

38. Peter Murray, "The Secret of Scale," *Stanford Social Innovation Review* (Fall 2013), http://ssir.org/articles/entry/the_secret_of_scale.

39. Ibid.; see also Morris, *The AARP*.

40. LeaMond, interview.

41. Lynch, *One Nation under AARP*, 132.

42. LeaMond, interview.

43. Certner, Lewin, and Mika, interview.

44. Julie Kosterlitz, "The World According to AARP," *National Journal*, March 10, 2007, 28–35; Vaida, "AARP's Big Bet."

45. Baumgartner, et al., *Lobbying and Policy Change*; Burdett A. Loomis and Allan J. Cigler, "Introduction: The Changing Nature of Interest Group Politics," in *Interest Group Politics*, 7th ed., ed. Allan J. Cigler and Burdett A. Loomis (Washington, DC: CQ Press, 2007), 1–36.

46. Christine L. Day, *What Older Americans Think: Interest Groups and Aging Policy* (Princeton, NJ: Princeton University Press, 1990); Christine L. Day, "Old-Age Interest Groups in the 1990s: Coalition, Competition, and Strategy," in *New Directions in Old-Age Policies*, ed. Janie S. Steckenrider and Tonya M. Parrott (Albany: State University of New York Press, 1998): 131–150.

47. Center for Responsive Politics, "Lobbyists Representing AARP," 2016, https://www.opensecrets.org/lobby/clientlbs.php?id=D000023726&year=2016. The Lobbying Disclosure Act of 1995 requires paid lobbyists at the federal level to register with the Clerk of the U.S. House of Representatives and the Secretary of the U.S. Senate, and to report on lobbying activities and expenditures. The Center for Responsive Politics obtains these data from Congress and reports them in user-friendly formats on their website, www.opensecrets.org, which contains a wealth of information about lobbying as well as campaign contributions to candidates for national office.

48. Grossmann, *The Not-So-Special Interests*, 79.

49. Laura Meckler, "Why John Rother, AARP's Policy Chief, Is Leaving," *Wall Street Journal*, September 8, 2011, http://blogs.wsj.com/washwire/2011/09/08/why-john-rother-aarps-policy-chief-is-leaving/.

50. William Novelli, Professor, McDonough School of Business, Georgetown University, and former CEO, AARP, telephone interview, January 22, 2016.

51. Kosterlitz, "Test of Strength," 2653–2656.

52. Morris, *The AARP*, 43, 60.

53. Certner, Lewin, and Mika, interview.

54. Center for Responsive Politics, https://www.opensecrets.org/lobby/.

55. Ibid.

56. Alec Goodwin and Emma Baccellieri, "Number of Registered Lobbyists Plunges as Spending Declines Yet Again," Center for Responsive Politics, August 9, 2016, https://www.opensecrets.org/news/2016/08/number-of-registered-lobbyists-plunges-as-spending-declines-yet-again/.

57. Catherine Ho, "Lobbying Registrations Are Down, but the Influence Industry Is Flourishing," *Washington Post*, September 12, 2016, https://www.washingtonpost.com/news/powerpost/wp/2016/09/12/lobbying-registrations-are-down-but-the-influence-industry-is-flourishing/?utm_term=.439a32fb7ce4; see also Tim LaPira, "Lobbying in the Shadows: How Private Interests Hide from Public Scrutiny, and Why That Matters," in *Interest Group Politics*, 9th ed., ed. Allan J. Cigler, Burdett A. Loomis, and Anthony Nownes (Washington, DC: CQ Press, 2015), 224–248.

58. Grossmann, *The Not-So-Special Interests*, 80.

59. Mento, interview.

60. AARP's chapter locator and information site is available at http://www.aarp.org/giving-back/aarp-chapter-locator/.

61. Cheryl Matheis, former Senior Vice President of Policy, Strategy, and International Affairs, AARP, telephone interview, January 25, 2016.

62. Grossmann, *The Not-So-Special Interests*, 80.

63. AARP, "*2015 AARP Year in Review*," 2016, http://www.aarp.org/content/dam/aarp/about_aarp/about_us/2016/2015-annual-report-aarp.pdf; LeaMond, interview

64. Center for Responsive Politics, "AARP: Issues, 2015," https://www.opensecrets.org/lobby/clientissues.php?id=D000023726&year=2015.

65. LeaMond, interview.

66. William P. Browne, "Organized Interests and Their Issue Niches: A Search for Pluralism in a Policy Domain," *Journal of Politics* 52, no. 2 (1990): 477–509.

67. Grossmann, *The Not-So-Special Interests*, 112.

68. Certner, Lewin, and Mika, interview.

69. Richard L. Hall and Frank W. Wayman, "Buying Time: Moneyed Interests and the Mobilization of Bias in Congressional Committees," *American Political Science Review* 84, no. 3 (1990): 797–820; Lawrence Lessig, *Republic, Lost: How Money Corrupts Congress—And a Plan to Stop It* (New York: Twelve, 2011); Lynda W. Powell, "The Influence of Campaign Contributions on Legislative Policy," *The Forum* 11, no. 3 (2013): 339–355.

70. Grossmann, *The Not-So-Special Interests*; Schlozman, Verba, and Brady, *The Unheavenly Chorus*, chapter 14.

71. Paul S. Herrnson, *Congressional Elections: Campaigning at Home and in Washington*, 7th ed. (Washington, DC: CQ Press, 2015).

72. Certner, Lewin, and Mika, interview.

73. Center for Responsive Politics, "AARP: Total Contributions" (2016), https://www.opensecrets.org/orgs/totals.php?id=D000023726&cycle=2016.

74. Kosterlitz, "Test of Strength," 2653.

75. Robert A. Dahl, "The Concept of Power," *Behavioral Science* 2, no. 3 (1957): 201–215, quote on 202–203.

76. Peter Bachrach and Morton S. Baratz, "The Two Faces of Power," *American Political Science Review*, 56, no. 4 (1962): 947–952.

77. Robert H. Binstock, "The Aged as Scapegoat," *Gerontologist* 23, no. 2 (1983): 136–143.

78. Robert B. Hudson and Judith G. Gonyea, "The Shifting Political Construction of Older Americans as a Target Population," in *The New Politics of Old Age Policy*, 3rd ed., ed. Robert B. Hudson (Baltimore: Johns Hopkins University Press, 2014), 99–116; Robert B. Hudson and Judith G. Gonyea, "Baby Boomers and the Shifting Political Construction of Old Age," *Gerontologist* 52, no. 2 (2012): 272–282; Anne Schneider and Helen Ingram, "Social Construction of Target Populations: Implications for Politics and Policy," *American Political Science Review* 87, no. 2 (1993): 334–347.

79. Robert H. Binstock, "From Compassionate Ageism to Intergenerational Conflict?" *Gerontologist* 50, no. 5 (2010): 574–585.

80. Andrea Louise Campbell, *How Policies Make Citizens: Senior Political Activism and the American Welfare State* (Princeton, NJ: Princeton University

Press, 2003); Hudson and Gonyea, "The Shifting Political Construction of Older Americans."

81. Michael B. Katz, *The Undeserving Poor: America's Enduring Confrontation with Poverty*, 2nd ed. (New York: Oxford University Press, 2013).

82. Daniel Béland, *Social Security: History and Politics from the New Deal to the Privatization Debate* (Lawrence, KS: University of Kansas Press, 2005); James H. Schulz and Robert H. Binstock, *Aging Nation: The Economics and Politics of Growing Older in America* (Baltimore: Johns Hopkins University Press, 2006).

83. Theodore R. Marmor, *The Politics of Medicare*, 2nd ed. (Hawthorne, NY: Aldine de Gruyter, 2000); Colleen M. Grogan and Christina M. Andrews, "The Politics of Aging within Medicaid," in *The New Politics of Old Age Policy*, 2nd ed., ed. Robert B. Hudson (Baltimore: Johns Hopkins University Press, 2010), 275–306.

84. Béland, *Social Security*; Fay Lomax Cook and Edith J. Barrett, *Support for the American Welfare State: The Views of Congress and the Public* (New York: Columbia University Press, 1992).

85. Jack L. Walker, "The Origins and Maintenance of Interest Groups in America," *American Political Science Review* 77, no. 2 (1983): 390–406, quote on p. 403.

86. Binstock, "Interest-Group Liberalism"; Demkovich, "There's a New Kick"; Pratt, *The Gray Lobby*.

87. Morris, *The AARP*; Kosterlitz, "Test of Strength."

88. Campbell, *How Policies Make Citizens*, 25–32.

89. Campbell, *How Policies Make Citizens*.

90. Campbell, *How Policies Make Citizens*, 7.

91. Campbell, *How Policies Make Citizens*.

92. Ibid.

93. Cook and Barrett, *Support for the American Welfare State*; Day, *What Older Americans Think*; Linda L. Fowler and Ronald G. Shaiko, "The Graying of the Constituency: Active Seniors in Congressional District Politics," presented at the annual meeting of the American Political Science Association, 1987, Chicago; Neal R. Peirce and Peter C. Choharis, "The Elderly as a Political Force—26 Million Strong and Well Organized," *National Journal*, September 11, 1982, 1559–1562.

94. Campbell, *How Policies Make Citizens*; Schlozman, Verba, and Brady, *The Unheavenly Chorus*.

95. Grossmann, *The Not-So-Special Interests*, chapter 2.

96. Hudson and Gonyea, "The Shifting Political Construction of Older Americans"; Campbell, *How Policies Make Citizens*.

97. Christine L. Day, "Aging Policy: A Partisan Paradox," in *Polarized Politics: The Impact of Divisiveness in the U.S. Political System*, ed. William Crotty (Boulder, CO: Lynne Rienner, 2014), 285–307; Hudson and Gonyea, "The Shifting Political Construction of Older Americans."

98. Martha Derthick, *Policymaking for Social Security* (Washington, DC: Brookings, 1979); Robert B. Hudson, "The 'Graying' of the Federal Budget and Its Consequences for Old Age Policy," *Gerontologist* 18, no. 4 (1978): 428–440.

99. Joseph White, *False Alarm: Why the Greatest Threat to Social Security and Medicare Is the Campaign to "Save" Them* (Baltimore: Johns Hopkins University Press, 2001).

100. Jacob S. Hacker, *The Great Risk Shift: The New Economic Insecurity and the Decline of the American Dream* (New York: Oxford University Press, 2006); Hudson and Gonyea, "The Shifting Political Construction of Older Americans."

101. Grossmann, *The Not-So-Special Interests.*

102. Craig Walker and Bret Bradigan, "The Age of Reformation: Dr. Ethel Percy Andrus and the Founding of the AARP," *Ojai History*, Winter, 2011–2012, 120–125.

103. Binstock, "Interest-Group Liberalism."

104. Day, *What Older Americans Think*, 122.

105. Lynch, *One Nation under AARP*, 171.

106. Jenkins and Donnellan, interview.

107. Mike Unger, "AARP Is Redefining What Aging Means for Its 38 Million Members," *Smart CEO*, 2016, http://www.smartceo.com/aarp-redefining-aging-means-38-million-members/.

108. Jo Ann Jenkins, *Disrupt Aging: A Bold New Path to Living Your Best Life at Every Age* (New York: Public Affairs, 2016).

109. Martin Gilens and Benjamin I. Page, "Testing Theories of American Politics: Elites, Interest Groups, and Average Citizens," *Perspectives on Politics* 12, no. 3 (2014): 564–581; Jacob S. Hacker, "Out of Balance: Medicare, Interest Groups, and American Politics," *Generations*, Summer 2015, asaging.org/blog/out-balance-medicare-interest-groups-and-american-politics; Schlozman and Tierney, *Organized Interests.*

110. Gilens, *Affluence and Influence.*

111. Ibid.; see also Campbell, *How Policies Make Citizens*; Day, *What Older Americans Think*; Susan A. MacManus, *Young v. Old: Generational Combat in the 21st Century* (Boulder, CO: Westview, 1996); Laurie A. Rhodebeck, "The Politics of Greed? Political Preferences among the Elderly," *Journal of Politics* 55, no. 2 (1993): 342–364.

112. R. Allen Hays, *Who Speaks for the Poor? National Interest Groups and Social Policy* (New York: Routledge, 2001); see also Grossmann, *The Not-So-Special-Interests.*

113. Larry M. Bartels, *Unequal Democracy: The Political Economy of the New Gilded Age* (New York and Princeton, NJ: Russell Sage Foundation and Princeton University Press, 2008).

114. Campbell, *How Policies Make Citizens.*

115. Gilens, *Affluence and Influence*, 123.

116. Gregory Korte, "Here's the Truth About Meals on Wheels in Trump's Budget," *USA Today*, March 18, 2017, http://www.usatoday.com/story/news/

politics/2017/03/18/meal-on-wheels-trump-budget-proposal-cuts/99308928/; Wendy Fox-Grage and Kathleen Ujvari, "The Older Americans Act," *Insight on the Issues* 92, May, 2014, AARP Public Policy Institute, Washington, DC.

117. John Rother, Chief Executive Officer, National Coalition on Health Care, telephone interview, September 18, 2014.

118. Rother, interview.

119. Walker and Bradigan, "The Age of Reformation"; Morris, *The AARP.*

120. On those three questionable business decisions, see Brian Viner, "The Man Who Rejected the Beatles," *The Independent*, February 12, 2012, http://www.independent.co.uk/arts-entertainment/music/news/the-man-who-rejected-the-beatles-6782008.html.

121. Pratt, *The Gray Lobby*, 96.

122. Alexander Guerin, Media Relations Associate, AARP, e-mail message to author, July 11, 2016.

123. Walker and Bradigan, "The Age of Reformation"; Pratt, *The Gray Lobby*, 51.

124. Morris, *The AARP*, 9; see, for example, John Tierney, "Old Money, New Power," *New York Times Magazine*, October 23, 1988, www.nytimes.com/1988/10/23/magazine/old-money-new-power.html?pagewanted=all.

125. Dorothy Crippen, Ruth Lana, Jean Lipman Block, Thomas E. Zetkov, and Gordon Elliott, eds., *The Wisdom of Ethel Percy Andrus* (Long Beach, CA: National Retired Teachers Association, 1968), 303, quoted in Jason G. Roe, "From the Impoverished to the Entitled: The Experience and Meaning of Old Age in America since the 1950s," PhD diss., University of Kansas, 2016, https://kuscholarworks.ku.edu/bitstream/handle/1808/10438/Roe_ku_0099D_12090_DATA_1.pdf;sequence=1,6.

126. Pratt, *The Gray Lobby*, 91.

127. Marmor, *The Politics of Medicare*; Marilyn Moon, *Medicare: A Policy Primer* (Washington, DC: The Urban Institute Press, 2006); Jonathan Oberlander, *The Political Life of Medicare* (Chicago: University of Chicago Press, 2003); Paul Starr, *Remedy and Reaction: The Peculiar American Struggle over Health Care Reform* (New Haven, CT: Yale University Press, 2013).

128. Day, *What Older Americans Think*, 25–26; Demkovich, "There's a New Kick," 1386; Pratt, *The Gray Lobby*, 90–91.

129. Morris, *The AARP*, 25–27.

130. Walker and Bradigan, "The Age of Reformation," 125.

131. Pratt, *The Gray Lobby*, 94.

132. Pratt, *The Gray Lobby*; Henry J. Pratt, *Gray Agendas: Interest Groups and Public Pensions in Canada, Britain, and the United States* (Ann Arbor: University of Michigan Press, 1993)

133. Campbell, *How Policies Make Citizens*, 16.

134. Demkovich, "There's a New Kick"; Pratt, *The Gray Lobby*, chapters 9–10; Laursen, *The People's Pension*, 2012).

135. Binstock, "Interest-Group Liberalism."

136. Demkovich, "There's a New Kick."

137. Pratt, *The Gray Lobby*, 155.

138. Demkovich, "There's a New Kick."

139. *AARP Bulletin,* June 1978, 6, quoted in Pratt *Gray Agendas*, 186.

140. Pratt, *Gray Agendas*, 186–190.

141. Demkovich, "There's a New Kick," 1389.

142. Morris, *The AARP*; Kosterlitz, "Test of Strength."

143. Peirce and Choharis, "The Elderly as a Political Force"; Robert B. Samuelson, "Benefit Programs for the Elderly—Off Limits to Federal Budget Cutters?" *National Journal*, October 3, 1981, 1757–1762.

144. Peirce and Choharis "The Elderly as a Political Force"; Campbell *How Policies Make Citizens*; Paul Light, *Artful Work: The Politics of Social Security Reform* (New York: Random House, 1985).

145. William Safire, "Language: Tracking the Source of the 'Third Rail' Warning," *International Herald Tribune*, February 18, 2007, http://www.nytimes.com/2007/02/18/opinion/18iht-edsafmon.4632394.html?_r=0.

146. Safire, "Language: Tracking the Source."

147. Béland, *Social Security*, 162; see also Light, *Artful Work*.

148. Day, *What Older Americans Think*; Kosterlitz, "Test of Strength."

149. LeaMond, interview; Novelli, interview.

150. A. J. P. Taylor, *Bismarck: The Man and the Statesman* (New York: Vintage, 1967).

151. Richard Himelfarb, *Catastrophic Politics: The Rise and Fall of the Medicare Catastrophic Coverage Act of 1988* (University Park, PA: Penn State University Press, 1995); Moon, *Medicare: A Policy Primer* 82–87; Pratt, *Gray Agendas*, 193–196; Fernando Torres-Gil, "The Politics of Catastrophic and Long-Term Care Coverage," *Journal of Aging and Social Policy* 1, no. 1/2 (1989): 61–86.

152. Himelfarb, *Catastrophic Politics*, 44; see also Julie Rovner, "Catastrophic-Insurance Law: Costs vs. Benefits," *Congressional Quarterly Weekly Report*, December 3, 1988, 3450–3452.

153. Himelfarb, *Catastrophic Politics*; Moon, *Medicare: A Policy Primer*; Debra Street, "Maintaining the Status Quo: The Impact of Old-Age Interest Groups on the Medicare Catastrophic Coverage Act of 1988," *Social Problems* 40, no. 4 (1993): 431–444.

154. Tierney, "Old Money, New Power"; Samuelson, "AARP's America Is a Mirage."

155. Birnbaum, "Washington's Power 25"; Birnbaum and Graves, "Follow the Money."

156. Steven A. Holmes, "The World According to AARP," *New York Times*, March 21, 2001. http://www.nytimes.com/2001/03/21/jobs/the-world-according-to-aarp.html; see also Lynch, *One Nation under AARP*; Pratt, *Gray Agendas*; Joshua M. Wiener, Carroll L. Estes, Susan M. Goldenson, and Sheryl C. Goldberg, "What Happened to Long-Term Care in the Health Reform Debate of 1993–1994? Lessons for the Future," *Milbank Quarterly* 79, no. 2 (2001): 207–252.

157. Wiener, et al., "What Happened to Long-Term Care," 212.

158. Himelfarb, *Catastrophic Politics*, 99–101; Marmor, *The Politics of Medicare*, 131–135.

159. Howard, *The Welfare State Nobody Knows*; Clifford Krauss, "Clinton's Health Plan: Interest Groups, Lobbyists of Every Stripe Turning to the Grass Roots," *New York Times*, September 24, 1993, http://www.nytimes.com/1993/09/24/us/clinton-s-health-plan-interest-groups-lobbyists-every-stripe-turning-grass-roots.html?pagewanted=all.

160. Jeffrey H. Birnbaum, "Washington's Second Most Powerful Man Horace Deets Heads the Most Fearsome Force in Politics, the American Association of Retired Persons," *Fortune*, May 12, 1997, http://archive.fortune.com/magazines/fortune/fortune_archive/1997/05/12/226236/index.htm; Holmes, "The World According to AARP."

161. Kosterlitz, "Test of Strength," 2654.

162. Philip Brasher, "Baby-Boom Think Tank Silenced," *Los Angeles Times*, April 1, 1990, articles.latimes.com/1990–04–01/news/mn-731_1_generational-equity.

163. Lynch, *One Nation under AARP*, 131; see also Laursen, *The People's Pension*, 303–305; Morris, *The AARP*, xi–xiv.

164. Grossmann, *The Not-So-Special-Interests*, 121; Morris, *The AARP*, 5.

165. Jeff Shear, "The Untouchables," *National Journal*, July 16, 1994, 1681–1685, quote on 1682; see also Schulz and Binstock, *Aging Nation*, 17.

166. Matheis, interview.

167. Roger A. Lohmann, "An Interview: Horace Deets of AARP," *Nonprofit Management and Leadership* 12, no. 1 (2001): 87–94, quote on 91.

168. Holmes, "The World According to AARP."

169. Marilyn Werber Serafini, "AARP's New Direction," *National Journal*, January 5, 2002, 28–31. Novelli changed the title of executive director to chief executive officer (CEO).

170. Kosterlitz, "The World According to AARP"; Paul Schwartzman, "At 50, AARP Enters Its Golden Years; with Boomers on Board, Seniors Lobby Flexes Its Muscle," *Washington Post*, September 4, 2008, http://www.washingtonpost.com/wp-dyn/content/article/2008/09/03/AR2008090303785.html; Serafini, "AARP's New Direction."

171. Schwartzman, "At 50, AARP Enters Its Golden Years."

172. Kosterlitz, "The World According to AARP," 29.

173. Lynch, *One Nation under AARP*, 136.

174. Novelli, interview; Rother, interview.

175. Novelli, interview.

176. Serafini, "AARP's New Direction," 29.

177. Ibid.

178. Vaida, "AARP's Big Bet," 800.

179. Mary Agnes Carey, "Medicare Deal Goes to Wire in Late-Night House Vote," *Congressional Quarterly Weekly Report*, November 22, 2003, 2879; John K. Iglehart, "The New Medicare Prescription-Drug Benefit—A Pure Power Play,"

New England Journal of Medicine 350, no. 8 (2004): 826–833; Thomas R. Oliver, Philip R. Lee, and Helene L. Lipton, "A Political History of Medicare and Prescription Drug Coverage," *Milbank Quarterly* 82, no. 2 (2004): 283–354; Schulz and Binstock, *Aging Nation*, 215–217.

180. Barbara T. Dreyfuss, "The Seduction: The Shocking Story of How AARP Backed the Medicare Bill," *American Prospect* 15, no. 6 (2004): 18–23; Schulz and Binstock, *Aging Nation*.

181. Courtney Mabeus, "The Battle Ahead: The Lobbying over Social Security Heats Up," Center for Responsive Politics, *Money in Politics Alert* 8, No. 2 (January 25, 2005), http://www.capitaleye.org/inside.asp?ID=153.

182. Ibid.

183. Andrea Louise Campbell and Ryan King, "Social Security: Political Resilience in the Face of Conservative Strides," in *The New Politics of Old Age Policy*, 2nd ed., ed. Robert B. Hudson (Baltimore: Johns Hopkins University Press, 2010), 234–254.

184. Andrea Louise Campbell and Robert H. Binstock, "Politics and Aging in the United States," in *Handbook of Aging and the Social Sciences*, 7th ed., ed. Robert H. Binstock and Linda K. George (London: Elsevier, 2011), 265–279; Fay Lomax Cook and Rachel L. Moskowitz, "The Great Divide: Elite and Mass Opinion about Social Security," in *The New Politics of Old Age Policy*, 3rd ed., ed. Robert B. Hudson (Baltimore: Johns Hopkins University Press, 2014), 69–96.

185. Schwartzman, "At 50, AARP Enters Its Golden Years."

186. Schulz and Binstock, *Aging Nation*; Glenn Kessler, "Fact Checker: The Strange Tale of How a False 2009 Obamacare Claim Ended Up in a Viral 2017 Video," *Washington Post*, February 14, 2017, https://www.washingtonpost.com/news/fact-checker/wp/2017/02/14/the-strange-tale-of-how-a-false-2009-obamacare-claim-ended-up-in-a-viral-2017-video/?utm_term=.0c7084054bec.

187. Lynch, *One Nation under AARP*, 175.

188. Lynch, *One Nation under AARP*; Jacobs and Skocpol, *Health Care Reform and American Politics*, 74; Starr, *Remedy and Reaction*, 224.

189. Kimberley A. Strassel, "The Love Song of AARP and Obama," *Wall Street Journal*, September 20, 2012, https://www.wsj.com/articles/SB10000872396390444165804578008413907642282.

190. Jacobs and Skocpol, *Health Care Reform and American Politics*, 187.

191. See, for example, A. Barry Rand, "Rebuilding the Middle Class: A Blueprint for the Future," *Vital Speeches of the Day*, 79, no. 3 (2013): 72–76.

192. Robert Pear, "Repeal of Health Law Faces a New Hurdle: Older Americans," *New York Times*, March 5, 2017, https://www.nytimes.com/2017/03/05/us/politics/health-care-law-obamacare-repeal-older-americans.html/.

193. Sy Mukherjee, "These Three Powerful Groups Are Slamming the GOP's Obamacare Replacement Plan," *Fortune*, March 8, 2017, http://fortune.com/2017/03/08/gop-healthcare-plan-aarp-ama-aha/.

194. Eli Watkins, "AARP Comes Out against House GOP Health Care Bill," cnn.com, March 8, 2017, https://www.google.com/#q=eli+watkins+cnn+aarp+comes+out+against+house+gop&*.

195. Jennifer Rubin, "If the GOP's Obamacare Alternative Fails, We Might See Real Reforms," *Washington Post*, March 8, 2017, https://www.washingtonpost.com/blogs/right-turn/wp/2017/03/08/if-the-gops-obamacare-alternative-fails-we-might-see-real-reforms/?utm_term=.f14fd7f98c4b.

196. Quinnipiac University Poll, "U.S. Voters Oppose GOP Health Plan 3–1," Quinnipiac University, Hamden, CT., March 23, 2017, https://poll.qu.edu/national/release-detail?ReleaseID=2443.

197. Starr, *Remedy and Reaction*, 277.

198. LeaMond, interview.

199. Lynch, *One Nation under AARP*, 148; "Special Report: Caregiving in America," *AARP Bulletin*, November, 2015.

200. Denise Bottcher, State Director, Louisiana State AARP, telephone interview, March 20, 2015; LeaMond, interview; Matheis, interview. For an example of an AARP state office, this one in Louisiana, filming interviews with gubernatorial candidates on their views about Medicaid funding for home and community based services, see Marsha Shuler, "Expand Bobby Jindal's Medicaid Privatization? John Bel Edwards Says Yes; David Vitter TBD," *The Advocate*, November 17, 2015, http://www.theadvocate.com/baton_rouge/news/politics/elections/article_bf03c460–9e69–52ab-80bb-ea5035996930.html.

201. Matheis, interview.

202. Bottcher, interview.

203. Gilens, *Affluence and Influence*; Serafini, "AARP's New Direction"; Theda Skocpol, *The Missing Middle: Working Families and the Future of American Social Policy* (New York: W. W. Norton, 2000).

204. Lynch, *One Nation under AARP*, 189.

205. Edmund Andrews, "AARP Looms as Key Player in Deficit Panel Debate," *Fiscal Times*, August 31, 2010, www.thefiscaltimes.com/Articles/2010/08/31/AARP-Looms-as-Key-Player-in-Deficit-Panel-Debate.

206. "The Moment of Truth: Report of the National Commission on Fiscal Responsibility and Reform" (Washington, DC: White House, December 2010), http://www.washingtonpost.com/wp-srv/politics/documents/TheMomentofTruth.pdf.

207. Andrea Louise Campbell, "Social Security, the Great Recession, and the Entitlement Problem," in *The New Politics of Old Age Policy*, 3rd ed., ed. Robert B. Hudson (Baltimore: Johns Hopkins University Press, 2014), 183–200.

208. Andrews, "AARP Looms as Key Player."

209. Campbell, "Social Security"; Nancy Cook and Chris Frates, "Thanks to AARP, Grandma's Got Influence," *National Journal*, October 1, 2011, 5; Michael A. Fletcher and Zachary A. Goldfarb, "AARP Uses Its Power to Oppose Social Security, Medicare Benefit Cuts for Retirees," *Washington Post*, November 17, 2012,

https://www.washingtonpost.com/business/economy/aarp-uses-its-power-to-oppose-social-security-medicare-benefit-cuts-for-retirees/2012/11/17/affb5874-2aa6-11e2-bab2-eda299503684_story.html?utm_term=.d3340ebabcf6.

210. Cook and Frates, "Thanks to AARP," 5.

211. Russell Berman, "Will Trump Cut Medicare and Social Security?" *The Atlantic*, January 24, 2017, https://www.theatlantic.com/politics/archive/2017/01/will-trump-cut-medicare-and-social-security/514298/; John Wasik, "How GOP, Trump Will Take Backdoor Route to Slash Social Security, Medicare," *Forbes*, January 30, 2017, https://www.forbes.com/sites/johnwasik/2017/01/30/how-gop-trump-will-take-backdoor-route-to-slash-social-security-medicare/#f4750a568ad1.

212. Jessie Hellmann, "AARP Launches Ad Campaign Urging Republicans to 'Protect' Medicare," *The Hill*, January 20, 2017, http://thehill.com/policy/healthcare/316799-aarp-launches-ad-campaign-urging-republicans-to-protect-medicare.

213. Howard Gleckman, "Trump's Budget Framework Points to Big Cuts in Programs for Seniors," *Forbes*, March 17, 2017, https://www.forbes.com/sites/howardgleckman/2017/03/17/trumps-budget-framework-points-to-big-cuts-in-programs-for-seniors/#7513eb2212c9; Korte, "Here's the Truth About Meals on Wheels."

214. Christopher Ingraham, "Meals on Wheels Is 'Not Showing Any Results' Only If You Ignore All These Results," *Washington Post*, March 16, 2017, https://www.washingtonpost.com/news/wonk/wp/2017/03/16/trump-budget-chief-says-meals-on-wheels-is-not-showing-any-results-hes-wrong/?utm_term=.d323dce54f16.

215. Ibid.; Huichen Zhu and Ruopeng An, "Impact of Home-Delivered Meal Programs on Diet and Nutrition Among Older Adults: A Review," *Nutrition and Health* 22, no. 2 (2013): 89–103.

216. Kali S. Thomas and David Dosa, "More Than a Meal: Pilot Research Study," Meals on Wheels America, Arlington, VA, 2015, http://www.mealsonwheelsamerica.org/docs/default-source/News-Assets/mtam-full-report—-march-2–2015.pdf?sfvrsn=6.

217. Ingraham, "Meals on Wheels."

218. AARP, *2015 AARP Services, Inc. Annual Report*, 2016, http://www.aarp.org/content/dam/aarp/about_aarp/about_us/2016/services-2015-annual-report-aarp.pdf, 1.

219. Ibid., 13.

220. Jilenne Gunther, "AARP's BankSafe Initiative: A Comprehensive Approach to Better Serving and Protecting Consumer," AARP Public Policy Institute, Washington, DC, February 2016, http://www.aarp.org/content/dam/aarp/ppi/2016–02/AARP-Banksafe-Initiatiive-Serving-Protecting-Communities.pdf.

221. Jenkins and Donnellan, interview; LeaMond, interview.

222. AARP, "2015 AARP Services, Inc. Annual Report," 13.

223. LeaMond, interview.

224. AARP Media Sales, "7 Reasons Boomers Will Grow Your Bottom Line," https://res.cloudinary.com/advertise-aarp/image/upload/v1481232699/AARP_Media_Sales_-_7_Reasons_Boomers_Will_Grow_Your_Bottom_Line.pdf, 3.

225. Birnbaum and Graves, "Follow the Money"; Grossmann, *The Not-So-Special Interests*; Leach, "10 Most Powerful Special Interest Groups."

226. Baumgartner, et al., *Lobbying and Policy Change.*

227. Rother, interview.

228. Hudson and Gonyea, "The Shifting Political Construction of Older Americans."

229. Howard, *The Welfare State Nobody Knows*, 137.

Chapter 6 Business, Advocacy, and Service: Conflict or Convergence?

1. AARP, "Our Mission," http://www.aarp.org/about-aarp/ (accessed April 4, 2017).

2. AARP, "About Us," *2016 AARP Year in Review*, annual report, http://www.aarp.org/content/dam/aarp/about_aarp/about_us/2017/01/2016-AARP-Year-in-Review.pdf.

3. Frederick R. Lynch, *One Nation under AARP: The Fight over Medicare, Social Security, and America's Future* (Berkeley: University of California Press, 2011), 136–149.

4. AARP, "About AARP Foundation," http://www.aarp.org/aarp-foundation/about-us/.

5. Wayne Thomas, "What Is the Difference between a 501c3 & 501c4?" LegalZoom, info.legalzoom.com/difference-between-501c3-501c4–26450.html (accessed July 17, 2016); Internal Revenue Service, "Types of Organizations Exempt Under Section 501(c)(4)," https://www.irs.gov/charities-non-profits/other-non-profits/types-of-organizations-exempt-under-section-501-c-4.

6. Anthony Johnstone. "Politics and the Public Benefit Corporation," Columbia University Academic Commons, 2013, http://dx.doi.org/10.7916/D8XD0ZNN; Michael Franz, "Attack of the Super PACs? Interest Groups in the 2012 Elections," in *New Directions in Interest Group Politics*, ed. Matt Grossmann (New York: Routledge, 2014), 144–164.

7. All budget information comes from *Consolidated Financial Statements Together with Report of Independent Certified Public Accountants, AARP, December 31, 2015 and 2014*, 2016. www.aarp.org/content/dam/aarp/about_aarp/annual_reports/2016/2015-financial-statements-AARP.pdf.

8. Roger L. Martin and Sally R. Osberg, "Two Keys to Sustainable Social Enterprise," *Harvard Business Review* 93, no. 5 (2015): 86–94; Marthe Nyssens, *Social Enterprise: At the Crossroads of Market, Public Policies and Civil Society* (New York: Routledge, 2006).

9. Lynch, *One Nation under AARP*, 129–130.

10. Martin and Osberg, "Two Keys to Sustainable Social Enterprise."

11. Peter Murray, "The Secret of Scale," *Stanford Social Innovation Review* (Fall, 2013), http://ssir.org/articles/entry/the_secret_of_scale.

12. Roger A. Lohmann, "An Interview: Horace Deets of AARP," *Nonprofit Management and Leadership* 12, no. 1 (2001): 87–94, quote on 92–93.

13. Lawrence P. Flanagan, "Letter from the President and CEO," *2015 AARP Services Annual Report* (Washington, DC: AARP, 2016), http://www.aarp.org/content/dam/aarp/about_aarp/about_us/2016/services-2015-annual-report-aarp.pdf, 2.

14. See, for example, Fred Lucas, "AARP: Advocacy Group or Crony Capitalists?" Capital Research Center, 2012, https://capitalresearch.org/article/aarp-advocacy-group-or-crony-capitalists/.

15. Julie Kosterlitz, "The World According to AARP," *National Journal*, March 10, 2007, 28–35

16. Andy Rooney, *Sincerely, Andy Rooney* (New York: Public Affairs, 2009), 217.

17. Julie Kosterlitz, "Test of Strength," *National Journal*, October 24, 1987, 2652–2657, quote is on 2653.

18. Charles R. Morris, *The AARP: America's Most Powerful Lobby and the Clash of Generations* (New York: Times Books, 1996), 30–35.

19. U.S. Senate, Committee on Finance, "Business and Financial Practices of the AARP: Hearings before the Subcommittee on Social Security and Family Policy," 104th Congress, First Session, June 13–20, 1995, https://www.finance.senate.gov/imo/media/doc/Hrg104–109.pdf.

20. Morris, *The AARP*, 237–242.

21. U.S. Senate, "Business and Financial Practices of the AARP," 64–65.

22. David Cay Johnston, "A.A.R.P. Sets Up a Taxable Subsidiary," *New York Times*, July 15, 1999, http://www.nytimes.com/1999/07/15/business/aarp-sets-up-a-taxable-subsidiary.html; see also Colette Fraley, "Lobbying: Simpson Zeroes In on AARP and Its Tax Exemption," *Congressional Quarterly Weekly Report*, June 17, 1995, 1749; Kosterlitz, "The World According to AARP"; Morris, *The AARP*; Bara Vaida, "AARP's Big Bet," *National Journal*, March 13, 2004, 796–802.

23. Morris, *The AARP*, 41, 241–242; see also Dale Van Atta, *Trust Betrayed: Inside the AARP* (Washington, DC: Regnery, 1998), 66; U.S. Senate, "Business and Financial Practices of the AARP," 49–52.

24. Jonathan D. Salant and Robert Marshall Wells, "Lobbies: AARP's Federal Funds Endangered," *Congressional Quarterly Weekly Report*, July 29, 1995, 2240; Joshua M. Wiener, Carroll L. Estes, Susan M. Goldenson, and Sheryl C. Goldbert, "What Happened to Long-Term Care in the Health Reform Debate of 1993–1994? Lessons for the Future," *Milbank Quarterly* 79, no. 2 (2001): 207–252.

25. U.S. Senate, "Business and Financial Practices of the AARP," 47.

26. Ibid., 46.

27. Ibid., 6.

28. Ibid., 1.
29. Ibid., 3.
30. Ibid., 1–2.
31. Ibid., 7.
32. Ibid., 64.
33. Fraley, "Lobbying: Simpson Zeroes In," 1749.
34. Eric Laursen, *The People's Pension: The Struggle to Defend Social Security Since Reagan* (Oakland, CA: AK Press, 2012), 303.
35. Salant and Wells, "Lobbies: AARP's Federal Funds Endangered," 2240.
36. Lynch, *One Nation under AARP*, 131–133.
37. Jo Ann Jenkins, Chief Executive Officer, AARP, and Kevin Donnellan, Executive Vice President and Chief of Staff, AARP, personal interview, Washington, DC, July 22, 2015.
38. U.S. Senate, "Business and Financial Practices of the AARP," 46–47.
39. Matt Grossmann, *The Not-So-Special Interests: Interest Groups, Public Representation, and American Governance* (Stanford: Stanford University Press, 2012), 121; Morris, *The AARP*, 4.
40. Peter Overby, "Conflict of Interest for AARP in Health Bill Debate?" Morning Edition, National Public Radio, November 4, 2009, http://www.npr.org/templates/story/story.php?storyId=120069183.
41. Kimberly J. Morgan and Andrea Louise Campbell, *The Delegated Welfare State: Medicare, Markets, and the Governance of Social Policy* (New York: Oxford University Press, 2011); Kimberly J. Morgan, "The Medicare Challenge: Clients, Cost Controls, and Congress," in *The New Politics of Old Age Policy*, 3rd ed., ed. Robert B. Hudson (Baltimore: Johns Hopkins University Press, 2014), 201–220.
42. Lynch, *One Nation under AARP*, 140–142; Vaida, "AARP's Big Bet."
43. Barbara T. Dreyfuss, "The Seduction: The Shocking Story of How AARP Backed the Medicare Bill," *American Prospect* 15, no. 6 (2004): 18–23, quote on 19.
44. Milt Freudenheim, "Opponents of Medicare Bill Say AARP Has Conflicts," *New York Times*, November 21, 2003, http://www.npr.org/templates/story/story.php?storyId=120069183.
45. Jerry Markon, "AARP Lobbies against Cuts That May Hurt Its Bottom Line," *Washington Post*, December 4, 2012, https://www.washingtonpost.com/politics/aarp-lobbies-against-medicare-changes-that-could-hurt-its-bottom-line/2012/12/03/aa3e509e-3a8c-11e2-b01f-5f55b193f58f_story.html?utm_term=.37c678e983dd. The 4.95 percent figure was verified by AARP CEO A. Barry Rand in congressional testimony in 2011.
46. AARP, *Consolidated Financial Statements*; Rebecca Adams, "AARP's Medicare Drug Benefit," *Congressional Quarterly Weekly Report*, December 12, 2005, 3295; Kosterlitz, "The World According to AARP."
47. Freudenheim, "Opponents of Medicare Bill."
48. Adams, "AARP's Medicare Drug Benefit," 3295.

49. William Novelli, Professor, McDonough School of Business, Georgetown University, and former CEO, AARP, telephone interview, January 22, 2016.

50. John Rother, Chief Executive Officer, National Coalition on Health Care, telephone interview, September 18, 2014.

51. James H. Schulz and Robert H. Binstock, *Aging Nation: The Economics and Politics of Growing Older in America* (Baltimore: Johns Hopkins University Press, 2006), 217.

52. Freudenheim, "Opponents of Medicare Bill."

53. Vaida, "AARP's Big Bet," 801.

54. U.S. House of Representatives, Committee on Ways and Means, "Behind the Veil: The AARP America Doesn't Know," investigative report prepared by Representative Wally Herger and Representative Dave Reichert, March 29, 2011, https://waysandmeans.house.gov/UploadedFiles/AARP_REPORT_FINAL_PDF_3_29_11.pdf. Representatives Herger and Reichert, chairs of two Ways and Means subcommittees, prepared the report, which was released by the Ways and Means Subcommittee on Oversight, chaired by Representative Charles Boustany.

55. Ibid., 1.

56. David Certner, Legislative Counsel and Legislative Policy Director for Government Affairs, AARP; Cindy Lewin, Executive Vice President and General Counsel, AARP; and Sarah Mika, Senior Vice President, AARP Services, Inc., personal interview, Washington, DC, July 22, 2015.

57. AARP, "AARP Responds to Congressional Inquiries," November 1, 2012, http://www.aarp.org/about-aarp/info-03–2011/website_overview.html.

58. Jonathan Allen, "GOP Calls for IRS Probe of AARP," *Politico*, April 8, 2011, http://www.politico.com/story/2011/04/gop-calls-for-irs-probe-of-aarp-052829.

59. U.S. House of Representatives, "Behind the Veil," 17; Ricardo Alonso-Zaldivar and Stephen Ohlemacher, "House Republicans Seek IRS Probe of AARP," boston.com, March 30, 2011, http://archive.boston.com/news/nation/articles/2011/03/30/house_republicans_seek_irs_probe_of_aarp/; Dan Eggen, "AARP Could Benefit from the Health Insurance Reforms It Advocates," *Washington Post*, October 27, 2009, http://www.washingtonpost.com/wp-dyn/content/article/2009/10/26/AR2009102603392.html; Angie Drobnic Holan, "AARP Profits from Insurance Sales; GOP Calls It a Health Reform Conflict," *Politifact*, September 29, 2009, http://www.politifact.com/truth-o-meter/statements/2009/sep/29/ginny-brown-waite/aarp-insurance-health-reform-conflict/.

60. Gary Cohn and Darrell Preston, "AARP Collects Royalties, Fees from Insurance It Endorses," boston.com, December 5, 2008, http://archive.boston.com/news/nation/articles/2008/12/05/aarp_collects_royalties_fees_from_insurers_it_endorses/.

61. Holan, "AARP Profits from Insurance Sales."

62. Eggen, "AARP Could Benefit."

63. U.S. House of Representatives, "Behind the Veil," 17.

64. Jenkins and Donnellan, interview; Certner, Lewin, and Mika, interview.

65. Markon, "AARP Lobbies against Cuts."

66. Ibid.

67. Sidney M. Wolfe, "AARP: A Profitable Nonprofit Organization," Public Citizen, June, 2014, www.citizen.org/Page.aspx?pid=6325.

68. Jenkins and Donnellan, interview.

69. AARP, "AARP Responds to Congressional Inquiries," 3.

70. Cheryl Matheis, former Senior Vice President of Policy, Strategy, and International Affairs, AARP, telephone interview, January 25, 2016.

71. Certner, Lewin, and Mika, interview; Jenkins and Donnellan, interview; Matheis, interview; Novelli, interview; Rother, interview.

72. Bruce D. Collins, "Fundamentally Flawed: Recent GOP Report about AARP Plays It Fast and Loose with the Facts," *Inside Counsel*, August, 2011, http://www.insidecounsel.com/2011/08/01/recent-gop-report-criticizes-aarp, 71.

73. Jenkins and Donnellan, interview; Novelli, interview.

74. U.S. House of Representatives, "Behind the Veil," 3.

75. Charity Watch, "Top Compensation Packages," 2017, https://www.charitywatch.org/top-charity-salaries.

76. Charity Navigator, "2014 Charity CEO Compensation Study," October, 2014, https://www.charitynavigator.org/docs/2014_CEO_Compensation_Study.pdf.

77. AARP "AARP Responds to Congressional Inquiries"; Bennett Roth, "GOP Probe of AARP Could Ensnare Other Nonprofits," *Roll Call*, April 1, 2011, http://www.rollcall.com/news/gop_probe_of_aarp_could_ensnare_other_nonprofits-204534–1.html.

78. Internal Revenue Service, Form 990, AARP, 2015, http://www.aarp.org/content/dam/aarp/about_aarp/annual_reports/2016/aarp-amended-990-public-disclosure-2015.pdf.

79. Brian Eastwood, "Top Health Insurance CEO Pay Exceeds $10 Million in 2014," *Fierce Healthcare*, April 10, 2015, http://www.fiercehealthcare.com/payer/top-health-insurance-ceo-pay-exceeds-10-million-2014.

80. Eggen, "AARP Could Benefit."

81. Matheis, interview.

82. U.S. House of Representatives, "Behind the Veil," 2; Lucas, "AARP: Advocacy Group or Crony Capitalists?"; Alonso-Zaldiver and Ohlemacher, "House Republicans Seek IRS Probe."

83. The Harris Poll, "American Red Cross, Nature Conservancy, Consumers Union and AARP Are Organizations Inside the Beltway Most Trusted by Public," January 17, 2012, http://www.theharrispoll.com/search?keywords=most+trusted+beltway.

84. Overby, "Conflict of Interest."

85. Barbara Shipley, Senior Vice President of Brand Integration, AARP, personal interview, July 23, 2015.

86. Jenkins and Donnellan, interview.

87. Ibid.

88. Novelli, interview.

89. Jenkins and Donnellan, interview.

90. Rother, interview.

91. Morris, *The AARP*, 30–35.

92. Ibid., Kosterlitz, "Test of Strength."

93. Robert Pear, "Rates Are Rising on Policies That Cover Gaps in Medicare," *New York Times*, December 20, 1995, http://www.nytimes.com/1995/12/20/us/rates-are-rising-on-policies-that-cover-gaps-in-medicare.html.

94. Morris, *The AARP*.

95. Ibid., 213.

96. Ibid., 209–242.

97. Pear, "Rates Are Rising."

98. Milt Freudenheim, "Prudential, Outbid, Loses $4 Billion of A.A.R.P. Work," *New York Times*, September 12, 1996, http://www.nytimes.com/1996/09/12/business/prudential-outbid-loses-4-billion-of-aarp-work.html.

99. Howard Gleckman, Mike McNamee, and David Henry, "By Raising Its Voice, AARP Raises Questions," *Bloomberg Businessweek*, March 13, 2005, https://www.bloomberg.com/news/articles/2005–03–13/by-raising-its-voice-aarp-raises-questions; Anne Tergesen, "Sure, It's from AARP. But Is It a Good Deal?" *Bloomberg Businessweek*, February 13, 2008, https://www.bloomberg.com/news/articles/2008–02–13/sure-its-from-aarp-dot-but-is-it-a-good-deal.

100. Lynch, *One Nation under AARP*, 142.

101. Bob Trebilcock, "Life Insurance and Annuities: Is AARP Looking Out for You?" CBS Moneywatch, October 9, 2009, http://www.cbsnews.com/news/life-insurance-and-annuities-is-aarp-looking-out-for-you/.

102. Morris, *The AARP*, 242.

103. Ibid., 211.

104. AARP, "Our Mission," http://www.aarp.org/about-aarp/ (accessed July 31, 2016).

105. Novelli, interview.

106. Kosterlitz, "The World According to AARP," 33.

107. Morris, *The AARP*.

108. David Cay Johnston, "A.A.R.P. Sets Up a Taxable Subsidiary," *New York Times*, July 15, 1999, http://www.nytimes.com/1999/07/15/business/aarp-sets-up-a-taxable-subsidiary.html.

Chapter 7 Conclusion

1. Julie Kosterlitz, "The World According to AARP," *National Journal*, March 10, 2007, 28–35, quote on 32.

2. Sara Edelstein, Heather Hahn, Julia Isaacs, Ellen Steele, and C. Eugene Steuerle, *Kids' Share 2016: Federal Expenditures on Children Through 2015 and Future Projections* (Washington, DC: Urban Institute, 2016), http://www.urban.org/research/publication/kids-share-2016federal-expenditures-children-through-2015-and-future-projections.

3. John Rother, Chief Executive Officer, National Coalition on Health Care, telephone interview, September 18, 2014.

4. William Novelli, Professor, McDonough School of Business, Georgetown University, and former CEO, AARP, telephone interview, January 22, 2016.

5. J. Gabriel Ware, "Why AARP Is Backing a New Lobbying Group for Millennials," *Yes! Magazine*, April 20, 2017, http://www.yesmagazine.org/people-power/why-aarp-is-backing-a-new-lobbying-group-for-millennials-20170420.

6. Jo Ann Jenkins, Chief Executive Officer, AARP, and Kevin Donnellan, Executive Vice President and Chief of Staff, AARP, personal interview, Washington, DC, July 22, 2015.

7. Nancy LeaMond, Executive Vice President and Chief Advocacy and Engagement Officer, AARP, personal interview, Washington, DC, July 23, 2015.

8. "Jo Ann Jenkins, Age Disruptor," *Insight News*, November 7, 2016, http://www.insightnews.com/2016/11/07/jo-ann-jenkins-age-disruptor/.

9. AARP, "AARP History," May 10, 2010, http://www.aarp.org/about-aarp/company/info-2016/history.html.

References

60 Plus Association. "Seniors Group Responds to Ominous Social Security and Medicare Trust Fund Report." June 22, 2016. https://60plus.org/seniors-group-responds-to-ominous-social-security-and-medicare-trust-fund-report/.

AARP. "2015 AARP Services, Inc. Annual Report." 2016. http://www.aarp.org/content/dam/aarp/about_aarp/about_us/2016/services-2015-annual-report-aarp.pdf.

AARP. "2015 AARP Year in Review." 2016. http://www.aarp.org/content/dam/aarp/about_aarp/about_us/2016/2015-annual-report-aarp.pdf.

AARP. "Trump and Clinton: Find Out Where They Stand on Social Security." *AARP Bulletin*, June 27, 2016.

AARP. "AARP History." May 10, 2010. http://www.aarp.org/about-aarp/company-info-2016/history.html.

AARP. "AARP Ramps Up Grassroots Advertising in Opposition to Fast Track Debt Commission." *AARP Media Relations/Press Center.* January 26, 2010. http://www.aarp.org/about-aarp/press-center/info-03-2010/aarp_activities_conrad_gregg.html.

AARP. "AARP Responds to Congressional Inquiries." November 1, 2012. http://www.aarp.org/about-aarp/info-03-2011/website_overview.html.

AARP. "About AARP Foundation." http://www.aarp.org/aarp-foundation/about-us/ (accessed April 4, 2017).

AARP Bulletin. "Special Report: Caregiving in America." November 2015.

AARP. "Consolidated Financial Statements Together with Report of Independent Certified Public Accountants, AARP, December 31, 2015 and 2014." 2016. www.aarp.org/content/dam/aarp/about_aarp/annual_reports/2016/2015-financial-statements-AARP.pdf.

AARP. "Our Mission." http://www.aarp.org/about-aarp/ (accessed April 4, 2017).

AARP. "Updating Social Security for the 21st Century: 12 Proposals You Should Know About." October 2015. http://www.aarp.org/work/social-security/info-05-2012/future-of-social-security-proposals.html.

Abramowitz, Alan A. *The Disappearing Center: Polarization and American Democracy.* New Haven: Yale University Press, 2010.

Achenbaum, W. Andrew. *Old Age in the New Land: The American Experience Since 1790.* Baltimore: Johns Hopkins University Press, 1978.

Achenbaum, W. Andrew, and Vern L. Bengtson. "Re-engaging the Disengagement Theory of Aging: On the History and Assessment of Theory Development in Gerontology." *Gerontologist* 34, no. 6 (1994): 756–763.

Adams, Rebecca. "AARP's Medicare Drug Benefit." *Congressional Quarterly Weekly Report*, December 12, 2005: 3295.

Aldrich, John H., and David W. Rohde. "The Consequences of Party Organization in the House: The Role of the Majority and Minority Parties in Conditional Party Government." In *Polarized Politics: Congress and the President in a Partisan Era*, edited by Jon R. Bond and Richard Fleisher, 31–72. Washington, DC: CQ Press, 2000.

"ALEC and AARP." *AARP Online Community.* http://community.aarp.org/t5/Introduce-Yourself/ALEC-and-AARP/td-p/1747998 (accessed August 2, 2016).

Allen, Jonathan. "GOP Calls for IRS Probe of AARP." *Politico*, April 8, 2011. http://www.politico.com/story/2011/04/gop-calls-for-irs-probe-of-aarp-052829.

Alonso-Zaldivar, Ricardo, and Stephen Ohlemacher. "House Republicans Seek IRS Probe of AARP." *boston.com.* March 30, 2011. http://archive.boston.com/news/nation/articles/2011/03/30/house_republicans_seek_irs_probe_of_aarp/.

Alstott, Anne L. *A New Deal for Old Age.* Cambridge, MA: Harvard University Press, 2016.

Altman, Nancy J., and Eric R. Kingson. *Social Security: How Expanding It Will Help Us All.* New York: The New Press, 2015.

Amenta, Edwin. *When Social Movements Matter: The Townsend Plan and the Rise of Social Security.* Princeton, NJ: Princeton University Press, 2005.

American Political Science Association. "Toward a More Responsible Party System: A Report of the Committee on Political Parties." *American Political Science Review* 44 (Supplement) (1950).

Andrews, Edmund. "AARP Looms as Key Player in Deficit Panel Debate." *Fiscal Times*, August 31, 2010. www.thefiscaltimes.com/Articles/2010/08/31/AARP-Looms-as-Key-Player-in-Deficit-Panel-Debate.

Andrus, Ethel Percy. "The Aged and Retired." In *Who Is My Neighbor?*, edited by Esther Pike, 119–136. Greenwich, CT: Seabury Press, 1960.

Association of Mature American Citizens. "AARP's Rival Has Good Social Security Plan." January 15, 2014. www.amac.us/aarps-rival-good-social-security-plan/.

Axelrod, Joel N. "Attitude Measures That Predict Purchase." *Journal of Advertising Research* 8 (1968): 3–17.

Bachrach, Peter, and Morton S. Baratz. "The Two Faces of Power." *American Political Science Review* 56, no. 4 (1962): 947–952.

Barakso, Maryann, and Brian F. Schaffner. "Exit, Voice, and Interest Group Governance." *American Politics Research* 36, no. 2 (2008): 186–209.

Barry, Dave. *Dave Barry Turns 50.* New York: Ballantine Books, 1998.

Bartels, Larry M. *Unequal Democracy: The Political Economy of the New Gilded Age.* New York and Princeton: Russell Sage Foundation and Princeton University Press, 2008.

Baumgartner, Frank R., Jeffry M. Berry, Marie Hojnacki, David C. Kimball, and Beth L. Leech. *Lobbying and Policy Change: Who Wins, Who Loses, and Why.* Chicago: University of Chicago Press, 2009.

Beard, Reneé L., and John B. Williamson. "Symbolic Politics, Social Policy, and the Senior Rights Movement." *Journal of Aging Studies* 25, no. 1 (2011): 22–33.

Béland, Daniel. *Social Security: History and Politics from the New Deal to the Privatization Debate.* Lawrence, KS: University of Kansas Press, 2005.

Berman, Russell. "Will Trump Cut Medicare and Social Security?" *The Atlantic*, January 24, 2017. https://www.theatlantic.com/politics/archive/2017/01/will-trump-cut-medicare-and-social-security/514298/.

Berry, Jeffrey M., and Clyde Wilcox. *The Interest Group Society.* 5th ed. New York: Routledge, 2008.

Bimber, Bruce, Andrew Flanagin, and Cynthia Stohl. *Collective Action in Organizations: Interaction and Engagement in an Era of Technological Change.* Cambridge: Cambridge University Press, 2012.

Binder, Sarah. *Stalemate: Causes and Consequences of Legislative Gridlock.* Washington, DC: Brookings, 2003.

Binstock, Robert H. "From Compassionate Ageism to Intergenerational Conflict?" *Gerontologist* 50, no. 5 (2010): 574–585.

Binstock, Robert H. "Interest-Group Liberalism and the Politics of Aging." *Gerontologist* 12, no. 3, Part 1 (1972): 265–280.

Binstock, Robert H. "Older Voters and the 2008 Election." *Gerontologist* 49, no. 5 (2009): 697–701.

Binstock, Robert H. "Older Voters and the 2010 U.S. Election: Implications for 2012 and Beyond?" *Gerontologist* 52, no. 3 (2012): 408–417.

Binstock, Robert H. "The Aged as Scapegoat." *Gerontologist* 23, no. 2 (1983): 136–143.

Birnbaum, Jeffrey H. "Washington's Power 25: Which Pressure Groups Are Best at Manipulating the Laws We Live By?" *Fortune*, December 8, 1997. http://archive.fortune.com/magazines/fortune/fortune_archive/1997/12/08/234927/index.htm.

Birnbaum, Jeffrey H. "Washington's Second Most Powerful Man Horace Deets Heads the Most Fearsome Force in Politics, the American Association of Retired Persons." *Fortune*, May 12, 1997. http://archive.fortune.com/magazines/fortune/fortune_archive/1997/05/12/226236/htm.

Birnbaum, Jeffrey H., and Russell Newell. "Fat and Happy in D.C." *Fortune*, May 28, 2001: 94–100.

Birnbaum, Jeffry H., and Natasha Graves. "Follow the Money." *Fortune*, December 6, 1999: 206–208.

Blahous, Charles P. *Reforming Social Security: For Ourselves and Our Posterity.* New York: Praeger, 2000.

Brasher, Philip. "Baby-Boom Think Tank Silenced." *Los Angeles Times*, April 1, 1990.

Broder, David. "Budget Funds for Elderly Grow Rapidly." *Washington Post*, January 30, 1973: A-16.

Browne, William P. "Organized Interests and Their Issue Niches: A Search for Pluralism in a Policy Domain." *Journal of Politics* 52, no. 2 (1990): 477–509.

Campbell, Andrea Louise. *How Policies Make Citizens: Senior Political Activism and the American Welfare State.* Princeton, NJ: Princeton University Press, 2003.

Campbell, Andrea Louise. "Social Security, the Great Recession, and the Entitlement Problem." In *The New Politics of Old Age Policy*, edited by Robert B. Hudson, 183–200. Baltimore: Johns Hopkins University, 2014.

Campbell, Andrea Louise. *Trapped in America's Safety Net: One Family's Struggle.* Chicago: University of Chicago Press, 2014.

Campbell, Andrea Louise, and Julia Lynch. "Whose 'Gray Power'? Elderly Voters, Elderly Lobbies, and Welfare Reform in Italy and the United States." *Italian Politics and Society* 53 (2000): 11–39.

Campbell, Andrea Louise, and Robert H. Binstock. "Politics and Aging in the United States." In *Handbook of Aging and the Social Sciences*, edited by Robert H. Binstock and Linda K. George, 265–280. New York: Elsevier, 2011.

Campbell, Andrea Louise, and Ryan King. "Social Security: Political Resilience in the Face of Conservative Strides." In *The New Politics of Old Age Policy*, edited by Robert B. Hudson, 234–254. Baltimore: Johns Hopkins University Press, 2010.

Card, Jean. "'Shut Up' Politics: AARP's Decision to Leave ALEC Due to Left-Wing Bullying Means Leaving the Political Conversation." *U.S. News*, August 11, 2016. http://www.usnews.com/opinion/articles/2016-08-11/aarp-yielded-to-shut-up-politics-by-ending-its-alec-membership.

Carey, Mary Agnes. "Medicare Deal Goes to Wire in Late-Night House Vote." *Congressional Quarterly Weekly Report*, November 22, 2003: 2879.

Carlie, Michael Kaye. "The Politics of Age: Interest Group or Social Movement?" *Gerontologist* 9, no. 4, Part 1 (1969): 259–264.

Center for Responsive Politics. "AARP: Issues, 2015." *opensecrets.org.* 2015. https://www.opensecrets.org/lobby/clientissues.php?id=D000023726&year=2015.

Center for Responsive Politics. "AARP: Total Contributions." *opensecrets.org.* 2016. https://www.opensecrets.org/orgs/totals.php?id=D000023726&cycle=2016.

Center for Responsive Politics. "Lobbyists Representing AARP." *opensecrets.org.* 2016. https://www.opensecrets.org/lobby/clientlbs.php?id=D000023726&year=2016.

Centers for Medicare and Medicaid Services. "President Signs Medicare Legislation: Remarks by the President at Signing of the Medicare Prescription Drug, Improvement and Modernization Act of 2003." https://www.cms.gov/about-cms/agency-information/history/downloads/bushsignmma2003.pdf.

Charity Navigator. "2014 Charity CEO Compensation Study." October 2014. https://www.charitynavigator.org/docs/2014_CEO_Compensation_Study.pdf.

Charity Watch. "Top Compensation Packages." 2017. https://www.charitywatch.org/top-charity-salaries.

Church, George J., and Richard Lacayo. "Social Insecurity." *Time*, March 20, 1995. http://content.time.com/time/magazine/article/0,9171,982700,00.html.

Cigler, Allan J., and Burdett C. Loomis, *Interest Group Politics*. 4th ed. Washington, DC: CQ Press, 1995.

Clark, Peter B., and James Q. Wilson. "Incentive Systems: A Theory of Organizations." *Administrative Science Quarterly* 6 (1961): 129–166.

Cohn, Gary, and Darrell Preston. "AARP Collects Royalties, Fees from Insurance It Endorses." *boston.com*. December 5, 2008. http://archive.boston.com/news/nation/articles/2008/12/05/aarp_collects_royalties_fees_from_insurers_it_endorses/.

Collins, Bruce D. "Fundamentally Flawed: Recent GOP Report about AARP Plays It Fast and Loose with the Facts." *Inside Counsel*, August 2011. http://www.insidecounsel.com/2011/08/01/recent-gop-report-criticizes-aarp.

Committee for a Responsible Federal Budget. "Op-Ed: Reforming Social Security Is Easy—But It Won't Be for Long." June 4, 2013. http://www.crfb.org/papers/op-ed-reforming-social-security-easy-%E2%80%94-it-wont-be-long.

Condon, Stephanie. "Alan Simpson: Social Security Is Like a 'Milk Cow with 310 Million Tits'." *CBS News*, August 25, 2010. http://www.cbsnews.com/news/alan-simpson-social-security-is-like-a-milk-cow-with-310-million-tits/.

Cook, Fay Lomax, and Edith J. Barrett. *Support for the American Welfare State: The Views of Congress and the Public*. New York: Columbia University Press, 1992.

Cook, Fay Lomax, and Rachel L. Moskowitz. "The Great Divide: Elite and Mass Opinion about Social Security." In *The New Politics of Old Age Policy*, edited by Robert B. Hudson, 69–96. Baltimore: Johns Hopkins University, 2014.

Cook, Nancy, and Chris Frates. "Thanks to AARP, Grandma's Got Influence." *National Journal*, October 1, 2011: 5.

Crotty, William, ed. *Polarized Politics: The Impact of Divisiveness in the U.S. Political System*. Boulder, CO: Lynne Rienner, 2014.

Crystal, Stephen, and Dennis Shea. "Cumulative Advantage, Cumulative Disadvantage, and Inequality among Elderly People." *Gerontologist* 30, no. 4 (1990): 437–443.

Cutler, Neal E. "Demographic, Social-Psychological, and Political Factors in the Politics of Aging: A Foundation for Research in Political Gerontology." *American Political Science Review* 71, no. 3 (1977): 1011–1025.

Cutler, Neal E. "Political Characteristics of Elderly Cohorts in the Twenty-First Century." In *Aging: Social Change*, edited by Sarah B. Kiesler, James N. Morgan and Valerie Kincaid Oppenheimer. New York: Academic Press, 1981.

Dahl, Robert A. "The Concept of Power." *Behavioral Science* 2, no. 3 (1957): 201–215.

Dahl, Robert A. *Who Governs?* New Haven: Yale University Press, 1961.

Davis, Julie Hirschfeld. "The Influence Game: Labor and Business, Joined in Health Care Cause, Now at Odds on Specifics." *Chicago Tribune*, February 16, 2009. http://www.chicagotribune.com/news/nationworld/sms-ap-health-care-strange-bedfellows,0,6877237.story.

Day, Christine L. "Aging Policy: A Partisan Paradox." In *Polarized Politics: The Impact of Divisiveness in the U.S. Political System*, edited by William Crotty, 285–307. Boulder, CO: Lynne Rienner, 2014.

Day, Christine L. "Old-Age Interest Groups in the 1990s: Coalition, Competition, and Strategy." In *New Directions in Old-Age Policies*, edited by Janie S. Steckenrider and Tonya M. Parrott, 131–150. Albany: State University of New York Press, 1998.

Day, Christine L. "Older Americans' Attitudes Toward the Medicare Catastrophic Coverage Act of 1988." *Journal of Politics* 55, no. 1 (1993): 167–177.

Day, Christine L. *What Older Americans Think: Interest Groups and Aging Policy.* Princeton, NJ: Princeton University Press, 1990.

Delli Carpini, Michael X. "Baby Boomers." *The Forum* 12, no. 3 (2014): 417–445.

Demkovich, Linda E. "There's a New Kick in the Step of the Senior Citizen Lobbies." *National Journal*, October 2, 1976: 1382–1389.

DeNavas-Watt, Carmen, and Bernadette D. Proctor. *Income and Poverty in the United States: 2014.* U.S. Census Bureau, Current Population Reports, P60–252, Washington, DC: U.S. Government Printing Office, 2015. https://www.census.gov/content/dam/Census/library/publications/2015/demo/p60-252.pdf.

Derthick, Martha. *Policymaking for Social Security.* Washington, DC: Brookings, 1979.

DeVoss, David. "Who Will Pay? Two Views on How—or Whether—America Can Afford a Rapidly Aging Population." *Los Angeles Times Magazine*, May 25, 1986. http://www.articles.latimes.com/1986-05-25/magazine/tm-7032_1_social-security-benefits.

Domhoff, G. William. *Who Rules America: The Triumph of the Corporate Rich.* 7th ed. New York: McGraw-Hill, 2013.

Dreyfuss, Barbara T. "The Seduction: The Shocking Story of How AARP Backed the Medicare Bill." *American Prospect* 15, no. 6 (2004): 18–23.

Dukhovnov, Denys, and Emilio Zagheni. "Who Takes Care of Whom in the United States? Time Transfers by Age and Sex." *Population and Development Review* 41, no. 2 (2015): 183–206.

Eastwood, Brian. "Top Health Insurance CEO Pay Exceeds $10 Million in 2014." *Fierce Healthcare*, April 10, 2015. http://www.fiercehealthcare.com/payer/top-health-insurance-ceo-pay-exceeds-10-million-2014.

Edelstein, Sara, Heather Hahn, Julia Isaacs, Ellen Steele, and C. Eugene Steuerle. *Kids' Share 2016: Federal Expenditures on Children through 2015 and Future Projections*. Washington, DC: Urban Institute, 2016. http://www.urban.org/research/publication/kids-share-2016federal-expenditures-children-through-2015-and-future-projections.

Edmondson, Brad. "A Comeback Story in New Orleans." *AARP Bulletin*, August 23, 2010. http://www.aarp.org/home-garden/livable-communities/info-08-2010/a_comeback_in_new_orleans.html.

Edsall, Thomas B. "High Drug Prices Return as Issue That Stirs Voters." *Washington Post*, October 15, 2002. https://www.washingtonpost.com/archive/politics/2002/10/15/high-drug-prices-return-as-issue-that-stirs-voters/d528c46b-1a89-4da7-8d08-aeb6d94ef002/.

Eggen, Dan. "AARP Could Benefit from the Health Insurance Reforms It Advocates." *Washington Post*, October 27, 2009. http://www.washingtonpost.com/wp-dyn/content/article/2009/10/26/AR2009102603392.html.

Estes, Carroll L. *The Aging Enterprise*. San Francisco: Jossey-Bass, 1979.

Eulau, Heinz. "The Legislator as Representative: Representational Roles." In *The Legislative System: Explorations in Legislative Behavior*, edited by John C. Wahlke, Heinz Eulau, William Buchanan and LeRoy C. Ferguson. New York: John Wiley, 1962.

Evans, Linda, and John B. Williamson. "Social Control of the Elderly." In *Readings in the Political Economy of Aging*, edited by Meredith Minkler and Carroll L. Estes, 47–72. Farmingdale: Baywood, 1984.

Fairlie, Henry. "Talkin' 'Bout My Generation." *New Republic*, March 28, 1988: 19–22.

Fineman, Howard. "Can Social Security Be Cut?" *Newsweek*, May 13, 1985.

Fischer, David Hackett. "The Politics of Aging in America: A Short History." *Journal of the Institute for Socioeconomic Studies* 4 (1979): 51–66.

Flanagan, Lawrence P. "Letter from the President and CEO." *2015 AARP Services Annual Report*. 2016. http://www.aarp.org/content/dam/aarp/about_aarp/about_us/2016/services-2015-annual-report-aarp.pdf.

Fletcher, Michael A., and Zachary A. Goldfarb. "AARP Uses Its Power to Oppose Social Security, Medicare Benefit Cuts for Retirees." *Washington Post*, November 17, 2012. https://www.washingtonpost.com/business/economy/aarp-uses-its-power-to-oppose-social-security-medicare-benefit-cuts-for-retirees/2012/11/17/affb5874-2aa6-11e2-bab2-eda299503684_story.html?utm_term=.d3340ebabcf6.

Fowler, Linda L., and Ronald G. Shaiko. "The Graying of the Constituency: Active Seniors in Congressional District Politics." *Annual Meeting of the American Political Science Association*. Chicago, 1987.

Fox-Grage, Wendy, and Kathleen Ujvari. "The Older Americans Act." *Insight on the Issues*, May 2014.

Fraley, Colette. "Lobbying: Simpson Zeroes In on AARP and Its Tax Exemption." *Congressional Quarterly Weekly Report*, June 17, 1995: 1749.

Franz, Michael. "Attack of the Super PACs? Interest Groups in the 2012 Elections." In *New Directions in Interest Group Politics*, edited by Matt Grossmann, 144–164. New York: Routledge, 2014.

Freudenheim, Milt. "Opponents of Medicare Bill Say AARP Has Conflicts." *New York Times*, November 21, 2003. http://www.nytimes.com/2003/11/21/business/opponents-of-medicare-bill-say-aarp-has-conflicts.html.

Freudenheim, Milt. "Prudential, Outbid, Loses $4 Billion of A.A.R.P. Work." *New York Times*, September 12, 1996. http://www.nytimes.com/1996/09/12/business/prudential-outbid-loses-4-billion-of-aarp-work.html.

Fried, Carla. "Did AARP Really Sell Out Seniors on Social Security?" *CBS News*, June 21, 2011. http://www.cbsnews.com/news/did-aarp-really-sell-out-seniors-on-social-security/.

Gais, Thomas, Mark A. Peterson, and Jack L. Walker. "Interest Groups, Iron Triangles, and Representative Institutions in American National Government." *British Journal of Political Science* 14 (1984): 161–185.

Geist, Bill. *The Big Five-Oh! Facing, Fearing, and Fighting Fifty.* New York: William Morrow, 1997.

Gelman, Andrew, Daniel Lee, and Yair Ghitza. "Public Opinion on Health Care Reform." *The Forum* 8, no. 1 (2010): article 8. http://www.bepress.com/forum/vol8/iss1/art8.

Gibbs, Nancy. "Living: Grays on the Go." *Time*, February 22, 1988, 66–75.

Gilens, Martin. *Affluence and Influence: Economic Inequality and Political Power in America.* Princeton, NJ: Princeton University Press, 2012.

Gilens, Martin, and Benjamin I. Page. "Testing Theories of American Politics: Elites, Interest Groups, and Average Citizens." *Perspectives on Politics* 12, no. 3 (2014): 564–581.

Gleckman, Howard. "Trump's Budget Framework Points to Big Cuts in Programs for Seniors." *Forbes*, March 17, 2017. https://www.forbes.com/sites/howardgleckman/2017/03/17/trumps-budget-framework-points-to-big-cuts-in-programs-for-seniors/#7513eb2212c9.

Gleckman, Howard, Mike McNamee, and David Henry. "By Raising Its Voice, AARP Raises Questions." *Bloomberg Businessweek*, March 13, 2005. https://www.bloomberg.com/news/articles/2005-03-13/by-raising-its-voice-aarp-raises-questions.

Godwin, Ken, Scott H. Ainsworth, and Erik Godwin. *Lobbying and Policymaking: The Public Pursuit of Private Interests.* Washington, DC: CQ Press, 2012.

Godwin, R. Kenneth. *The Direct Marketing of Politics: $1 Billion of Influence.* Chatham, NJ: Chatham House, 1988.

Godwin, R. Kenneth, and Robert Cameron Mitchell. "The Implications of Direct Mail for Political Organizations." *Social Science Quarterly* 65, no. 3 (1984): 829–845.

Gold, Matea. "Koch-Backed Political Network, Built to Shield Donors, Raised $400 Million in 2012 Elections." *Washington Post*, January 4, 2014. https://www.washingtonpost.com/politics/koch-backed-political-network-built-to-shield-donors-raised-400-million-in-2012-elections/2014/01/05/9e7cfd9a-719b-11e3-9389-09ef9944065e_story.html.

Goodwin, Alec, and Emma Baccellieri. "Number of Registered Lobbyists Plunges as Spending Declines Yet Again." *Center for Responsive Politics, opensecrets.org.* August 9, 2016. https://www.opensecrets.org/news/2016/08/number-of-registered-lobbyists-plunges-as-spending-declines-yet-again/.

Gough, Paul. "AARP to Combine Modern Maturity, My Generation." *Online Media Daily*, August 28, 2002. http://www.mediapost.com/publications/article/3337/aarp-to-combine-modern-maturity-my-generation.html.

Goyer, Amy. *Juggling Work and Caregiving.* Washington, DC: AARP and the American Bar Association, 2013.

Greenhouse, Stephen. "Passing the Buck from One Generation to the Next." *New York Times*, August 17, 1986. http://www.nytimes.com/1986/08/17/weekinreview/passing-the-buck-from-one-generation-to-the-next.html.

Grogan, Colleen M., and Christina M. Andrews. "The Politics of Aging within Medicaid." In *The New Politics of Old Age Policy*, edited by Robert B. Hudson, 275–306. Baltimore: Johns Hopkins University Press, 2010.

Grossmann, Matt. *The Not-So-Special Interests: Interest Groups, Public Representation, and American Governance.* Stanford: Stanford University Press, 2012.

Grossmann, Matt, and David Hopkins. *Asymmetric Politics: Ideological Republicans and Group Interest Democrats.* New York: Oxford University Press, 2016.

Gunther, Jilenne. *AARP's BankSafe Initiative: A Comprehensive Approach to Better Serving and Protecting Consumers.* Washington, DC: AARP Public Policy Institute, 2016. http://www.aarp.org/content/dam/aarp/ppi/2016-02/AARP-Banksafe-Initiatiive-Serving-Protecting-Communities.pdf.

Haas, Lawrence. "Fiscal Catastrophe." *National Journal*, October 7, 1989: 2453–2456.

Hacker, Jacob S. "Out of Balance: Medicare, Interest Groups, and American Politics." *Generations*, Summer 2015.

Hacker, Jacob S. *The Great Risk Shift: The New Economic Insecurity and the Decline of the American Dream.* New York: Oxford University Press, 2006.

Hall, Richard L., and Alan V. Deardorff. "Lobbying as Legislative Subsidy." *American Political Science Review* 100, no. 1 (2006): 69–84.

Hall, Richard L., and Frank W. Wayman. "Buying Time: Moneyed Interests and the Mobilization of Bias in Congressional Committees." *American Political Science Review* 84, no. 3 (1990): 797–820.

The Harris Poll. "American Red Cross, Nature Conservancy, Consumers Union and AARP Are Organizations inside the Beltway Most Trusted by Public." January 17, 2012. http://www.theharrispoll.com/search?keywords=most+trusted+beltway.

Harrison, David. "Advocates for Seniors Fight Potential CPI Shift." *CQ Today Online News*, October 21, 2011. http://public.cq.com/docs/news/news-000003967448.html.

Hasan, Shafaq. "AARP Bars Right-to-Die Group from Annual Exposition in San Diego." *Nonprofit Quarterly*, September 4, 2014. https://nonprofitquarterly.org/2014/09/04/aarp-bars-right-to-die-group-from-annual-exposition-in-san-diego/.

Hays, R. Allen. *Who Speaks for the Poor? National Interest Groups and Social Policy*. New York: Routledge, 2001.

Heaney, Michael T. "Identity Crisis: How Interest Groups Struggle to Define Themselves in Washington." In *Interest Group Politics*, edited by Allan J. Cigler and Burdett A. Loomis, 279–300. Washington, DC: CQ Press, 2006.

Heclo, Hugh. "Issue Networks and the Executive Establishment." In *The New American Political System*, edited by Anthony King, 87–124. Washington, DC: American Enterprise Institute, 1978.

Hellmann, Jessie. "AARP Launches Ad Campaign Urging Republicans to 'Protect' Medicare." *The Hill*, January 20, 2017. http://thehill.com/policy/healthcare/316799-aarp-launches-ad-campaign-urging-republicans-to-protect-medicare.

Herrnson, Paul S. *Congressional Elections: Campaigning at Home and in Washington*. 7th ed. Washington, DC: CQ Press, 2015.

Hertel-Fernandez, Alexander. "Who Passes Business's 'Model Bills'? Policy Capacity and Corporate Influence in U.S. State Politics." *Perspectives on Politics* 12, no. 3 (2014): 582–602.

Himelfarb, Richard. *Catastrophic Politics: The Rise and Fall of the Medicare Catastrophic Coverage Act of 1988*. University Park, PA: Pennsylvania State University Press, 1995.

Hitzik, Michael. "A Shamed AARP Withdraws from Right-wing Lobbying Organization." *Los Angeles Times*, August 5, 2016. http://www.latimes.com/business/hiltzik/la-fi-hiltzik-aarp-alec-20160805-snap-story.html.

Hitzik, Michael. "The GOP Unveils a 'Permanent Save' for Social Security—with Massive Benefit Cuts." *Los Angeles Times*, December 9, 2016. http://www.latimes.com/business/hiltzik/la-fi-hiltzik-social-security-gop-20161209-story.html.

Ho, Catherine. "Lobbying Registrations Are Down, but the Influence Industry Is Flourishing." *Washington Post*, September 12, 2016. https://www.washingtonpost.com/news/powerpost/wp/2016/09/12/lobbying-registrations-are-down-but-the-influence-industry-is-flourishing/?utm_term=.439a32fb7ce4.

Hochschild, Arlie Russell. "Disengagement Theory: A Critique and Proposal." *American Sociological Review* 40, no. 5 (1975): 553–569.

Holan, Angie Drobnic. "AARP Profits from Insurance Sales; GOP Calls It a Health Reform Conflict." *PolitiFact*, September 29, 2009. http://www

.politifact.com/truth-o-meter/statements/2009/sep/29/ginny-brown-waite/aarp-insurance-health-reform-conflict/.

Holan, Angie Drobnic. "PolitiFact's Life of the Year: 'Death Panels'." *PolitiFact*, December 18, 2009. http://www.politifact.com/truth-o-meter/article/2009/dec/18/politifact-lie-year-death-panels/.

Holan, Angie Drobnic. "The PolitiFact Guide to Medicare Attack Lines." *PolitiFact*, May 6, 2012. http://www.politifact.com/truth-o-meter/article/2012/may/06/politifact-guide-medicare-attack-lines/.

Holmes, Steven A. "The World According to AARP." *New York Times*, March 21, 2001. http://www.nytimes.com/2001/03/21/jobs/the-world-according-to-aarp.html.

Holtzman, Abraham. "Analysis of Old Age Politics in the United States." *Journal of Gerontology* 9, no. 1 (1954): 56–66.

Holtzman, Abraham. *The Townsend Movement: A Political Study.* New York: Bookman, 1963.

Holyoke, Thomas T. *Competitive Interests: Competition and Compromise in American Interest Group Politics.* Washington, DC: Georgetown University Press, 2011.

Hooyman, Nancy R., and Judith G. Gonyea. "A Feminist Model of Family Care: Practice and Policy Directions." *Journal of Women and Aging* 11, no. 2–3 (1999): 149–169.

Hornblower, Margot. "AARP's Gray Power!" *Time*, January 4, 1988, 36–37.

Howard, Christopher. *The Welfare State Nobody Knows: Debunking Myths about U.S. Social Policy.* Princeton, NJ: Princeton University Press, 2008.

Hudson, Robert B. "The 'Graying' of the Federal Budget and Its Consequences for Old Age Policy." *Gerontologist* 18, no. 4 (1978): 428–440.

Hudson, Robert B., and Judith G. Gonyea. "Baby Boomers and the Shifting Political Construction of Old Age." *Gerontologist* 52, no. 2 (2012): 272–282.

Hudson, Robert B., and Judith G. Gonyea. "The Shifting Political Construction of Older Americans as a Target Population." In *The New Politics of Old Age Policy*, edited by Robert B. Hudson, 99–116. Baltimore: Johns Hopkins University Press, 2014.

Iglehart, John K. "The New Medicare Prescription-Drug Benefit—A Pure Power Play." *New England Journal of Medicine* 350, no. 8 (2004): 826–833.

Ingraham, Christopher. "Meals on Wheels Is 'Not Showing Any Results' Only if You Ignore All These Results." *Washington Post*, March 16, 2017. https://www.washingtonpost.com/news/wonk/wp/2017/03/16/trump-budget-chief-says-meals-on-wheels-is-not-showing-any-results-hes-wrong/?utm_term=.d323dce54f16.

Insight News. "Jo Ann Jenkins, Age Disruptor." November 7, 2016. http://www.insightnews.com/2016/11/07/jo-ann-jenkins-age-disruptor/.

Isaacs, Julia, Sara Edelstein, Heather Hahn, Ellen Steele, and C. Eugene Steuerle. *Kids' Share 2015: Report on Federal Expenditures on Children in 2014 and Future Projections.* Washington, DC: Urban Institute, 2015. http://www

.urban.org/sites/default/files/alfresco/publication-pdfs/2000422-Kids-Share-2015-Report-on-Federal-Expenditures-on-Children-Through-2014.pdf.

Jacobs, Lawrence R., and Theda Skocpol. *Health Care Reform and American Politics: What Every American Needs to Know.* New York: Oxford University Press, 2016.

Jain World. "Elephant and the Blind Men." *Jainism Global Resource Center.* http://www.jainworld.com/education/stories25/asp (accessed June 25, 2016).

Jalonick, Mary Clare. "Sam Johnson, Key Republican on House Ways and Means Subcommittee, Looks to Overhaul Social Security." *Washington Times*, December 13, 2016. http://www.washingtontimes.com/news/2016/dec/13/republican-lawmaker-floats-social-security-overhaul/.

Jenkins, Jo Ann. "After the Storm, We All Need to Get to Work." *AARP Bulletin*, December 2016, 38.

Jenkins, Jo Ann. *Disrupt Aging: A Bold New Path to Living Your Best Life at Every Age.* New York: Public Affairs, 2016.

Jenkins, Jo Ann. "Own Your Age—and Resist Ageism." *AARP blog.* May 14, 2015. http://blog.aarp.org/2015/05/14/own-your-age-and-fight-back-against-ageism/.

Jenkins, Jo Ann. "Walking the Walk: Renewal in New Orleans Ten Years After Katrina." *AARP blog.* August 25, 2015. http://blog.aarp.org/2015/08/25/walking-the-walk-renewal-in-new-orleans-10-years-after-katrina/.

Johannes, Laura. "AARP Faces Competition from Conservative Leaning Groups." *Wall Street Journal*, March 30, 2014. http://www.wsj.com/articles/SB10001424052702304704504579433435918919\48.

Johnston, David Cay. "A.A.R.P. Sets Up a Taxable Subsidiary." *New York Times*, July 15, 1999. http://www.nytimes.com/1999/07/15/business/aarp-sets-up-a-taxable-subsidiary.html.

Johnstone, Anthony. "Politics and the Public Benefit Corporation." *Columbia University Academic Commons.* 2013. http://dx.doi.org/10.7916/D8XD0ZNN.

Karpf, David. "How Will the Internet Change American Interest Groups?" In *New Directions in Interest Group Politics*, edited by Matt Grossmann, 122–143. New York: Routledge, 2014.

Karpf, David. *The MoveOn Effect: The Unexpected Transformation of American Political Advocacy.* New York: Oxford University Press, 2012.

Katz, Michael B. *The Undeserving Poor: America's Enduring Confrontation with Poverty.* 2nd. New York: Oxford University Press, 2013.

Kessler, Glenn. "Fact Checker: The Strange Tale of How a False 2009 Obamacare Claim Ended Up in a Viral 2017 Video." *Washington Post*, February 14, 2017. https://www.washingtonpost.com/news/fact-checker/wp/2017/02/14/the-strange-tale-of-how-a-false-2009-obamacare-claim-ended-up-in-a-viral-2017-video/?utm_term=.0c7084054bec.

Kessler, Glenn. "Paul Ryan's False Claim That 'Because of Obamacare, Medicare Is Going Broke.'" *Washington Post*, November 14, 2016. https://www

.washingtonpost.com/news/fact-checker/wp/2016/11/14/paul-ryans-false-claim-that-because-of-obamacare-medicare-is-going-broke/.

Khan, Naureen. "Is the AARP the '900-Pound Invisible Gorilla' in the Room?" *Aljazeera America*, March 22, 2014. http://alj.am/1hSz1xt.

Kingson, Eric R., Barbara A. Hirshorn, and John M. Cornman. *The Ties That Bind: The Interdependence of Generations.* Washington, DC: Seven Lockis Press, 1986.

Korte, Gregory. "Here's the Truth about Meals on Wheels in Trump's Budget." *USA Today*, March 18, 2017. http://www.usatoday.com/story/news/politics/2017/03/18/meal-on-wheels-trump-budget-proposal-cuts/99308928/.

Kosterlitz, Julie. "Test of Strength." *National Journal*, October 24, 1987: 2652–2657.

Kosterlitz, Julie. "The World According to AARP." *National Journal*, March 10, 2007: 28–35.

Kotlikoff, Lawrence. *Generational Accounting: Knowing Who Pays, and When, for What We Spend.* New York: Free Press, 1992.

Kotlikoff, Lawrence J., and Scott Burns. *The Clash of Generations: Saving Ourselves, Our Kids, and Our Economy.* Cambridge: MIT Press, 2014.

Krauss, Clifford. "Clinton's Health Plan: Interest Groups, Lobbyists of Every Stripe Turning to the Grass Roots." *New York Times*, September 24, 1993. http://www.nytimes.com/1993/09/24/us/clinton-s-health-plan-interest-groups-lobbyists-every-stripe-turning-grass-roots.html?pagewanted=all.

Kroll-Smith, Steve, Vern Baxter, and Pam Jenkins. *Left to Chance: Hurricane Katrina and the Story of Two New Orleans Neighborhoods.* Austin: University of Texas Press, 2015.

Kunkle, Fredrick. "Mid-Life Crisis Becomes 'Life Reimagined' with AARP Program." *Washington Post*, March 16, 2015. https://www.washingtonpost.com/news/local/wp/2015/03/16/mid-life-crisis-becomes-life-reimagined-with-aarp-program/?utm_term=.60740c2a6e1e.

Kuttner, Robert. "Why Social Security Beats All Rivals—And the Case for Expanding It." *Huffington Post*, July 26, 2015. http://huffingtonpost.com/robert-kuttner/why-social-security-beats-all-rivals_b_7876090.html.

LaCapria, Kim. "Is the AARP Funding ALEC?" *Snopes.com.* August 4, 2016. http://www.snopes.com/2016/08/04/is-the-aarp-funding-alec/.

LaPira, Tim. "Lobbying in the Shadows: How Private Interests Hide from Public Scrutiny, and Why That Matters." In *Interest Group Politics*, edited by Allan J. Cigler, Burdett A. Loomis and Anthony Nownes, 224–248. Washington, DC: CQ Press, 2015.

"Largest U.S. Magazines by Circulation." *Statistic Brain.* http://www.statisticbrain.com/largest-u-s-magazines-by-circulation (accessed April 2, 2017).

Laursen, Eric. *The People's Pension: The Struggle to Defend Social Security Since Reagan.* Oakland, CA: AK Press, 2012.

Leach, Michelle. "10 Most Powerful Special Interest Groups in America." *Listosaur.com.* July 2, 2014. http://listosaur.com/politics/1-powerful-special-interest-groups-america/.

Lessig, Lawrence. *Republic, Lost: How Money Corrupts Congress—and a Plan to Stop It.* New York: Twelve, 2011.

Light, Paul C. *Artful Work: The Politics of Social Security Reform.* New York: Random House, 1985.

Light, Paul C. *Baby Boomers.* New York: W. W. Norton, 1990.

Little, Lyneka. "AARP Wobbles on Social Security Benefits." *ABC News*, June 17, 2011. http://abcnews.go.com/Business/aarp-denies-social-security-cuts/story?id=13859214.

Lohmann, Roger A. "An Interview: Horace Deets of AARP." *Nonprofit Management and Leadership* 12, no. 1 (2001): 87–94.

Longman, Phillip. "Justice between Generations." *Atlantic Monthly*, June 1985: 73–91.

Longman, Phillip. *Born to Pay: The New Politics of Aging in America.* Boston: Houghton-Mifflin, 1987.

Loomis, Burdett A., and Allan J. Cigler. "Introduction: The Changing Nature of Interest Group Politics." In *Interest Group Politics*, 1–36. Washington, DC: CQ Press, 2007.

Lucas, Fred. "AARP: Advocacy Group or Crony Capitalists?" *Capital Research Center.* 2012. https://capitalresearch.org/article/aarp-advocacy-group-or-crony-capitalists/.

Lynch, Frederick R. "How AARP Can Get Its Groove Back." *New York Times*, June 23, 2011. http://www.nytimes.com/2011/06/24/opinion/24lynch.html?_r=2.

Lynch, Frederick R. *One Nation under AARP: The Fight over Medicare, Social Security, and America's Future.* Berkeley: University of California Press, 2011.

Mabeus, Courtney. "The Battle Ahead: The Lobbying over Social Security Heats Up." *Money in Politics Alert*, January 25, 2005. http://www.capitaleye.org/inside.asp?ID=153.

MacManus, Susan A. *Young v. Old: Generational Combat in the 21st Century.* Boulder, CO: Westview, 1996.

Madison, James, Alexander Hamilton, and John Jay. *The Federalist Papers.* Auckland, New Zealand: Floating Press, 2011 [1787].

Mann, Thomas E., and Norman J. Ornstein. *It's Even Worse Than It Looks: How the American Constitutional System Collided with the New Politics of Extremism.* 2nd ed. New York: Basic Books, 2016.

Mann, Thomas E., and Raymond E. Wolfinger. "Candidates and Parties in Congressional Elections." *American Political Science Review* 74, no. 3 (1980): 617–632.

Marans, Daniel. "AARP to Withdraw from Controversial Conservative Group amid Rising Pressure." *Huffington Post*, August 5, 2016. http://www.huffingtonpost.com/entry/aarp-to-withdraw-from-alec_us_57a4c72de4b03ba6801233e5.

Marans, Daniel. "Nation's Largest Seniors Group Is Using Conservative Scare Tactics on Social Security." *Huffington Post*, October 16, 2016. http://

www.huffingtonpost.com/entry/aarp-conservative-social-security_us_57fbe10be4b068ecb5e0d0f3.

Marans, Daniel. "Why AARP's New Social Security Campaign Is Upsetting Progressives." *Huffington Post*, February 16, 2016. http://www.huffingtonpost.com/entry/aarp-social-security-campaign_us_56c3854fe4b0c3c55052e81e.

Marans, Daniel. "Why AARP's New Social Security Campaign Is Upsetting Progressives." *Huffington Post*, February 16, 2016. http://www.huffingtonpost.com/entry/aarp-social-security-campaign_us_56c3854fe4b0c3c55052e81e.

Marans, Daniel, Ryan Grim, and Arthur Delaney. "Barack Obama Once Proposed Cutting Social Security. Here's What Changed His Mind." *Huffington Post*, June 3, 2016. http://www.huffingtonpost.com/entry/barack-obama-grand-bargain-social-security-expansion_us_5751f92de4b0eb20fa0e0142.

Markon, Jerry. "AARP Lobbies against Cuts That May Hurt Its Bottom Line." *Washington Post*, December 4, 2012. https://www.washingtonpost.com/politics/aarp-lobbies-against-medicare-changes-that-could-hurt-its-bottom-line/2012/12/03/aa3e509e-3a8c-11e2-b01f-5f55b193f58f_story.html?utm_term=.37c678e983dd.

Marmor, Theodore R. *The Politics of Medicare*. 2nd ed. New York: Aldine deGruyter, 2000.

Marmor, Theodore R., Fay Lomax Cook, and Stephen Scher. "Social Security and the Politics of Generational Conflict." In *The Generational Equity Debate*, edited by John B. Williamson and Diane M. Watts-Roy, 185–203. New York: Columbia University Press, 1999.

Martin, Roger L., and Sally R. Osberg. "Two Keys to Sustainable Social Enterprise." *Harvard Business Review* 93, no. 5 (2015): 86–94.

McCarthy, Meaghan. "The GOP's Senior Moment." *National Journal*, September 29, 2012: 41.

McCarty, Nolan, Keith T. Poole, and Howard Rosenthal. *Polarized America: The Dance of Ideology and Unequal Riches*. 2nd ed. Cambridge: MIT Press, 2016.

McFarland, Andrew S. *Neopluralism: The Evolution of Political Process Theory*. Lawrence, KA: University of Kansas Press, 2004.

Meckler, Laura. "Key Seniors Association Pivots on Benefit Cut." *Wall Street Journal*, June 17, 2011. http://www.wsj.com/articles/SB10001424052702304186404576389760955403414.

Meckler, Laura. "Why John Rother, AARP's Policy Chief, Is Leaving." *Wall Street Journal*, September 8, 2011. http://blogs.wsj.com/washwire/2011/09/08/why-john-rother-aarps-policy-chief-is-leaving/.

Meyers, Jim. "Wall Street Journal: AARP Flips Position, Agrees to Social Security Cuts." *Newsmax*, June 17, 2011. http://www.newsmax.com/Newsfront/AARP-socialsecurity-cuts-benefits/2011/06/17/id/400411/.

Miller v. Davis. 464 F. Supp. 458 (United States District Court, District of Columbia, November 18, 1978).

Miller, Arthur H., Patricia Gurin, and Gerald Gurin. "Age Consciousness and Political Mobilization of Older Americans." *Gerontologist* 20 (1980): 691–700.

Minkler, Meredith, and Carroll L. Estes. *Critical Gerontology: Perspectives from Political and Moral Economy*. New York: Baywood, 1999.

Mintz, Morton. "Two Groups for Elderly May Lose Nonprofit Postal Status." *Washington Post*, January 3, 1979: 2A.

Mitchell, Alison. "Clinton Has $10 Million Wish for Birthday Bash." *New York Times*, August 19, 1996. http://www.nytimes.com/1996/08/19/us/clinton-has-10-million-wish-for-birthday-bash.html.

The Moment of Truth: Report of the National Commission on Fiscal Responsibility and Reform. Washington, DC: White House, 2010. http://www.washingtonpost.com/wp-srv/politics/documents/TheMomentofTruth.pdf.

Moon, Marilyn. *Medicare: A Policy Primer*. Washington, DC: The Urban Institute Press, 2006.

Morgan, Kimberly J. "The Medicare Challenge: Clients, Cost Controls, and Congress." In *The New Politics of Old Age Policy*, edited by Robert B. Hudson, 201–220. Baltimore: Johns Hopkins University Press, 2014.

Morgan, Kimberly J., and Andrea Louise Campbell. *The Delegated Welfare State: Medicare, Markets, and the Governance of Social Policy*. New York: Oxford University Press, 2011.

Morris, Charles R. *The AARP: America's Most Powerful Lobby and the Clash of Generations*. New York: Times Books, 1996.

Mukherjee, Sy. "These Three Powerful Groups Are Slamming the GOP's Obamacare Replacement Plan." *Fortune*, March 8, 2017. http://fortune.com/2017/03/08/gop-healthcare-plan-aarp-ama-aha/.

Murray, Peter. "The Secret of Scale." *Stanford Social Innovation Review*, Fall 2013. http://www.ssir.org/articles/entry/the_secret_of_scale.

Novelli, William. *Voices of Social Change: Selected Speeches of Bill Novelli*. Washington, DC: AARP, 2009.

Nyssens, Marthe. *Social Enterprise: At the Crossroads of Market, Public Policies and Civil Society*. New York: Routledge, 2006.

Oberlander, Jonathan. *The Political Life of Medicare*. Chicago: University of Chicago Press, 2003.

Ohlemacher, Stephen. "AARP in the Midst of Social Security Controversy." *Fort Wayne News-Sentinel*, June 18, 2011. www.news-sentinel.com/apps/pbcs.dll/article?AID=/SE/20110618/NEWS/106180343.

Ohlemacher, Stephen. "AARP Slammed for Not Fighting Social Security Cuts." *NBC News*, June 17, 2011. http://www.nbcnews.com/id/43445777/ns/politics/t/aarp-slammed-not-fighting-social-security-cuts/%20-%20.WD-mXtIrLcs#.WPuG6zdgncs.

Oliver, Thomas R., Philip R. Lee, and Helene L. Lipton. "A Political History of Medicare and Prescription Drug Coverage." *Milbank Quarterly* 82, no. 2 (2004): 283–354.

Olson, Laura Katz. *The Not-So-Golden Years.* New York: Rowman & Littlefield, 2003.

Olson, Mancur. *The Logic of Collective Action.* Cambridge, MA: Harvard University Press, 1965.

Overby, Peter. "Conflict of Interest for AARP in Health Bill Debate?" *Morning Edition, National Public Radio*, November 4, 2009. http://www.npr.org/templates/story/story.php?storyId=120069183.

Pace, Julie. "Obama Celebrates 50th Birthday at White House." *Seattle Times*, August 4, 2011. http://www.seattletimes.com/seattle-news/politics/obama-celebrates-50th-birthday-at-white-house/.

Pampel, Fred C. "Population Aging, Class Context, and Age Inequality in Public Spending." *American Journal of Sociology* 100, no. 1 (1994): 153–195.

Pear, Robert. "AARP, Eye on Drug Costs, Urges Change in New Law." *New York Times*, January 17, 2004: A12.

Pear, Robert. "In Ads, AARP Criticizes Plan on Privatizing." *New York Times*, December 30, 2004. www.nytimes.com/2004/12/30/politics/in-ads-aarp-criticizes-plan-on-privatizing.html.

Pear, Robert. "Rates Are Rising on Policies That Cover Gaps in Medicare." *New York Times*, December 20, 1995. http://www.nytimes.com/1995/12/20/us/rates-are-rising-on-policies-that-cover-gaps-in-medicare.html.

Pear, Robert. "Repeal of Health Law Faces a New Hurdle: Older Americans." *New York Times*, March 5, 2017. https://www.nytimes.com/2017/03/05/us/politics/health-care-law-obamacare-repeal-older-americans.html/.

Peirce, Neal R., and Peter C. Choharis. "The Elderly as a Political Force—26 Million Strong and Well Organized." *National Journal*, September 11, 1982: 1559–1562.

Peterson, Peter G. "The Morning After." *Atlantic Monthly*, October 1987: 44.

Peterson, Peter G. *Gray Dawn: How the Coming Age Wave Will Transform America—and the World.* New York: Times Books, 1999.

Peterson, Peter G. "How Will America Pay for the Retirement of the Baby Boom Generation?" In *The Generational Equity Debate*, edited by John B. Williamson and Diane M. Watts-Roy, 41–57. New York: Columbia University Press, 1999.

Peterson, Peter G. *Running on Empty: How the Democratic and Republican Parties Are Bankrupting Our Future and What Americans Can Do about It.* New York: Farrar, Straus and Giroux, 2004.

Peterson, Peter G. *Will America Grow Up before It Gets Old? How the Coming Social Security Crisis Threatens You, Your Family, and Your Country.* New York: Random House, 1996.

Pew Research Center for People and the Press. "The Generation Gap and the 2012 Election." November 3, 2011. www.people-press.org/2011/11/03/section-2-generations-and-the-2012-election.

Pew Research Center. "Partisanship and Political Animosity in 2016." *Pew Research Center.* June 22, 2016. http://www.people-press.org/2016/06/22/partisanship-and-political-animosity-in-2016/.

Pitkin, Hannah F. *The Concept of Representation*. Berkeley: University of California Press, 1967.

Plumb, Tierney. "AARP Loses 300,000 Members over Health Care Reform Debate." *Washington Business Journal*, April 8, 2011. http://www.bizjournals.com/washington/print-edition/2011/04/08/aarp-loses-300000-members-over-health.html.

Polivka, Larry, and Carroll L. Estes. "The Economic Meltdown and Old Age Politics." *Generations* 33, no. 3 (2009): 56–62.

Poo, Al-Jen, and Ariane Conrad. *The Age of Dignity: Preparing for the Elder Boom in a Changing America*. New York: New Press, 2015.

Powell, Lynda W. "The Influence of Campaign Contributions on Legislative Policy." *The Forum* 11, no. 3 (2013): 339–355.

Pratt, Henry J. *Gray Agendas: Interest Groups and Public Pensions in Canada, Britain, and the United States*. Ann Arbor: University of Michigan Press, 1993.

Pratt, Henry J. *The Gray Lobby*. Chicago: University of Chicago Press, 1976.

Preston, Samuel H. "Children and the Elderly in the United States." *Scientific American* 251, no. 6 (1984): 44–49.

Prisuta, Robert. "Enhancing Volunteerism among Aging Boomers." *Conference on Baby Boomers and Retirement: Impact on Civic Engagement*. Cambridge, MA, 2003. www.agingsociety.org/agingsociety/links/AARPboomers.pdf.

Putnam, Robert D. "Bowling Alone: America's Declining Social Capital." *Journal of Democracy* 6, no. 1 (1995): 65–78.

Putnam, Robert D. *Bowling Alone: The Collapse and Revival of American Community*. New York: Simon and Schuster, 2000.

Quadagno, Jill. "Generational Equity and the Politics of the Welfare State." *Politics and Society* 17, no. 3 (1989): 353–376.

Quadagno, Jill. "Social Security and the Myth of the Entitlement Crisis." In *The Generational Equity Debate*, edited by John B. Williamson and Diane M. Watts-Roy, 140–156. New York: Columbia University Press, 1999.

Quattrone, George A., and Amos Tversky. "Contrasting Rational and Psychological Analyses of Political Choice." *American Political Science Review*, 1988: 718–736.

Quinnipiac University Poll. "U.S. Voters Oppose GOP Health Plan 3–1." *Quinnipiac University*. March 23, 2017. https://poll.qu.edu/national/release-detail?ReleaseID=2443.

Rand, A. Barry. "Our Age of Possibilities." *AARP Bulletin*, July-August 2014: 38.

Rand, A. Barry. "Rebuilding the Middle Class: A Blueprint for the Future." *Vital Speeches of the Day* 79, no. 3 (2013): 72–76.

Reinhard, Susan C., Lynn Friss Feinberg, Rita Choula, and Ari Houser. "Valuing the Invaluable: 2015 Update." *Insight on the Issues*, 2015. http://www.aarp.org/content/dam/aarp/ppi/2015/valuing0the-invaluable-2015-update-new.pdf.

Rhodebeck, Laurie A. "The Politics of Greed? Political Preferences among the Elderly." *Journal of Politics* 55, no. 2 (1993): 342–364.

Robb, Bob. "Does AARP Still Want Your Guns?" *NRA American Rifleman*, April 10, 2013. https://www.americanrifleman.org/articles/2013/4/10/does-the-aarp-still-want-your-guns/.

Roe, Jason G. "From the Impoverished to the Entitled: The Experience and Meaning of Old Age in America since the 1950s." PhD dissertation, University of Kansas, 2016. https://kuscholarworks.ku.edu/bitstream/handle/1808/10438/Roe_ku_0099D_12090_DATA_1.pdf;sequence=1.

Rooney, Andy. *Sincerely, Andy Rooney*. New York: Public Affairs, 2001.

Rose, Max, and Frank R. Baumgartner. "Framing the Poor: Media Coverage and U.S. Poverty Policy, 1960–2008." *Policy Studies Journal* 41, no. 1 (2013): 22–53.

Roth, Bennett. "GOP Probe of AARP Could Ensnare Other Nonprofits." *Roll Call*, April 1, 2011. http://www.rollcall.com/news/gop_probe_of_aarp_could_ensnare_other_nonprofits-204534-1.html.

Rother, John. "Closing Remarks." In *Justice Across Generations: What Does It Mean?*, edited by Lee M. Cohen, 291–292. Washington, DC: Public Policy Institute, American Association of Retired Persons, 1993.

Rovner, Julie. "Catastrophic-Costs Conferees Irked by Lobbying Assault." *Congressional Quarterly Weekly Report*, March 26, 1988: 777.

Rovner, Julie. "Catastrophic-Insurance Law: Costs vs. Benefits." *Congressional Quarterly Weekly Report*, December 3, 1988: 3450–3452.

Rovner, Julie. "The Catastrophic-Costs Law: A Massive Miscalculation." *Congressional Quarterly Weekly Report*, October 14, 1989: 2712–2715.

Rubin, Jennifer. "If the GOP's Obamacare Alternative Fails, We Might See Real Reforms." *Washington Post*, March 8, 2017. https://www.washingtonpost.com/blogs/right-turn/wp/2017/03/08/if-the-gops-obamacare-alternative-fails-we-might-see-real-reforms/?utm_term=.f14fd7f98c4b.

Safire, William. "Language: Tracking the Source of the 'Third Rail' Warning." *International Herald Tribune*, February 18, 2007. http://www.nytimes.com/2007/02/18/opinion/18iht-edsafmon.4632394.html?_r=0.

Salant, Jonathan D., and Robert Marshall Wells. "Lobbies: AARP's Federal Funds Endangered." *Congressional Quarterly Weekly Report*, July 29, 1995: 2240.

Salisbury, Robert H. "An Exchange Theory of Interest Groups." *Midwest Journal of Political Science* 13 (1969): 1–32.

Salisbury, Robert H. "Interest Group Representation: The Dominance of Institutions." *American Political Science Review* 78 (1984): 64–76.

Samuelson, Robert J. "Benefit Programs for the Elderly—Off Limits to Federal Budget Cutters?" *National Journal*, October 3, 1981: 1757–1762.

Samuelson, Robert J. "Off Golden Pond." *National Review*, April 12, 1999: 44.

Samuelson, Robert J. "AARP's America Is a Mirage." *Washington Post*, November 16, 2005. http://www.washingtonpost.com/wp-dyn/content/article/2005/11/15/AR2005111501308.html.

Samuelson, Robert J. "It's the Welfare State, Stupid." *Washington Post*, November 11, 2012. https://www.washingtonpost.com/opinions/robert-samuelson-its-the-welfare-state-stupid/2012/11/11/e392868a-2ab0-11e2-bab2-eda299503684_story.html?utm_term=.797cdb90cd98.

Samuelson, Robert J. "Why Are We in This Debt Fix? It's the Elderly, Stupid." *Washington Post*, July 28, 2011. http://www.washingtonpost.com/opinions/why-are-we-in-this-debt-fix-its-the-elderly-stupid.

Sanjek, Roger. *Gray Panthers*. Philadelphia: University of Pennsylvania Press, 2009.

Schattschneider, E. E. *The Semi-Sovereign People: A Realist's View of Democracy in America*. New York: Holt, Rinehart, and Winston, 1960.

Schlozman, Kay Lehman, and John T. Tierney. *Organized Interests and American Democracy*. New York: Harper and Row, 1986.

Schlozman, Kay Lehman, and Philip Edward Jones. "How Membership Associations Change the Balance of Representation in Washington (and How They Don't)." In *New Directions in Interest Group Politics*, edited by Matt Grossmann, 22–43. New York: Routledge, 2014.

Schlozman, Kay Lehman, Sidney Verba, and Henry E. Brady. *The Unheavenly Chorus: Unequal Political Voice and the Broken Promise of American Democracy*. Princeton, NJ: Princeton University Press, 2012.

Schulz, James H., and Robert H. Binstock. *Aging Nation: The Economics and Politics of Growing Older in America*. Baltimore: Johns Hopkins University Press, 2006.

Schwartzman, Paul. "At 50, AARP Enters Its Golden Years; with Boomers on Board, Seniors Lobby Flexes Its Muscle." *Washington Post*, September 4, 2008. http://www.washingtonpost.com/wp-dyn/content/article/2008/09/03/AR2008090303785.html.

Schweber, Howard. "The Limits of Representation." *American Political Science Review* 110, no. 2 (2016): 382–396.

Serafini, Marilyn Werber. "AARP's New Direction." *National Journal*, January 5, 2002: 28–31.

Serafini, Marilyn Werber. "Senior Schism." *National Journal*, May 6, 1995: 1089–1093.

Shear, Jeff. "The Untouchables." *National Journal*, July 16, 1994: 1681–1685.

Shuler, Marsha. "Expand Bobby Jindal's Medicaid Privatization? John Bel Edwards Says Yes; David Vitter TBD." *The Advocate*, November 17, 2015. http://www.theadvocate.com/baton_rouge/news/politics/elections/article_bf03c460-9e69-52ab-80bb-ea5035996930.html.

Skocpol, Theda. *Diminished Democracy: From Membership to Management in American Civic Life*. Norman, OK: University of Oklahoma Press, 2013.

Skocpol, Theda. *The Missing Middle: Working Families and the Future of American Social Policy*. New York: W. W. Norton, 2000.

Smith, Lee. "The Tyranny of America's Old." *Fortune*, January 13, 1992: 68–72.

Smith, Wesley L. "AARP Excludes Suicide Pushers from Expo." *National Review*, September 6, 2014. http://www.nationalreview.com/human-exceptionalism/387294/aarp-exclude-suicide-pushers-expo-wesley-j-smith.

Social Security and Medicare Boards of Trustees. *Status of the Social Security and Medicare Programs: A Summary of the 2016 Annual Reports.* Washington, DC: Social Security Administration, 2016. https://www.ssa.gov/oact/TRSUM/index.html.

Soss, Joe, Richard C. Fording, and Sanford S. Schram. *Disciplining the Poor: Neoliberal Paternalism and the Persistent Power of Race.* Chicago: University of Chicago Press, 2011.

Starr, Paul. "What Happened to Health Care Reform?" *American Prospect*, Winter 1995: 20–31.

Starr, Paul. *Remedy and Reaction: The Peculiar American Struggle over Health Care Reform.* 2nd ed. New Haven, CT: Yale University Press, 2013.

Stoker, Laura. "Reflections on the Study of Generations in Politics." *The Forum* 12, no. 3 (2014): 377–396.

Stolberg, Sheryl Gay. "Ideas and Trends: An 800-Pound Gorilla Changes Partners over Medicare." *New York Times*, November 23, 2003. www.nytimes.com/2003/11/23/weekinreview/ideas-trends-an-800-pound-gorilla-changes-partners-over-medicare.html.

Stolberg, Sheryl Gay, and Milt Freudenheim. "A Final Push in Congress: AARP Support Came as Group Grew 'Younger'." *New York Times*, November 26, 2003. www.nytimes.com/2003/11/26/us/a-final-push-in-congress-the-endorsement-aarp-support-came-as-group-grew-younger.html.

Stonecash, Jeffrey M. "Changing American Political Parties." In *New Directions in American Political Parties*, edited by Jeffrey M. Stonecash, 3–10. New York: Routledge, 2010.

Stonecash, Jeffrey M., ed. *New Directions in American Political Parties.* New York: Routledge, 2010.

Strassel, Kimberley A. "The Love Song of AARP and Obama." *Wall Street Journal*, September 20, 2012. https://www.wsj.com/articles/SB10000872396390444165804578008413907642282.

Street, Debra. "Maintaining the Status Quo: The Impact of Old-Age Interest Groups on the Medicare Catastrophic Coverage Act of 1988." *Social Problems* 40, no. 4 (1993): 431–444.

Strolovich, Dara Z. *Affirmative Advocacy: Race, Class, and Gender in Interest Group Politics.* Chicago: University of Chicago Press, 2007.

Sundquist, James L. "For the Old, Health Care." In *Politics and Policy: The Eisenhower, Kennedy, and Johnson Years*, edited by James L. Sundquist. Washington, DC: Brookings, 1968.

Tanenbaum, Sandra J. "Work and Family, Round Two: The Political Construction of Elders' Working Daughters." *Presented at the Annual Meeting of the American Political Science Association.* San Francisco, 2015.

Taylor, A. J. P. *Bismarck: The Man and the Statesman.* New York: Vintage, 1967.

Taylor, Paul and Pew Research Center. *The Next America: Boomers, Millennials, and the Looming Generational Showdown.* New York: Public Affairs, 2016.

Tergesen, Anne. "Sure, It's from AARP. But Is It a Good Deal?" *Bloomberg Businessweek*, February 13, 2008.

Thomas, Kali S., and David Dosa. "More Than a Meal: Pilot Research Study." *Meals on Wheels America*. 2015. http://www.mealsonwheelsamerica.org/docs/default-source/News-Assets/mtam-full-report—march-2-2015.pdf?sfvrsn=6.

Thomas, Wayne. "What Is the Difference between a 501c3 & 501c4?" *LegalZoom*. info.legalzoom.com/difference-between-501c3-501c4-26450.html (accessed July 17, 2016).

Tierney, John. "Old Money, New Power." *New York Times Magazine*, October 23, 1988. www.nytimes.com/1988/10/23/magazine/old-money-new-power.html?pagewanted=all.

Tilove, Jonathan. "Seniors Group Says No to Demo Health Bills." *New Orleans Times Picayune*, November 17, 2009: A1, A6.

Tocqueville, Alexis de. *Democracy in America*. New York: Vintage Books, 1972 [1840].

Torres-Gil, Fernando M. "The Politics of Catastrophic and Long-Term Care Coverage." *Journal of Aging and Social Policy* 1, no. 1/2 (1989): 61–86.

Torrey, Barbara Boyle. "Guns vs. Canes: The Fiscal Implications of an Aging Population." *American Economic Review* 72, no. 2 (1982): 309–313.

Trainor, Charles. "AARP Conference Attendees Do a Little Learning, a Little Shopping." *Miami Herald*, May 15, 2015. www.miamiherald.com/news/local/community/miami-dade/article21118479.html.

Trebilcock, Bob. "Life Insurance and Annuities: Is AARP Looking Out for You?" *CBS Moneywatch*, October 9, 2009. http://www.cbsnews.com/news/life-insurance-and-annuities-is-aarp-looking-out-for-you/.

Truman, David B. *The Governmental Process*. 2nd ed. New York: Alfred A. Knopf, 1971.

U.S. Department of Health and Human Services, Administration for Children and Families, Office of Family Assistance. "TANF Caseload Data 2014." May 22, 2015. www.acf.hhs.gov/ofa/resource/caseload-data-2014.

U.S. House of Representatives, Committee on Ways and Means. "Behind the Veil: The AARP America Doesn't Know." Investigative report prepared by Representative Wally Berger and Representative Dave Reichert, Washington, DC, 2011. https://waysandmeans.house.gov/UploadedFiles/AARP_REPORT_FINAL_PDF_3_29_11.pdf.

U.S. Internal Revenue Service. "Types of Organizations Exempt under Section 501(c)(4)." https://www.irs.gov/charities-non-profits/other-non-profits/types-of-organizations-exempt-under-section-501-c-4 (accessed March 14, 2017).

U.S. Senate, Committee on Finance. "Business and Financial Practices of the AARP: Hearings before the Subcommittee on Social Security and Family Policy." 104th Congress, First Session, June 13–20, 1995. https://www.finance.senate.gov/imo/media/doc/Hrg104-109.pdf.

Unger, Mike. "AARP Is Redefining What Aging Means for Its 38 Million Members." *Smart CEO.* 2016. http://www.smartceo.com/aarp-redefining-aging-means-38-million-members/.

Vaida, Bara. "AARP's Big Bet." *National Journal*, March 13, 2004: 796–802.

Vaida, Bara. "AARP's Chief: Giving Back." *National Journal*, July 31, 2010: 43–44.

Van Atta, Dale. "This Isn't the Old AARP." *Los Angeles Times*, November 4, 2003. http://articles.latimes.com/print/2003/nov/24/opinion/oe-vanatta24.

Van Atta, Dale. *Trust Betrayed: Inside the AARP.* Washington, DC: Regnery, 1998.

Van Tassel, David Dirck, and Jimmy Elaine Wilkinson Meyer. *U.S. Aging Policy Interest Groups: Institutional Profiles.* Westport, CT: Greenwood, 1982.

Viner, Brian. "The Man Who Rejected the Beatles." *The Independent*, February 12, 2012. http://www.independent.co.uk/arts-entertainment/music/news/the-man-who-rejected-the-beatles-6782008.html.

Walker, Craig. "Ethel Andrus: How One Woman Changed America." *A talk given to the Ojai Valley Museum.* May 1, 2011. www.ojaihistory.com/ethel-percy-andrus-how-one-woman-changed-america/.

Walker, Craig, and Bret Bradigan. "The Age of Reformation: Dr. Ethel Percy Andrus and the Founding of the AARP." *Ojai History*, Winter 2011–2012: 120–125.

Walker, Jack L. *Mobilizing Interest Groups in America: Patrons, Professions, and Social Movements.* Ann Arbor: University of Michigan Press, 1991.

Walker, Jack L. "The Origins and Maintenance of Interest Groups in America." *American Political Science Review* 77, no. 2 (1983): 390–406.

Wall Street Journal. "Ryan at the AARP." September 26, 2012. http://www.wsj.com/articles/SB10000872396390444813104578014243421799324.

Ware, J. Gabriel. "Why AARP Is Backing a New Lobbying Group for Millennials." *Yes! Magazine*, April 20, 2017. http://www.yesmagazine.org/people-power/why-aarp-is-backing-a-new-lobbying-group-for-millennials-20170420.

Wasik, John. "How GOP, Trump Will Take Backdoor Route to Slash Social Security, Medicare." *Forbes*, January 30, 2017. https://www.forbes.com/sites/johnwasik/2017/01/30/how-gop-trump-will-take-backdoor-route-to-slash-social-security-medicare/#f4750a568ad1.

Wasson, Erik. "AARP Says Some Social Security Cuts Could Be Acceptable." *The Hill*, June 17, 2011. http://thehill.com/policy/healthcare/167125-aarp-says-some-social-security-cuts-acceptable.

Watkins, Eli. "AARP Comes Out against House GOP Health Care Bill." *CNN.com*, March 8, 2017. https://www.google.com/#q=eli+watkins+cnn+aarp+comes+out+against+house+gop&*.

Weaver, R. Kent. *Ending Welfare as We Know It.* Washington, DC: Brookings, 2000.

Weber, Katherine. "American Family Association Warns Christian Seniors Against Joining AARP." *Christian Post*, May 17, 2013. http://www.christianpost.com/news/american-family-association-warns-christian-seniors-against-joining-aarp-96139/.

Webster, Richard A. "$3.4M Hollygrove Senior Center Opens." *New Orleans Times-Picayune*, October 16, 2015. http://www.nola.com/politics/index.ssf/2015/10/34m_hollygrove_senior_center_o.html.

White, Joseph. *False Alarm: Why the Greatest Threat to Social Security and Medicare Is the Campaign to "Save" Them.* Baltimore: Johns Hopkins University Press, 2001.

Wiener, Joshua M., Carroll L. Estes, Susan M. Goldenson, and Sheryl C. Goldberg. "What Happened to Long-Term Care in the Health Reform Debate of 1993–1994? Lessons for the Future." *Milbank Quarterly* 79, no. 2 (2001): 207–252.

Williamson, John B., and Diane M. Watts-Roy. "Aging Boomers, Generational Equity, and the Framing of the Debate over Social Security." In *Boomer Bust? Economic and Political Issues of the Graying Society*, edited by Robert B. Hudson, 153–172. Westport, CT: Praeger, 2008.

Williamson, John B., and Diane M. Watts-Roy. "Framing the Generational Equity Debate." In *The Generational Equity Debate*, edited by John B. Williamson, Diane M. Watts-Roy and Eric R. Kingson, 3–38. New York: Columbia University Press, 1999.

Williamson, John B., and Diane M. Watts-Roy. "Introduction." In *The Generational Equity Debate*, edited by John B. Williamson and Diane M. Watts-Roy, 1–37. New York: Columbia University Press, 1999.

Williamson, John B., Linda Evans, and Lawrence A. Powell. *The Politics of Aging: Power and Policy.* Springfield, IL: Charles C. Thomas, 1982.

Wilson, James Q. *Political Organizations.* New York: Basic Books, 1973.

"The Wisdom of Ethel Percy Andrus." Edited by Dorothy Crippen, Ruth Lana, Jean Lipman Block, Thomas E. Zetkov and Gordon Elliott. Long Beach, CA: National Retired Teachers Association, 1968.

Wolfe, Sidney M. "AARP: A Profitable Nonprofit Organization." *Public Citizen.* June 2014. www.citizen.org/Page.aspx?pid=6325.

Wolfinger, Raymond E., and Steven J. Rosenstone. *Who Votes?* New Haven: Yale University Press, 1980.

Wong, Scott, and Mike Lillis. "Ten Public Policy Issues That Divide Trump and Ryan." *The Hill*, May 7, 2016. http://thehill.com/homenews/campaign/279067-10-issues-dividing-donald-trump-and-paul-ryan.

Wooton, Tom. *We Shall Not Be Moved: Rebuilding Home in the Wake of Katrina.* Boston: Beacon Press, 2012.

Zeiler, Shawn. "AARP Members: A Say Earned, But Foregone?" *Congressional Quarterly Weekly Report*, April 30, 2012: 846.

Zhu, Huichen, and Ruopeng An. "Impact of Home-Delivered Meal Programs on Diet and Nutrition among Older Adults: A Review." *Nutrition and Health* 22, no. 2 (2013): 89–103.

Index

Page numbers followed by *f* indicate figures.
Page numbers followed by *t* indicate tables.

About the Author

Christine L. Day is professor of political science at the University of New Orleans. She is the author of *What Older Americans Think: Interest Groups and Aging Policy* (1990), coauthor with Charles D. Hadley of *Women's PACs: Abortion and Elections* (2005), and author of numerous articles, primarily on aging and politics and gender and politics.